D0353490

# Essential thesaurus construction

Vanda Broughton

**f** facet publishing

© Vanda Broughton 2006

Published by
Facet Publishing
7 Ridgmount Street
London WC1E 7AE

Facet Publishing is wholly owned by CILIP: the Chartered Institute of Library and Information Professionals.

Vanda Broughton has asserted her right under the Copyright, Designs and Patents Act, 1988 to be identified as author of this work.

Except as otherwise permitted under the Copyright, Designs and Patents Act, 1988 this publication may only be reproduced, stored or transmitted in any form or by any means, with the prior permission of the publisher, or, in the case of reprographic reproduction, in accordance with the terms of a licence issued by The Copyright Licensing Agency. Enquiries concerning reproduction outside those terms should be sent to Facet Publishing, 7 Ridgmount Street, London WC1E 7AE.

First published 2006

*British Library Cataloguing in Publication Data*
A catalogue record for this book is available from the British Library.

ISBN-13: 978-1-85604-565-0
ISBN-10: 1-85604-565-X

025.49

Typeset in 11/14pt Aldine 721 and Humanist by Facet Publishing.
Printed and made in Great Britain by MPG Books Ltd, Bodmin, Cornwall.

# Contents

# Acknowledgements

I should like to thank Jean Aitchison for reading large sections of the text, for making some pertinent and useful suggestions, and for her invaluable help and advice in the area of all things thesaural. Her contribution to the development of the thesaurus over the last forty years cannot be overestimated, and I'm honoured to follow in that tradition.

I must also thank my colleague John Bowman for his keen eye for textual errors, and for his kindness in pointing these out diplomatically. He also made a number of helpful suggestions when my treatment of the more intractable parts of the subject had crossed the border into unintelligibility.

Needless to say, any errors that remain are my own.

Thanks are also due to those students of the School of Library, Archive & Information Studies at University College London who have undertaken the module in advanced cataloguing and classification over recent years. Their response to the teaching material has been an essential part of the development of the course on which this book is largely based. They have been a delight to teach, and their ingenuity in devising thesauri for the most unlikely of subjects is truly inspiring.

Vanda Broughton

# 1 Introduction

Today the thesaurus is a widely used retrieval tool, chosen by many information workers, particularly those concerned with the management of electronic resources. There is an abundance of technical papers about specific aspects of thesauri and their applications to retrieval in the journal literature, but there is a real dearth of more basic reading material on the subject. This is a book about the principles and practice of thesaurus construction with rather more emphasis than is usual on the latter. It is intended to serve as an introduction to the topic for students of library and information science (LIS), and also to provide a relatively simple manual for practitioners who need an indexing tool for a specific local situation and have little option but to create their own. These practitioners may be librarians, knowledge managers, records managers, or indeed anyone who needs to organize information in any format. It should be of particular interest to the archive community whose professional education possibly covers less of the area of vocabulary building and maintenance than do traditional LIS courses.

It is difficult to know how to identify the members of this diverse group in an economical manner. Throughout the text I've tended to refer to the practitioner as 'the indexer' and you may understand this to mean anyone concerned with the job of document analysis, description, and organization for retrieval. The term 'document' is also used in the widest possible sense to mean any kind of information-carrying item, in manuscript, print, or digital format, and in the form of books, papers, articles, reports, letters, websites, physical objects, and so on.

Although the book is entitled *Essential Thesaurus Construction*, because of the necessary preliminary of building a taxonomic structure from which to extract the thesaurus, there is an implicit subtitle . . . *and essential taxonomy construction*. Users will find that the book provides a basic method for building a structured vocabulary that can be used in more than one format for a range of subject retrieval purposes.

As was the case with my book *Essential Classification* (Facet Publishing, 2004), much of the material in this volume arises from the taught MA in Library and Information Studies at University College London, where the theoretical principles and construction techniques of vocabulary tools are taught as part of the optional module in advanced cataloguing and classification. Students design and build their own thesauri as part of the assessment and the choice of subjects is spectacularly diverse; in recent years there have been offerings on the themes of bereavement, opera, Latin grammar, cross-stitch, British regiments, ornithology, the Tour de France, church music, Chinese cookery, mediaeval castles, stars (of the astronomical sort), psychotherapy, Harry Potter, and the tango. The methodology has proved sufficiently robust to cope with all of these, and has thrown up some interesting problems along the way. I've used a number of examples of terms and relationships from these subject areas to illustrate the text.

The text covers three main aspects: a general introduction to the thesaurus, what it is, where it may be applied, and what its advantages are as a retrieval tool; an investigation of the general principles underlying the thesaurus, particularly in terms of its structure and navigational aids, and the formatting conventions used; and finally a detailed methodology for the creation of a thesaurus. The theoretical and practical chapters have been interspersed, so that the theory is introduced as needed to inform the practical process. The methodology takes the reader through all the stages in building a structured vocabulary for a particular subject, with worked examples, and a number of practical exercises. There is also a chapter on the maintenance of the thesaurus, including the use of thesaurus software, and a glossary of technical terms. Terms that are included in the glossary are printed in bold in the text, at least for the first few occasions of their use. Where examples of schedules and terms from the thesaurus are presented, the font of the main text is used for the systematic display, and Courier font for the alphabetic display.

This book owes much to the methods used in *Thesaurus Construction and Use: a practical manual* (2000) by Aitchison, Gilchrist and Bawden, and will be found to share the same general tradition and understanding of the thesaurus. In comparison with that work, this is a rather simpler version with more space devoted to the task of building a thesaurus, but readers of *Essential Thesaurus Construction* will find *Thesaurus Construction and Use* a very useful source of additional information should the need arise, with little risk of conflict in understanding.

# 2 What is a thesaurus?

[Captain] Hook and Peter [Pan] are now, as it were, alone on the island. Below, Peter is on the bed, asleep, no weapon near him; above, Hook, armed to the teeth, is searching noiselessly for some tree down which the nastiness of him can descend. ... Down this the pirate wriggles a passage. In the aperture below his face emerges and goes green as he glares at the sleeping child. Does no feeling of compassion disturb his sombre breast? The man is not wholly evil: he has a Thesaurus in his cabin, and is no mean performer on the flute.

J. M. Barrie, *Peter Pan*, Act IV

Reproduced with kind permission of Great Ormond Street Hospital for Children, London

## The nature of a thesaurus
### *The 'reference book' thesaurus*

The **thesaurus** as a reference tool dates back to 1852, and the publication of *Roget's Thesaurus*; this, or some modern equivalent, is probably what the majority of people have in mind when they think of a thesaurus. Captain Hook's thesaurus in the quotation at the top of the chapter is almost certainly a reference to *Roget*. But *Roget's Thesaurus* has a fundamentally different purpose from the sort of thesaurus which will be discussed in this book.

Most information professionals would consider *Roget* to be a type of classification scheme because it organizes its vocabulary in a systematic manner. In other words, it is a list of concepts or ideas, which are arranged so that similar concepts are next to each other. The example in Figure 2.1 (overleaf), taken from a digital version of *Roget*,[1] shows part of the list of conceptual classes; these are from the section on language. Underneath is the complete and detailed entry for one of these classes; as you can see, this consists of a list of synonyms or near-synonyms for the headword gathered together and arranged by parts of speech.

A thesaurus of this type is a guide to the English language organized conceptually, and incidentally it makes a map of knowledge. Thesauri on the *Roget* model are extremely useful reference tools because they constitute a

| | |
|---|---|
| 560. Language. | 568. Solecism. |
| 561. Letter. | 569. Style. |
| 562. Word. | 570. Perspicuity. |
| 563. Neologism. | 571. Obscurity. |
| 564. Nomenclature. | 572. Conciseness. |
| 565. Misnomer. | 573. Diffuseness. |
| 566. Phrase. | 574. Vigor. |
| 567. Grammar. | 575. Feebleness. |

### 562. Word.

N. word, term, vocable; name &c. 564; phrase &c. 566; root, etymon; derivative; part of speech &c. (grammar) 567; ideophone[obs3].

dictionary, vocabulary, lexicon, glossary; index, concordance; **thesaurus**; gradus[Lat], delectus[Lat].

etymology, derivation; glossology[obs3], terminology orismology[obs3]; paleology &c. (philology) 560[obs3].

lexicography; glossographer &c. (scholar) 492; lexicologist, verbarian[obs3].

Adj. verbal, literal; titular, nominal. conjugate[Similarly derived], paronymous[obs3]; derivative.

Adv. verbally &c. adj.; verbatim &c. (exactly) 494.

Phr. " the artillery of words" [Swift].

**Figure 2.1**   Structure of a typical reference thesaurus

complement to the dictionary; while the dictionary tells you the meanings of words you know, the thesaurus enables you to find words you don't know, but of which you do know the meaning. Essentially they are synonym and antonym finders. Nowadays most major reference book publishers include a thesaurus along with their dictionaries because it's such a useful tool for writers at any level, be they students, academics, journalists or professional writers of fiction or non-fiction. Interestingly, the very earliest dictionaries in English were organized in this systematic fashion, and it was only later that an alphabetic arrangement was adopted.

### The information retrieval thesaurus

The thesaurus as it occurs in information work is quite a different kind of tool, and the name thesaurus was applied to it only in the 1950s, a hundred years after *Roget*. It is essentially a tool used for the **subject indexing** of documents. It consists of a structured list of **terms** (usually in one particular subject field) that an **indexer** or **records manager** may use to describe documents so that end-users can retrieve relevant items when searching for material about a particular subject.

Unlike the reference thesaurus, the primary arrangement of the **information retrieval thesaurus** is alphabetical (although, just as the reference thesaurus has an alphabetical index, the retrieval thesaurus usually has a systematic arrangement of terms as an additional means of access to the **vocabulary**).

The essence of the retrieval thesaurus is that it is an organized and structured list of terms, and not just a random selection. Each term in the alphabetical sequence is accompanied by **cross-references** to other terms in the vocabulary. This helps the indexer **navigate** the vocabulary and select the most suitable terms for describing documents. When indexers look up a term in the thesaurus, the cross-references alert them to more general terms, more specific terms, and to terms related in other ways. The thesaurus also helps indexers choose between **synonyms** and **near synonyms** when these occur. These aids to navigating the content are a vital part of the thesaurus proper; without them it's only a word list, which is much less useful for indexing.

## What does a thesaurus look like?

Figure 2.2 shows an example of two entries from a very simple thesaurus which I compiled with students on the MA Library and Information Studies programme. The **display** uses a standard format for thesauri, and you can see the way in which the user is referred to other terms in the vocabulary. (We shall look at what the different codes mean in a later chapter.)

**Film**

    BT  Audiovisual media
    NT  Moving images
    NT  Photographs
    NT  Slides
    RT  Film libraries
    RT  Sound recordings

**Film libraries**

    UF  Film archives
    BT  Libraries
    RT  Film

**Figure 2.2**  Entries from a simple thesaurus

The extract from the much larger *DH/DSS-Data Thesaurus*[2] (Figure 2.3, overleaf), which is used at the Department of Health Library, also employs a typical format.

The thesaurus is particularly associated with a word-based or alphabetic approach to information retrieval, and is often contrasted with the classification scheme with its systematic structure. In a word-based system, the terms themselves are used for

**BOYS**
>BT Children
>RT Men

**Boys [physiology]**
>USE Male physiology

**BRACES**
>BT Orthotic devices

**BRACHIAL ARTERIES**
>UF Ante brachial arteries
>BT Arteries

**BRACKEN**
>BT Ferns
>.. Poisonous plants

**BRACKNELL**
>BT Berkshire

**Figure 2.3** Alphabetic display in the *DH/DSS-Data Thesaurus*

labelling the documents, and for searching and retrieval, whereas the classification scheme uses notational codes as labels. Classification schemes, subject heading lists, and thesauri are all different examples of **structured vocabularies**, which are also known as **controlled indexing languages** (see Chapter 3).

## Applications of the thesaurus

Nowadays the thesaurus is the preferred indexing tool for archivists and records managers, and also for librarians working with digital resources, whether this is in a local information service or in a more widely accessible digital resource.

The thesaurus may be used wherever there is a need for terms to describe the subject content of documents. This may be by adding **descriptors** to the subject field of a record in an automated catalogue or bibliographic database, or other tool used to manage a specific collection of documents. Figure 2.4 shows part of a record from the database of an online abstracting service with thesaurus terms in the 'Index term' section.

This is one of the commonest uses of the thesaurus today. Such applications of the thesaurus can be seen in catalogues, online databases, and in bibliographical tools such as **abstracting and indexing services**. A recent development of this kind of **indexing** is the use of thesauri to provide subject **keywords** in various metadata schemes for web published documents. Figure 2.5 shows the application of a thesaurus called the *Integrated Public Sector Vocabulary* (*IPSV*), which is used to provide subject terms in the UK e-Government Metadata System (eGMS).

**Abstract:** The first section of the report presents quotes from the gun lobby regarding efforts to recruit children and youth into America's gun culture. The second section contains copies of advertisements, articles, and photographs illustrating efforts by the NRA and the firearms industry to engage youth in the gun culture. The third section reviews the details of school shootings over the past 2 years, while the fourth section provides a brief overview of Colorado's gun laws, as well as statistics on firearms deaths in the State. 21 footnotes

**Main Term:** Violent juvenile offenders

**Index Term:** Violent crime statistics ; Gun control ; Weapon offenses ; Crime in schools ; Natl Rifle Association ; Citizen gun ownership ; Firearm-crime relationships ; Colorado

**Figure 2.4** Terms from a thesaurus on a database record, *National Criminal Justice Reference Service online database*

```
<title>Defra, UK - News stories - 2005 stories - Clean Neighbourhoods and Environment
Bill</title>
<!— #EndEditable —>
<meta http-equiv="content-type" content="text/html;charset=iso-8859-1">

<!— Document-specific Defra DC metadata —>
<!— #BeginEditable "DC" —>
<meta name="DC.Title" lang="en" content="Defra, UK - News stories - 2005 stories - Clean
Neighbourhoods and Environment Bill">
<meta name="DC.Date.created" scheme="W3CDTF" content="2005-01-07">
<meta name="DC.Date.modified" scheme="W3CDTF" content="2005-mm-dd">
<meta name="eGMS.Subject.Category" scheme="GCL" lang="en" content="Urban
communities; Rural communities; Environmental protection">
<meta name="DC.Creator" lang="en" content="Department for Environment, Food and
Rural Affairs (Defra), Communications Directorate, webmaster@defra.gsi.gov.uk">
<meta name="DC.Subject.keyword" lang="en" content="local environment, environmental
protection, environment
public space, litter">
<meta name="DC.Description" lang="en" content=" ">
<meta name="DC.Contributor" lang="en" content=" ">
<meta name="DC.Coverage" lang="en" content="UK; United Kingdom">
<meta name="DC.Identifier" scheme="URI" content=" ">
<meta name="DC.Relation" lang="en" content=" ">
<meta name="DC.Source" lang="en" content=" ">
<meta name="DC.Type" lang="en" content=" ">
```

eGovernment metadata descriptors

**Figure 2.5** Metadata on a news item on the website of the Department for Environment, Food and Rural Affairs (DEFRA). Subject terms are taken from the *Integrated Public Sector Vocabulary*, a thesaurus for UK government documentation (www.defra.gov.uk/news/latest/2005/localenv-0107.htm). © Crown copyright.

## Summary

- Reference thesauri are systematically arranged lists of concepts, used as synonym and antonym finders
- Information retrieval thesauri employ an alphabetical display of terms, often complemented by a systematic display
- A thesaurus must have a proper system of cross-referencing
- A thesaurus can be used wherever there is a need to describe the subject content of resources
- It is often used for indexing in databases, or as a source of subject metadata.

## The origin and development of the thesaurus

Information retrieval using subject words in the form of headings was popular from the nineteenth century onwards, as can be seen from the early proliferation of printed subject indexes and catalogues of libraries. Formal standards for subject indexing began to appear in the early twentieth century in the form of published subject heading lists, such as the *Library of Congress Subject Headings*, or *Sears' Subject Headings for a Small Library*.

Such lists provided an external standard for libraries to use, avoiding the need for much in-house work, and encouraging uniformity of practice. They were, however, intended for use principally in catalogues of book collections, and they exhibit a number of features that reflect that purpose. Often the headings are required to represent quite complex subjects and as a result they may consist of combinations of concepts rather than single subjects. These examples of modern subject headings taken from the Library of Congress system show the complexity and the high level of combination of terms that can occur in subject headings:

```
Religion and poetry
Dogs as carriers of disease
Motion picture actors and actresses
Civilization, Classical
Nineteenth century fiction
Photography in aircraft accident investigation
African American women college administrators
```

Systems like these, which combine simple concepts into more complicated subject descriptions, are often known as **pre-coordinate indexing** systems.

This is because the concepts have been combined, or coordinated, before they are applied to the document or its record. This is nearly always necessary when arranging items physically or organizing a printed list, since decisions must be made about the order of concepts for a multi-concept document so that it can be placed in a linear sequence. Sometimes it is done as a matter of convenience, to provide ready-made headings or notations for compound concepts. Library classifications and subject heading lists are usually pre-coordinated to a greater or lesser extent, and their application to documents is sometimes known as **pre-coordinate indexing**.

Even from the early days of the twentieth century, some information workers managing technical reports and other specialist documentation took an alternative approach to their material. They preferred to create their own headings from a basic vocabulary, rather than using pre-compounded headings like those above. When automation arrived in libraries and information centres in the mid-twentieth century, this simpler approach to subject indexing was seen as much more appropriate to the management of documentation. Where all the work of subject description, storage and retrieval took place within the automated catalogue or database, and there was no physical arrangement of documents, or printed catalogue to consider, there was no need to combine or coordinate concepts on the document or its record. When a search was made for a compound subject, the search software could identify the individual concepts and retrieve any items which contained them all (rather in the same way in which a search engine searches). Thus the concepts were not combined or coordinated until after they had been assigned to the document.

Indexing that assigns individual concepts to documents, but does not organize or combine them in any way until somebody makes a search for the document, is known as **post-coordinate indexing**. A vocabulary consisting of individual concepts of this kind may be known as a **post-coordinate indexing** system.

Post-coordinate indexing languages, therefore, only needed to consist of single concepts, and mainly these were single terms, although compound terms or phrases might also be used. During the 1950s a number of **keyword systems** of this kind were developed, and it was at that time that the term 'thesaurus' was first used for such a system. An important example from that period was the Uniterm[3] indexing system, which was regarded as a major development in information retrieval. As the name suggests, it used a language consisting of individual concepts or terms and was designed specifically for machine indexing. Uniterm, and other comparable systems of the period, used index terms derived from the documentation itself, either titles or abstracts. These keyword lists were always arranged alphabetically, but they didn't attempt to show any relationships between terms and didn't exhibit much in the way of internal structure. That came later with the development of the thesaurus proper.

Thesauri devised during the 1960s began to incorporate structural principles and to display the typical cross-references that we are familiar with today. The *Thesaurus of Engineering and Scientific Terms*[4] published in 1967, established this format, and also set out the rules on which it had been constructed. These would later be formalized in the various national and international **standards** for thesaurus construction[5] that appeared from the 1970s onwards.

As the thesaurus continued to develop, the predominantly **alphabetical display** of terms was sometimes accompanied by a **systematic display**, rather like a classification scheme. Initially this was regarded as a supplement to the alphabetical part of the thesaurus rather than an integral part of it, but eventually the two parts came to be seen as equally important. The modern thesaurus, with interdependent alphabetical and systematic displays, originates in the work of Jean Aitchison at English Electric in the 1960s, and the development of *Thesaurofacet*,[6] a thesaurus built on facet analytical principles.

**Facet analysis** is a methodology for building classification schemes which was invented by the librarian S. R. Ranganathan, and it involves a careful linguistic analysis of the concepts in a subject field. It creates a controlled vocabulary with a very logical and consistent structure, which is readily converted to a thesaurus format. The methodology for doing this is simple and elegant. The resulting thesaurus is thus one that has a sound theoretical structure, and that consists of both a systematic and an alphabetic display of indexing terms. Such a thesaurus is known as a **faceted thesaurus**; this style of thesaurus is widely used today.

This is the model that we shall follow in constructing a thesaurus. The logical structure of the thesaurus makes it much easier to identify the necessary cross-references, and also to add terms and to maintain, edit and revise the vocabulary in other ways.

## Summary

* Subject indexing using verbal descriptors dates back to the nineteenth century
* Early systems designed for cataloguing book collections normally included many ready-made headings for compound subjects
* These are described as pre-coordinate indexing systems because the terms are already combined, or coordinated, before indexing takes place
* Later systems designed for use with automated catalogues and databases used simple descriptors that were not combined until searching occurred
* Such systems are described as post-coordinate
* The thesaurus evolved from unstructured keyword lists of the 1950s into a more sophisticated tool built on theoretical principles, and controlled by national and international standards.

## Notes

1   ARTFL Project (1911) *Roget's Thesaurus*, http://machaut.uchicago.edu/cgi-in/ROGET.sh?word=thesaurus (accessed October 2005).

2   Aitchison, J., Brewin, P. M. R. and Cotton, J. E. (comps.) (1993) *DH/DSS-Data Thesaurus: the thesaurus of the Departments of Health and Social Security Libraries, London*, 2nd edn, edited by E. D. Dua, London, Departments of Health and Social Security.

3   Taube, M. (1952) *Unit Terms in Coordinate Indexing*, Washington, DC, Documentation Incorporated.

4   *Thesaurus of Engineering and Scientific Terms: a list of engineering and related scientific terms and their relationships for use as a vocabaulary reference in indexing and retrieving technical information* (1967) New York, NY, Engineers Joint Council.

5   There are various national and international standards for monolingual and multilingual thesaurus construction, of which the following is a sample:
    *American National Standard Guidelines for Thesaurus Structure, Construction, and Use: approved June 30, 1980, American National Standards Institute, Inc. / secretariat* (1980) Council of National Library and Information Associations, New York, NY, ANSI.
    *Guidelines for the Construction, Format, and Management of Monolingual Thesauri: an American national standard, developed by the National Information Standards Organization* (1994) Bethesda, MD, NISO Press.
    BS 8723-1:2005 *Structured Vocabularies for Information Retrieval. Part 1: Definitions, symbols and abbreviations*, London, British Standards Institution.

BS 8723-2:2005 *Structured Vocabularies for Information Retrieval. Part 2: Thesauri*, London, British Standards Institution.

[These replace BS 5723, ISO 2788 (1987) *British Standard Guide to the Establishment and Development of Monolingual Thesauri*, London, British Standards Institution.]

BS 6723, ISO 5964 (1985) *British Standard Guide to the Establishment and Development of Multilingual Thesauri*, London, British Standards Institution.

6   Aitchison, J., Gomersall, A. and Ireland, R. (comps) (1961) *Thesaurofacet: a thesaurus & faceted classification for engineering & related subjects*, Leicester, English Electric Co. Ltd.

# 3 Tools for subject access and retrieval

The thesaurus is only one of a variety of tools that are used to index or tag documents for the purpose of information storage and retrieval. The term 'thesaurus' is often applied fairly loosely to a number of these, with the general sense of some kind of a subject-related vocabulary. In this chapter I shall try to identify the main types of **vocabulary tool** which you may come across, and to determine their significant characteristics. Despite the existence of published standards for many of these tools, in practice the terminology is not applied very precisely, and it is easy to be confused by the different understanding of these names. We have already mentioned **classification schemes** and **subject heading lists** used in conventional library and document collections, and **keyword lists** used for post-coordinate indexing, as well as the thesaurus proper. More recently conceived types of subject tool include the **taxonomy**, the **concept map**, and the **ontology**. These sorts of system are sometimes referred to collectively as **controlled vocabularies,** or **controlled indexing languages,** to contrast them with the use of natural, or uncontrolled, language in subject indexing. They may also be described as **knowledge organization systems**, or **knowledge organization** structures, by those whose primary interest is in the analysis and structure of subject fields or domains, and the conceptual relationships between subjects.

Like natural languages such as English, Chinese or Arabic, the indexing language has a vocabulary (the terms used for indexing) and **syntax,** or operating rules. The 'control' is imposed by the compiler of the vocabulary, and consists of limits placed on the number and form of words or terms that can be used in indexing. This enables synonyms and variant forms of words to be managed in a way that supports more efficient indexing and retrieval, and avoids overlap and confusion in the use of similar concepts. Strictly speaking, **vocabulary control** refers only to this process of linguistic management, but controlled vocabularies commonly exhibit other features, such as the identification of relationships between terms, and rules for combining terms when necessary (the system **syntax** mentioned above). The advantages of using controlled languages are discussed in Chapter 5.

A brief examination of these different types of indexing tool and how they work will help to show how the thesaurus proper fits into the context of subject tools generally, and how to some extent it forms a bridge between them. Like the two types of thesaurus, vocabularies fall into two groups: those whose primary arrangement is systematic, and those whose arrangement is alphabetical.

## Systematically organized controlled languages

We'll begin by considering those categories of vocabulary tools that have a systematic arrangement of the indexing terms.

### Classification schemes

The bibliographic, or library, **classification scheme** is the earliest example of a controlled language in the modern documentation world, most of those in current use dating from the late 19th or early 20th century. You will probably be familiar with the end-user view of a scheme such as the *Dewey Decimal Classification* or the *Library of Congress Classification* through the classmarks allocated to books and used to arrange them in library collections. Non-librarian readers may never have seen the structure of the classification as it appears in the published schedules. Figure 3.1 provides an example of such a **schedule** from the second edition of the *Bliss Bibliographic Classification*.

The essence of a classification is that it groups related topics, and attempts to provide a natural linear sequence of topics. This is because the original purpose of classifications (and the one that is still dominant) was physically to organize the material and to allow retrieval through browsing the shelves. This purpose determines the structure of the classification; related **classes** of subjects appear next to each other, and **sub-classes** follow on immediately from the more general class of which they are part. The relationships between classes are usually displayed in the page layout with sub-classes indented to their containing classes. The inter-relationships between subjects are obviously complicated and often hard to establish in terms of a single linear sequence, and much of the work of constructing and maintaining classifications centres on this. Because the order of classes is conceptual and intellectual (and sometimes apparently rather arbitrary) some device must be used to keep the classes in the

| | |
|---|---|
| **Hadrons (general)** | **BNQQN** |
| | **BNRRF** |

|  | [Elementary particles types BNB] |
|---|---|
|  | [By mass] |
|  | [Hadrons general BNQ] |
|  |  |
|  | (*Types of hadrons*) |
|  | By part |
| BNQ RBW | Composite models |
|  | *By special and quantum property* |
| RCB | Symmetrical |
|  | * For multiplets, see BNQ T |
|  | *By lifetime* |
| DT | Resonances |
| T | Multiplets, isospin multiplets |
|  |     * Hypothetical groups of particles in which all the particles are regarded as different states of the same particle. All have the same spin (J), parity (P) & baryon number (B). |
|  |     * See also Hadron symmetry BNQ MC |
| U | SU3 (multiplets) |
|  |     * Special unitary group of 3 x 3 matrices, predictive of hadronic multiplet structure. |
|  | Theory |
| U8U | Eightfold way (hadron theory), octet theory |
| BNR | Quarks |
|  |     * Hypothetical particles corresponding to the basic building blocks of the SU3 group. Their charge is not the usual electron charge (e) but integral multiples of 1/3e. |
|  | Theory |
| BNR 8M | Quantum chromodynamics, QCD (quarks) |
| 8MG | Quark confinement |

**Figure 3.1**   Classification schedule for particle physics in the *Bliss Bibliographic Classification*, 2nd edition[1]

required sequence. This is achieved by the **notation**, which usually consists of numbers or letters that have a recognized **filing order**.

More recently developed classifications may work in a more sophisticated manner, and may be used for retrieval as well as **browsing**, but they still share some fundamental common attributes. The classification scheme is characterized by the systematic order, by a close analysis of the relationships between terms, and by the use of a notation to maintain the sequence.

## Taxonomies

The term 'taxonomy' really has no clear definition. The Taxonomy Warehouse (www.taxonomywarehouse.com/), a freely accessible online directory of vocabularies and subject tools, uses it as a comprehensive term for thesauri, classifications, glossaries and dictionaries. I would prefer the term 'vocabulary' for such a broad interpretation, and I believe that 'taxonomy' is more often used for a structured language of a general classificatory type, sometimes where the term 'classification' is felt to be old-fashioned, and a more scientific sounding name is preferred.

Traditionally, taxonomy is the science of classifying biological organisms, and in the scientific community it is mainly used for the organization of entities, based on shared attributes. A taxonomy will therefore be very clear about the **hierarchical relationships** between entities, and there is usually no room for doubt about the location of items in a taxonomic structure. Translated into a visual form, the taxonomy has a **tree structure**, and in mathematics it is used in a technical sense to indicate a system of that type. Whereas in classification we talk about classes and sub-classes, or **subordinate, superordinate** and **coordinate classes,** the taxonomist may describe these as **'parent', 'child',** and **'sibling'** relationships.

The taxonomy is very popular as a general organizing tool for electronic resources, particularly in the commercial sector, where it is often encountered on intranets. It is also employed as a search tool for browsing an organized collection of documents or links. Figure 3.2 shows a taxonomic display which can be navigated using hypertext to access more specific sub-categories, or deeper levels of the hierarchy. Because there is no need for the physical arrangement of the resources, the classes are not given notational codes.

The use here of a combination of systematic and alphabetical arrangement (**alphabetico-classed**) is also very common in tools of this sort, and because the detail is arrived at hypertextually, a broad view of the subject

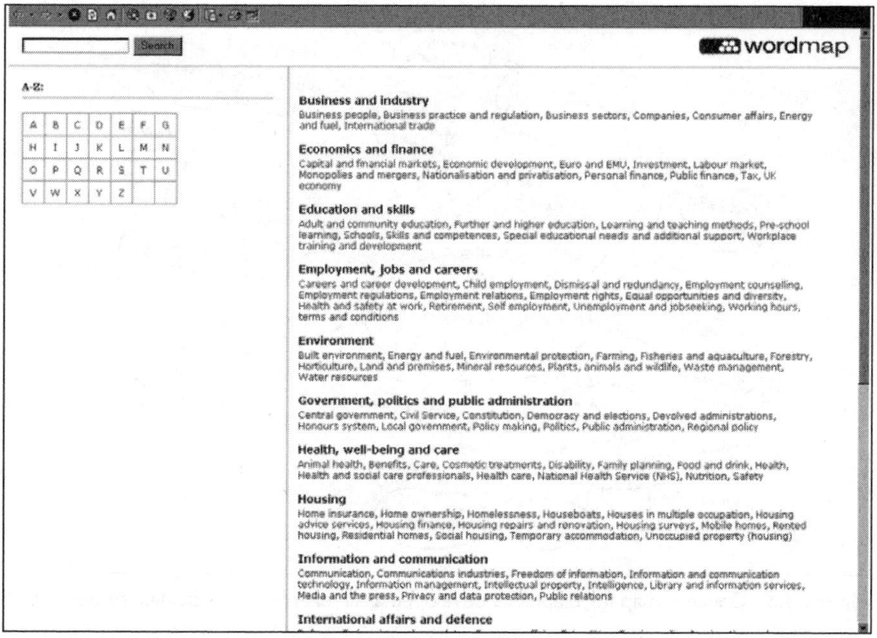

**Figure 3.2**   Display in the *Wordmap* taxonomy

domain can be provided. Such a broad and shallow 'classification' is sometimes referred to as a **'high-level'** tool. It can be a very helpful aid to browsing for the novice searcher, although it may still be no easier to predict where a very specific topic is located.

Despite the potential for a more general interpretation of the term 'taxonomy', a broad systematic structure of this kind, is, I think, what most people understand it to be.

## Concept maps, topic maps and ontologies

**Concept maps** and **ontologies** offer a graphic representation of topics and their relationships in a subject domain. They are usually restricted to a fairly narrow subject area because of the constraints imposed by the physical display.

The concept map varies a lot in its level of complexity, from a simple visual display of related topics, such as that shown in Figure 3.3, to a more sophisticated structure where the relationships between concepts are formalized and specified, and which is more properly known as a **topic map**.

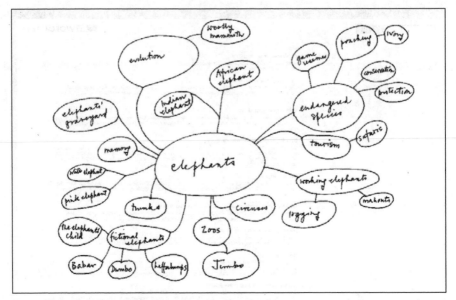

**Figure 3.3** Concept map for Elephants developed as an exercise in mapping a research area

An international standard exists for topic maps (ISO 13250), which describes them in the following manner:

> A topic map defines a multidimensional topic space – a space in which the locations are topics, and in which the distances between topics are measurable in terms of the number of intervening topics which must be visited in order to get from one topic to another, and the kinds of relationships that define the path from one topic to another, if any, through the intervening topics, if any.[2]

Topic maps are often regarded as more flexible than traditional classifications, although of course this depends on the syntax of the classification and its capacity to express compound subjects. Topic maps often deal with elements of a document other than **semantic content**, such as the originator of the document, and administrative **metadata elements**. The topic map in its developed form is not easily distinguishable from an ontology, which also aims to identify concepts and specify the relationships between them.

The relationships in topic maps and ontologies tend to be much wider in range and more subtle in nature than the straightforward hierarchical relationships of the taxonomy or classification. In the case of the ontology,

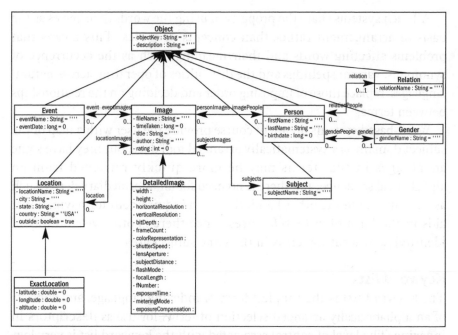

**Figure 3.4**  Ontology for digital image metadata management developed in a project at
California Polytechnic University
(http://counties.csc.calpoly.edu/~team_5fk/S03/ontology.jpg)

they may be formalized to the point where they can be manipulated
mathematically (Figure 3.4).

All the preceding tools take a structural view of a subject domain, and they
deal primarily with **concepts**. A concept is necessarily abstract in nature,
and in order to describe it more than one term may be required (although
this isn't invariably the case). For example, in Figure 3.1 the Bliss system
uses BNQ U8U to represent the concept 'Eightfold way (hadron theory), octet
theory'. The substitution of codes for descriptors or keywords is a useful tool
in handling such complicated verbal descriptions, and can also act as an
intermediary when mapping between different languages or systems.
Nevertheless there are a number of indexing tools that use words rather than
concepts, which we can describe as **alphabetical**, or **word-based** tools.

## Alphabetically arranged, word-based controlled languages

In Chapter 2 we looked at the evolution of the thesaurus from the simple
keyword lists of the 1950s and 1960s, and considered briefly other systems,
such as the **subject heading list**.

All such systems share the property of using the words themselves as the basis of arrangement rather than concepts or topics. This means that problems affecting words and their meaning, such as the occurrence of synonyms, variant spellings and the difficulties of operating across natural languages, replace those of imposing order and deciding on the relationships between terms.

Word-based systems do not of course provide the user with a map of the subject domain as a systematically arranged tool does, but they have some advantages in that terms may be more quickly retrieved from an alphabetical sequence, and there is no need for an intermediary device such as a notation. On the other hand, there is a requirement for navigational aids in the form of cross-references, since there is otherwise no way of identifying or locating terms in the same subject area.

## Keyword lists

The **keyword list** is the simplest form of indexing language, and consists of an alphabetically arranged selection of terms for use as **descriptors** in indexing. The level of control associated with the keyword list is very low, and the keywords are often derived from the text itself, either intellectually by the indexer, or by machine extraction from electronic text. Because the terms are so intimately associated with the documents indexed, they can reflect the content more closely than an intellectually built indexing language; new terms will be quickly incorporated, and obsolescent ones simply cease to be used.

The disadvantages are that synonyms are not identified, so that documents with similar subject content may not be indexed as such (and hence not retrieved), and there is usually no way for the indexer to navigate such a vocabulary to find alternative indexing terms.

The following is a section of a keyword list from a US health resource, the National Health Information Center:[3]

Family Services
Fanconi's Anemia
Farming
Fat
Fatherhood
Fecal Incontinence
Federal Clearinghouse

Federal Programs
Fellowships
Fen/Phen
Fertility
Fetal Alcohol Syndrome
Fetal Monitoring
Fever
Fever Blisters
Fibromyalgia
Financial Assistance
Fire Prevention
First Aid

The complete lack of cross-referencing shows how impossible it is for the indexer to identify other relevant terms, or indeed to know what terms are available except by scanning the entire list. In the case of this particular vocabulary, the terms were undoubtedly derived from the modest set of online resources to be organized, rather than from an intellectual breakdown of the subject of health sciences; terms would be added only as they become necessary.

Note that the key 'words' can, in practice, be compound terms ('Fire Prevention', 'Fetal Monitoring') or phrases ('Fetal Alcohol Syndrome').

## Subject heading lists
**Subject heading lists** are more sophisticated than keyword lists as regards the level of management of the terms, although the entries themselves may look very similar to keywords. (Examples here are taken from the *Library of Congress Subject Headings* (LCSH), the most widely used system in the English-speaking world, but many countries have their own similarly constructed national systems of subject headings.)

Snails
Snails as carriers of disease
Snails as pets
Snails, Edible
Snails, Fossil
Snaith family
Snake attacks
Snake bite

Snake bites
Snake blenny, Spotted
Snake Butte Dam
Snake Butte Reservoir Dam
Snake charmers

At first glance the entries in the subject heading list are very similar in form to the keyword list, but every term is supported by cross-references serving as navigational aids. An examination of the full entry for a term shows the much greater functionality of the subject heading lists:

**Snails**
    UF   Land snails
           Landsnails
    BT   Gastropoda
    NT   Edible snails
           Freshwater snails
           Introduced snails
           Limpets
           Prosobrachia

The cross-references here use the standard thesaural relaters, which make the indexer aware of synonyms (UF or Use For references), more general terms (BT or **broader terms**) and more specific terms (NT or **narrower terms**). RT (**related terms**) is also used for terms related in other ways. These relaters correspond to the superordinate, subordinate and coordinate classes of the classification, and the parent, child and sibling relations of the taxonomy. A subject heading list of the *LCSH* type can look very much like a thesaurus because of the similarity of format. Nevertheless, the subject heading list has often been developed in an impromptu manner, responding to the needs of the documents to be indexed, rather than being built logically as the thesaurus is. In the case of *LCSH*, the cross-references have been introduced retrospectively rather than being an integral part of the structure of the subject headings, but they nevertheless address various problems of vocabulary control and navigation of the vocabulary.

## The thesaurus proper

The thesaurus is the most fully developed form of the alphabetically presented indexing language, since it deals with vocabulary control and navigation in a systematic and logical manner. It achieves this by deriving the alphabetic display from an underlying systematic structure. The clearly identified subject structure and hierarchical relationships of the classification/taxonomy are used to generate the cross-references and navigational aids of the alphabetic display. The thesaurus with its dual format forms a bridge between the systematically organized indexing language and the word-based language. The example (Figure 3.5 overleaf) taken from the *UNESCO Thesaurus* shows the difference in layout and collocation of the two different parts of the thesaurus. The systematic display lays out all the hierarchical relationships between terms in a restricted subject area, in a similar fashion to a conventional classification. The alphabetical version lists terms A–Z, retaining a more limited part of the hierarchy (in *UNESCO* more detailed than in most thesauri), but also picking up associated terms from other areas of the vocabulary.

Because of this hybrid structure the thesaurus is able to fulfil a number of subject indexing roles. The systematic part can function as a map of the subject domain, and, if equipped with a notation, as a broad level classification tool. In an electronic version it can act as a browsing tool using hypertext to reveal the different levels of hierarchy. At the same time the alphabetic display functions as a list of descriptors for indexing and document description, and in combination the descriptors can be employed to generate subject headings.

Nowadays individual thesauri may adopt other forms of display, particularly graphical ones, so that it has become in many cases even more of a multi-purpose tool. It would not be uncommon to find some elements of all the various kinds of tool discussed in this chapter in examples of modern thesauri. This widening interpretation of the thesaurus is one of the reasons for its current use as a generic name for a vocabulary. Just as the term 'taxonomy' is very broadly interpreted, so 'thesaurus' may be applied to a range of vocabulary tools that do not meet the traditional thesaurus criteria.

**Systematic display**

**Marine biology**
  NT1    **Marine life**
         NT2    **Plankton**
                UF      *Marine bacteria*
                UF      *Marine microorganisms*
                UF      *Phytoplankton*
                UF      *Zooplankton*

**Oceanography**
         UF      *Marine science*
         UF      *Oceanology*
  NT1    **Oceanographic research**
         NT2    **Bathymetry**
                UF      *Bathymetric surveying*
                NT3     **Bathymetric charts**
         NT2    **Ocean exploration**
                UF      *Ocean expeditions*
         NT2    **Oceanographic data**
                UF      *Marine data*
         NT2    **Oceanographic measurement**
                UF      *Salinity measurement*
                UF      *Sea water measurement*

**Alphabetic display**

**Oceanography**
  MT     2.40    Geography and oceanography
         FR      Oceanographie
         SP      Oceanografia
  UF     Marine science
  UF     Oceanology
  NT1    **Oceanographic research**
         NT2    **Bathymetry**
                NT3     **Bathymetric charts**
         NT2    **Ocean exploration**
         NT2    **Oceanographic data**
         NT2    **Oceanographic measurement**
  RT     **Earth sciences**
  RT     **Hydrology**
  RT     **Marine biology**
  RT     **Marine engineering**
  RT     **Marine resources**
  RT     **Oceans**
  RT     **Seas**

*Continued on next page*

**Figure 3.5**  Systematic and alphabetical displays from the *UNESCO Thesaurus*

> **RT**      **Underwater technology**
>
> *Oceanography*:
>     **Chemical oceanography** (2.40)
>     **Dynamic oceanography** (2.40)
>     **Physical oceanography** (2.40)

**Figure 3.5**  *Continued*

## Summary

- There are several different sorts of vocabulary tool used for subject organization and access to resources
- These are primarily either systematic or alphabetical in arrangement
- Systematic arrangements include classifications, taxonomies, concept maps, topic maps and ontologies
- These provide a visual impression of topics and their inter-relationships in a subject domain and are good for browsing and navigation
- Alphabetically organized tools include keyword lists, subject heading lists and thesauri
- Relationships in the alphabetically organized tools are not explicit, and cross-referencing between terms is essential
- Terms such as 'taxonomy' and 'thesaurus' may be used imprecisely to refer to any kind of vocabulary tool.

## Notes

1   Mills, J. and Broughton, V. (eds) (1999) *Bliss Bibliographic Classification*, 2nd edn, Class AY/B General Science and Physics, London, Bowker-Saur.
2   ISO/IEC 13250 *Topic Maps* (1999), p. iii, www.y12.doe.gov/sgml/sc34/ document/ 0129.pdf (accessed July 2005).
3   Keyword listing. National Health Information Center resource database, www.health.gov/nhic/AlphaKeyword.htm (accessed July 2005).

# 4 What a thesaurus is used for

The last chapter showed us that the thesaurus is very much a multi-purpose vocabulary tool. As a consequence it has a number of potential applications, some of which have arisen only recently, within the context of electronic information management. In this chapter we will look at the ways in which the thesaurus can be used, primarily by the information professional for indexing and the organization of information, but also by the end-user to support retrieval through searching and browsing.

## The thesaurus as an indexing tool

As it was first developed, the thesaurus was an indexing tool for large technical document collections; that is to say it was used as a source of descriptors or indexing terms for attaching to the database or catalogue records for those documents. These assigned index terms would then form the 'text' which was searched in subject searches. Used in this way, the thesaurus almost presupposes the machine management of document collections.

### Thesaurus terms for subject headings

In fact the thesaurus can be used equally well in a print-based environment if the terms are combined to create alphabetical subject headings. A thesaurus used in this way will require clear instructions for the combination of terms, particularly for the order in which terms should be combined, if consistency is to be maintained. A good example of this sort of application of a thesaurus is in the paper version of *Library and Information Science Abstracts* (*LISA*) where 'every abstract in *LISA* is indexed with a general term taken from the *LISA Thesaurus*, to which qualifying terms are added to increase the specificity of the string'.[1] In other words, the thesaurus terms are combined to create subject headings for the printed list, as in this example, taken from the November/December 2005 edition of *LISA*:

**Classification: 13158–13162**
   Companies – Business information – Information work: 13604
   Documents – Searching: 13293
   Mapping – Cocitation – Visualization – Citation analysis: 12824
   Search engines – Online information retrieval: 13277

The subject index also uses *LISA Thesaurus* terms in a stand-alone manner so that they are cross-referenced to each other, although only downward references are given:

**Periodicals**
   *narrower terms*
      Core periodicals
      Electronic periodicals
      Library and information
         science periodicals
      Magazines

**Markup languages**
   *narrower term*
      HTML
      XML

## Thesaurus terms in commercial databases

A large number of current thesauri exist to underpin abstracting and indexing services for scholarly and research purposes, such as those produced by commercial abstracting organizations. It is easy to see examples of these terms on document records, and sometimes the thesaurus itself can be viewed. Figure 4.1 is an example of a record from Cambridge Scientific Abstracts' database *Library and Information Science Abstracts*, which shows thesaural terms in the descriptor field ('descriptor' here being used to mean 'subject descriptor').

You can see the range of thesaurus terms used in the descriptor field, and note that hypertext can be exploited to link to other sets of documents using any of these individual descriptors. This is a good example of thesaurus terms applied for post-coordinate indexing, since they appear to be in a random order with no attempt at combination. Only when combinations of these particular terms form part of a search query will this particular item be retrieved.

## Thesaurus for local collections

Probably the most frequent application of the thesaurus will be for the cataloguing or indexing of documents held in individual collections. Nowadays, with so many catalogues available on the web, it is quite likely

```
┌─────────────────────────────────────────────────────────────────┐
│  Sample Record                                                    │
│                                                                   │
│     TI:   Title                                                   │
│           An overview of readers' advisory service with           │
│           evaluations of related Websites                         │
│     AU:   Author                                                  │
│           Schultz, K                                              │
│     SO:   Source                                                  │
│           Acquisitions Librarian; (23) 2000, p.21-33              │
│     IS:   ISSN                                                    │
│           0896-3576                                               │
│     AB:   Abstract                                                │
│           Contribution to a thematic issue devoted to the Internet │
│           and acquisitions. As readers' advisors, librarians      │
│           attempt to match users with books they will enjoy.      │
│           (Original abstract – amended)                           │
│     FE:   Features                                                │
│           refs.                                                   │
│     LA:   Language                                                │
│           English                                                 │
│     PY:   Publication Year                                        │
│           2000                                                    │
│     DE:   Descriptors                                             │
│           Acquisitions; Selection aids; World Wide Web; Web        │
│           sites; Evaluation; Libraries; User services; Readers     │
│           advisory work                                           │
│     SH:   Shelfmark                                               │
│           0578.881170                                             │
│     UD:   Update                                                  │
│           20000725                                                │
│     AN:   Accession Number                                        │
│           95048                                                   │
└─────────────────────────────────────────────────────────────────┘
```

**Figure 4.1**   A sample bibliographic record from *Library and Information Science Abstracts*,[2] showing thesaurus terms in the descriptor field

that these records will be visible to a wider audience, but nevertheless the primary purpose will be to meet the retrieval needs of the local community. There is no substantial difference in practical application from the commercial indexing situation, although, of course, a published thesaurus may be customized to meet the local needs of a particular collection. The example in Figure 4.2 of a record from the catalogue of the Refugee Studies Centre in Oxford is the same in every significant way as the record from *LISA* in Figure 4.1.

Where documents are stored by **accession numbers** or some other

| | Type of record: IND | Shelfmark: RSC/NR-51 POT | ISBN/ISSN: | Language: ENG | Date of Publication: 19941000 | Date created: 19950424 |
|---|---|---|---|---|---|---|
| Publication Title: | Food security and agricultural rehabilitation in post-war Rwanda Aug - Sept 1994. Report to Save the Children (SCF) UK | | | | | |
| Author: | POTTIER, Johan ; WILDING, John | | | | | |
| Publisher: | SCF | | | | | |
| Place of Publication: | London | | | | | |
| Pages/Length: | 113p | | | | | |
| Subject terms: | FOOD / REHABILITATION / AGRICULTURE | | | | | |
| Geographic terms: | RWANDA | | | | | |

**Figure 4.2**  Subject descriptors from the *International Thesaurus of Refugee Terminology*[3] on a record from the Refugee Studies Centre, Oxford

kind of running number or filing device, the thesaurus terms will only be added to the catalogue or database record for the document, and physical retrieval will be effected using the storage number. This would usually be the case where documents are stored in **closed access** and have to fetched by staff, or where, for reasons of economy or convenience, documents are stored in boxes or other containers.

If the documents are stored in hanging files or use some similar means that make them accessible to users of the collection, the thesaurus terms can be used to create headings like those in the *LISA* printed list. Such headings can easily be mounted on tabs attached to the files to provide a subject guide to the material. This method is very suitable for traditional 'filing cabinet' collections, such as press cuttings, and photographs or other illustrations. In this situation, each item can have only one location, so there must be rules for the ordering and combination of the terms in the headings if the items are to be retrieved. Here the thesaurus would be used (untypically) pre-coordinately.

## The thesaurus as a source of metadata

Today the thesaurus is still mostly used as a source of indexing terms, or descriptors, in catalogues and bibliographic databases, but it has some broader, though related, applications. A frequently encountered use of thesauri is in the area of **subject metadata**. Strictly speaking, all cataloguing, classification and indexing information is metadata, since it is data about data, but it is fairly common practice to restrict the use of the term 'metadata' to that attached to digital resources. Often the metadata is not visible to the end-user because it is embedded in the source code. If you select the View menu on Internet Explorer or other browser, and click on 'Source', you will be able to see what has been hidden from the user, but is visible to a search engine. The use of metadata in this way is intended to improve the effectiveness of retrieval of web resources since it allows authors and designers of websites to include a range of terms that a searcher might use that are not necessarily wanted on the home page of the site. Our example of the eGMS metadata system looked at in Chapter 2 (Figure 2.5) is a fairly typical example of a controlled vocabulary used in this way.

Many metadata standards have been created in the last ten years or so. These standards usually consist of a set of 'attributes' of an item that should be specified for the description of that item, and which serve both to identify the item and to act as a basis for its retrieval. The best known metadata standard is that of the **Dublin Core**, which was developed by Online Computer Library Center (OCLC), in Dublin Ohio, specifically for the description of digital resources. Dublin Core contains the following fields, referred to as the Dublin Core, or DC, 'elements':

- title
- creator
- subject
- description
- publisher
- contributor
- date
- type

- format
- identifier
- source
- language
- relation
- coverage
- rights

These elements are intended to be filled out by the creator of the resource, and embedded in the HTML code for the item. In reality, metadata systems have not been very well taken up by the creators of resources, except where these are academic institutions or libraries, museums and archives.

The record from the Humbul Humanities Hub[4] in Figure 4.3 shows the DC applied to a resource (the National Railway Museum website) in the Humbul 'catalogue'. Clearly, the DC elements owe much to conventional cataloguing standards and bear a fairly close resemblance to **MARC** fields. As with descriptive cataloguing, most of the elements will contain data (more correctly metadata) derived from the resource itself. Thus the

| Main Title: | National railway museum |
|---|---|
| Web Address (URL): | http://www.nrm.org.uk/ |
| Description: | The web site of the United Kingdom's National Railway Museum in York provides access details, corporate information, special exhibitions, and details of many of the exhibits and features of the museum itself. (Original abstract amended) |
| Language: | English |
| Intended Audience: | General Public |
| Responsibility: | Author : National Railway Museum |
| Publisher: | National Railway Museum |
| Type of Resource: | Image<br>Text Document<br>Primary source<br>Organization<br>FAQ |
| Coverage – Start/End Date: | 1829 / 1989 |
| Coverage – Period: | 19th Century CE<br>20th Century CE |
| Makes Reference to: | National Grid for Learning.<br>http://www.ngfl.gov.uk/index.jsp<br>Learning on the Move.<br>http://www.learningonthemove.co.uk/ |
| Humbul Subjects: | History & Philosophy of Science   Museums, Libraries, Archives |

**Figure 4.3** Example of a Humbul record for a digital resource (the National Railway Museum website) using Dublin Core elements

names of the creators and contributors, the title of the resource, its date of creation, the language in which the text is written, and so on, are not normally open to interpretation. Although in theory they might be anything at all, in respect of a particular item the correct 'terms' are given.

The same is not true for the subject element. Here the indexers (or meta-taggers) are invited to enter whatever they wish. There is no generally agreed standard for subject description to which they can resort for an answer. Because those assigning metadata may not have access to, or be trained in the application of, classification schemes or subject heading lists, the thesaurus is an ideal alternative tool for this purpose.

If we examine the National Railway Museum website itself, we can see the source code with metadata embedded near the top of the code, but not made visible to the browser. The metadata scheme in Figure 4.4 is clearly not Dublin Core, but is close in conception, with comparable fields. The subject description differs a great deal from the Humbul subject description, since different standards are being drawn on. Humbul uses its own high-level classification, with just the major subject areas ('History and philosophy of science', 'Museums, libraries, archives'), but the Museum website uses thesaurus terms (National Railway Museum, NRM, trains, rail, eurotunnel) taken (probably) from the Museum Documentation Association, *Railway Object Name Thesaurus.*[5]

```
<HTML>
<HEAD>
<TITLE>NRM - National Railway Museum</TITLE>
<META HTTP-EQUIV="keywords" content="National Railway
Museum, NRM, trains, rail, eurotunnel">
<META NAME="author" content="Annett Jacob">
<META NAME="copyright" content="&copy: 1998 The Hub">
<META NAME="editor" content="Bbedit 4.5">
<META NAME="location" content="NRM/index.asp">
<META NAME="created" content="25/03/1998">
<META NAME="modified" content="25/03/1998">
</HEAD>
<FRAMESET cols="135,*" FRAMEBORDER=0 FRAMESPACING=0
BORDER=0>
   <FRAME SRC="nav.asp" NAME="NAV" MARGINHEIGHT=0
MARGINWIDTH=0 SCROLLING="NO">
```

Subject keywords in metadata

**Figure 4.4**   Metadata from the National Railway Museum website (www.nrm.org.uk)

## The thesaurus as a search tool

There are two different ways in which the thesaurus can be used directly as a search tool by modifying the way in which a search, or query, is put together: either the controlled vocabulary may be made visible to the end-user as an aid to **query formulation**, or the thesaurus may be 'embedded' in the search software and be used to support what is known as **query expansion**.

## Query formulation

In the past, in most indexing applications, the source of the indexing terms was not accessible to the end-user; only the indexer would be able to see it, and the searcher could only view terms as they were assigned to the subject field in specific records. With the development of online resources it has become easier to make the indexing vocabulary visible to the searcher through the use of hypertext links. This is immensely useful to searchers since it enables them to view the vocabulary, to see what terms have been used in indexing, to select appropriate terms for framing a search, and to modify searches through the cross-references in the thesaurus. The thesaurus used in this way may be termed a **search thesaurus**.

In the case of the *LISA* database, which we looked at to see the thesaurus in its indexing mode, the thesaurus itself can be accessed by the searcher, and used in a browse mode. In the example in Figure 4.5, the hypertext links take the searcher to the full thesaurus entry, with its cross-references to synonyms, and to broader, narrower, and related terms. You can also see options on the left-hand side of the screen that support the formulation, or construction, of more complicated queries.

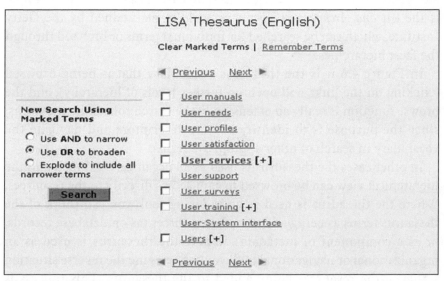

**Figure 4.5**  *LISA Thesaurus* navigation screen

## Query expansion

The thesaurus may also help to improve retrieval without ever being seen by the end-user. This occurs when the thesaurus forms part of the search software and terms in searches are mechanically matched against the controlled vocabulary. Alternative or additional terms can be entered into the query by the automatic use of the thesaurus cross-references. This can happen either as a matter of course, or in response to poor search results. The software can 'expand' the search by broadening the topic, adding a range of more specific topics, or searching on synonyms and related terms.

This sort of process is behind many **intelligent searching** systems. (Note that this is not necessarily the case with internet search engines where the query expansion may be achieved by running additional searches on commonly occurring terms in retrieved documents.) In the majority of cases where a thesaurus is used as a source of descriptors or metadata, it won't be available to the user, so it can seldom be used directly. In some cases the systematic structure of the thesaurus is evident, and then it can be used as a browsing aid.

## The thesaurus as a browse and navigation tool

In the digital environment the thesaurus is often used as an aid to navigation or browsing through the systematic display. A good example is the *Art and Architecture Thesaurus (AAT)*,[6] maintained by the Getty Institute, which can be searched for individual terms or browsed through the facet hierarchies.

In Figure 4.6 it is the thesaurus vocabulary that is being browsed (clicking on the links will open up further levels of hierarchy), and the browse function is really an extension of the search role of the thesaurus, since the purpose is to identify subject descriptors and navigate the vocabulary in search of other appropriate terms.

In other cases the thesaurus is used as an organizational tool, and the hierarchical view can be browsed to gain access directly to the resources. Where the thesaurus is used as an indexing tool, you can think of the thesaurus terms as being added to the resources (as on database records, or as a component of metadata). Where the thesaurus is used as an organizational or navigational tool, you can imagine the reverse situation – that of the resources being added to the thesaurus. This process is sometimes called the **population** of a knowledge organization system, since it fills out the theoretical framework of the vocabulary with real information. Used in this way, the thesaurus structure forms the browsing tool. The *Wordmap* example used in Chapter 3 shows how this may be done

(Figure 4.7). Here, clicking on a category in the display will reveal a list of resources allocated to that category. Because this is a virtual collection, resources can be assigned to several different categories and be retrievable from them all.

There is variation in the practice of displaying 'empty classes'. Some systems display the whole of the conceptual structure, with the consequence that some browsing may be unsuccessful. Others only display populated classes, which means that the view of the subject as a whole is incomplete. This is obviously less of a problem with larger collections where the occurrence of empty classes is likely to be lower.

........ Materials

............ materials

............... <material components> [N]

.................... atoms

.................... electrons

.................... ions

.................... molecules

............... <materials by composition>

.................... inorganic material

.................... organic material

.................... <combination inorganic/organic material>

............... <materials by form>

.................... dispersion (material)

.................... emulsion

.................... filament

.................... film (material)

.................... foam

.................... <materials by chemical form>

.................... <materials by physical form>

.................... membrane

**Figure 4.6**  *Art and Architecture Thesaurus®* (AAT) materials facet hierarchy
© 2006 J. Paul Getty Trust

**Business and industry**
Business people, Business practice and regulation, Business sectors, Companies, Consumer affairs, Energy and fuel, International trade

**Economics and finance**
Capital and financial markets, Economic development, Euro and EMU, Investment, Labour market, Monopolies and mergers, Nationalisation and privatisation, Personal finance, Public finance, Tax, UK economy

**Education and skills**
Adult and community education, Further and higher education, Learning and teaching methods, Pre-school learning, Schools, Skills and competences, Special educational needs and additional support, Workplace training and development

**Employment, jobs and careers**
Careers and career development, Child employment, Dismissal and redundancy, Employment counselling, Employment regulations, Employment relations, Employment rights, Equal opportunities and diversity, Health and safety at work, Retirement, Self employment, Unemployment and jobseeking, Working hours, terms and conditions

**Environment**
Built environment, Energy and fuel, Environmental protection, Farming, Fisheries and aquaculture, Forestry, Horticulture, Land and premises, Mineral resources, Plants, animals and wildlife, Waste management, Water resources

**Government, politics and public administration**
Central government, Civil Service, Constitution, Democracy and elections, Devolved administrations, Honours system, Local government, Policy making, Politics, Public administration, Regional policy

**Health, well-being and care**
Animal health, Benefits, Care, Cosmetic treatments, Disability, Family planning, Food and drink, Health, Health and social care professionals, Health care, National Health Service (NHS), Nutrition, Safety

**Housing**
Home insurance, Home ownership, Homelessness, Houseboats, Houses in multiple occupation, Housing advice services, Housing finance, Housing repairs and renovation, Housing surveys, Mobile homes, Rented housing, Residential homes, Social housing, Temporary accommodation, Unoccupied property (housing)

**Information and communication**
Communication, Communications industries, Freedom of information, Information and communication technology, Information management, Intellectual property, Intelligence, Library and information services, Media and the press, Privacy and data protection, Public relations

**International affairs and defence**

**Figure 4.7** Display in the *Wordmap* taxonomy

## Summary

- The thesaurus was originally intended as a source of descriptors for indexing documents
- Thesaurus terms can also be used in combination to create more complicated pre-coordinated subject headings
- Such headings can be used to organize physical files if required
- A more recent use of the thesaurus is as a source of subject metadata for digital resources
- A thesaurus can also be used as a search tool
- It can help to formulate and modify searches without being seen by the searcher
- The systematic display of a thesaurus can function as a browse and navigation tool.

## Notes

1 *Library and Information Science Abstracts*, 2005, Issue 11/12.
2 *Library and Information Science Abstracts (online)*, Oxford, Cambridge Scientific Abstracts.

3   Aitchison, J. (comp.) (1989) *International Thesaurus of Refugee Terminology*, London, Nijhoff.

4   Humbul Humanities Hub (www.humbul.ac.uk) is a JISC-funded resource for the UK higher education community. Its purpose is to identify, catalogue and provide access to quality digital resources across humanities disciplines (including archaeology, history of science and humanities computing).

5   Holm, S. (ed.) (2002) *Railway Object Name Thesaurus*, Cambridge, MDA.

6   Getty Vocabulary Program (1998–) *Art and Architecture Thesaurus* (AAT), Los Angeles, J. Paul Getty Trust, Vocabulary Program, www.getty.edu/research/conducting_research/vocabularies/aat/) (accessed October 2005).

# 5 Why use a thesaurus?

In the early development of the thesaurus, when it was essentially still a keyword list, the keywords or terms were usually drawn from the documents to be indexed. Later on this casual approach to term selection and use was abandoned in favour of much more control over the vocabulary. This was because there are some considerable advantages in using a controlled indexing language rather than 'uncontrolled' or **natural language**.

**Natural language indexing** means the selection and assignment of indexing terms, usually taken from the titles or text of the documents themselves, without any reference to a standard list of terms. The indexer chooses whatever seems appropriate for the material in hand (or in automatic indexing systems text analysis software identifies important terms based on their frequency and position, terms in the title or near the beginning of the document scoring more highly than others). Natural language can be seen to have several advantages: it is easy to use; no one has to be trained to use it; no one has to spend time compiling or maintaining an indexing vocabulary; the indexing terms match closely the vocabulary of the subject; new terms will be adopted naturally as they occur in the literature, and out-dated terms will equally naturally fall out of use; and there is reason to believe that the terms will match those chosen by searchers, particularly in technical or research literature.

Nevertheless, these advantages can be more than offset by the disadvantages of natural language use, and the effect it has on the efficiency of retrieval. For most people, the most familiar sort of searching in an uncontrolled environment is internet searching. Although retrieving some information is not difficult, performing an effective search can be tiresome and time-consuming, if not impossible. Usually search engines can only match search terms against the textual content, and all the possible forms and variations of a search term, including variant spellings and synonyms, must be entered individually if every relevant item is to be retrieved.

Added to this problem at the search stage is a comparable problem at the indexing stage, namely a lack of general agreement as to what individual documents might be about. Determining the content of documents (sometimes referred to as the aboutness of an item) is a very subjective process. Unlike the identification of the title, author, or date of publication of an item, about which there is usually general agreement, the identification of the subject is a much less exact science. In the 1960s, the Cranfield Project, the earliest large-scale piece of research into indexing and retrieval, found that consistency was very difficult to achieve. The index terms selected by an indexer for the same document on two different occasions displayed only 60% correspondence between the two sets. The situation was markedly worse when dealing with different indexers' interpretations of the same document, or when dealing with similar but not identical items.

The likelihood of searchers matching their search terms closely with the indexing terms also seems remote, so clearly some steps must be taken to reduce the potential chaos. There are several things that can be done to improve consistency in indexing, and to help achieve closer correspondence between indexing and search terms:

- At the most general level the use of a standard vocabulary will help to encourage uniformity of practice and easier exchange of information.
- The different forms and variants of indexing terms can be managed so that everybody uses the same term for the same idea – this is what is commonly understood by the notion of vocabulary control.
- The relationships between terms can be determined, and cross-references or other navigational aids can be introduced into the vocabulary so that users can identify additional or alternative terms that may have been used.

All these factors will tend to improve retrieval as compared with unmanaged systems. Naturally, there is a price to pay in terms of the construction and maintenance of vocabularies, and the time taken to analyse and index documents, but this is generally accounted worthwhile, particularly in spheres such as academia, research and development, and business. This is true whether the thesaurus is applied manually, or, as is increasingly the case, intellectually built and maintained vocabulary tools support retrieval and some degree of automatic indexing.

# 6 Types of thesaurus

In previous chapters we have looked at some of the different kinds of structure to be found in the thesaurus and related subject tools, and the purposes to which the thesaurus can be put. Other aspects of the thesaurus include the scope and range of the vocabulary, and the sort of material to which it is intended to be applied.

## General and special thesauri
### General thesauri: UNESCO and BSI Root

The thesaurus is unlike the bibliographic classification scheme, and more like contemporary taxonomic tools, in that it is more usually designed for a specific and limited subject field. Whereas several large general classification schemes and subject heading lists exist, there are no completely general thesauri. However, there are a few that cover a wide range of subjects. The two best known of those that are available are the *UNESCO Thesaurus*[1] and the British Standard Institution's *Root Thesaurus*.[2]

Although they are widely regarded as being general in scope, in reality neither deals with the whole of human knowledge in the way that, for example, the *Dewey Decimal Classification* does. The University of London Computing Centre hosts a browsable version of the *UNESCO Thesaurus* at www.ulcc.ac.uk/unesco/, of which it states:

> The *UNESCO Thesaurus* is a controlled vocabulary developed by the United Nations Educational, Scientific and Cultural Organisation which includes subject terms for the following areas of knowledge: education, science, culture, social and human sciences, information and communication, and politics, law and economics. It also includes the names of countries and groupings of countries: political, economic, geographic, ethnic and religious, and linguistic groupings.

This clearly relates to the economic, social, and cultural subjects which are UNESCO's remit. Although the thesaurus does contain some vocabulary for the sciences, this is largely related to economic and social aspects of those subjects, and there is no detailed terminology for, say, technology or the pure sciences.

The BSI *Root Thesaurus* was developed for BSI's in-house indexing of its own standards, and its descriptors are now entered into the BSI database available for online searching for British Standards. The scope of the thesaurus is potentially very broad, but, in practical terms, has something of a bias towards the scientific and technical since those are the subjects in which standards predominate. (There is a standard for making a cup of tea, but more usually standards are concerned with product and quality control in areas such as manufacturing or the construction industry.)

## Broadly based thesauri

There are a number of well known multi-disciplinary thesauri, which, while they do not cover the whole of knowledge, contain vocabulary for a range of different subject areas. Some of these are used by a number of organizations outside their own host institutions. Prominent examples include the *CAB Thesaurus*,[3] produced by CAB Publishing, and *Art and Architecture Thesaurus*,[4] managed by the Getty Institute.

The *CAB Thesaurus* is a substantial thesaurus of nearly 50,000 terms for use with applied life sciences – it covers agriculture, entomology, forestry, horticulture, mycology, nutrition, parasitology, rural studies, soil science and veterinary medicine. Originally developed for the indexing of *CAB Abstracts*, a commercial life sciences database, it's an excellent example of an in-house tool subsequently marketed in its own right. It is also available free of charge to non-commercial institutions such as academic and research organizations.

The *Art and Architecture Thesaurus (AAT)* is probably the most widely known specialist thesaurus, and a model of its kind. Its compilers were instrumental in implementing the principles of facet analysis in thesaurus construction, and for many years the Getty website was an excellent source of information about faceted systems. Sadly, the material about facet analysis has now disappeared from the website.

*AAT* provides a vocabulary of over 125,000 terms for the fine arts, decorative arts, architecture, and what is called material culture. The vocabulary is wider in scope than you might immediately expect because it makes extensive provision for manufactured objects (including such disparate items as transport vehicles and weapons) and materials, as well as for persons, periods, places, general organizational activities, and so on.

Figure 6.1 shows part of a sample record from *AAT* which demonstrates how extremely well organized the vocabulary is, with its detailed definitions, indication of context, and extensive cross-references. This detail is enabled by the strong structural principles of the vocabulary. As well as browsing and searching alphabetically, the user can view the complete **facet hierarchies** in each facet, as in Figure 6.2, which shows the expansion of a small array, or sub-facet, within the facet of objects.

Very similar in nature to *AAT* is the Museum Documentation Association's *Archaeological Objects Thesaurus*,[5] which also provides a rich vocabulary for artefacts and manufactured objects of all kinds, and which is widely used in the UK museums sector. This thesaurus is part of a suite of vocabulary tools in the area of cultural heritage produced by the Museum Documentation Association (MDA). Work by the organization has also produced the *British Museum Materials Thesaurus*,[6] the *British Museum Object Names Thesaurus*,[7] the *Railway Object Name Thesaurus*,[8] and the *Inland Waterways Object Name Thesaurus*.[9]

Another British thesaurus in this category is *HASSET*, *Humanities and Social Science Electronic Thesaurus*,[10] developed by the United Kingdom

---

**ID: 300015613**                                                    **Record Type:** concept

🔺  **graffiti** (<visual works by location or context>, <visual works>, … Visual and Verbal Communication)

**Note:** In archaeology and art history, refers to casual scribbles or pictographs on walls, stones, or other surfaces. In the context of ancient Greek vase painting, graffiti refers to marks incised or cut into the ceramic, usually on the underside of the foot of the vase; they were generally trademarks. In recent times the term is applied to humorous, satiric, obscene, or gang-related writings or drawings executed anonymously in public places.

**Terms:**
    **graffiti** (preferred, C,U,D,American English-P)
    **graffito** (C,U,AD)

**Facet/Hierarchy Code:**  V.VC

**Hierarchical Position:**
  🔺    Objects Facet
  🔺    …. Visual and Verbal Communication
  🔺    …….. Visual Works
  🔺    ……….. <visual works>
  🔺    …………… <visual works by location or context>
  🔺    ………………… graffiti

**Additional Parents:**
  🔺    Objects Facet
  🔺    …. Visual and Verbal Communication

**Figure 6.1**   Individual thesaurus record from *Art and Architecture Thesaurus*® (AAT)
© 2006 J. Paul Getty Trust

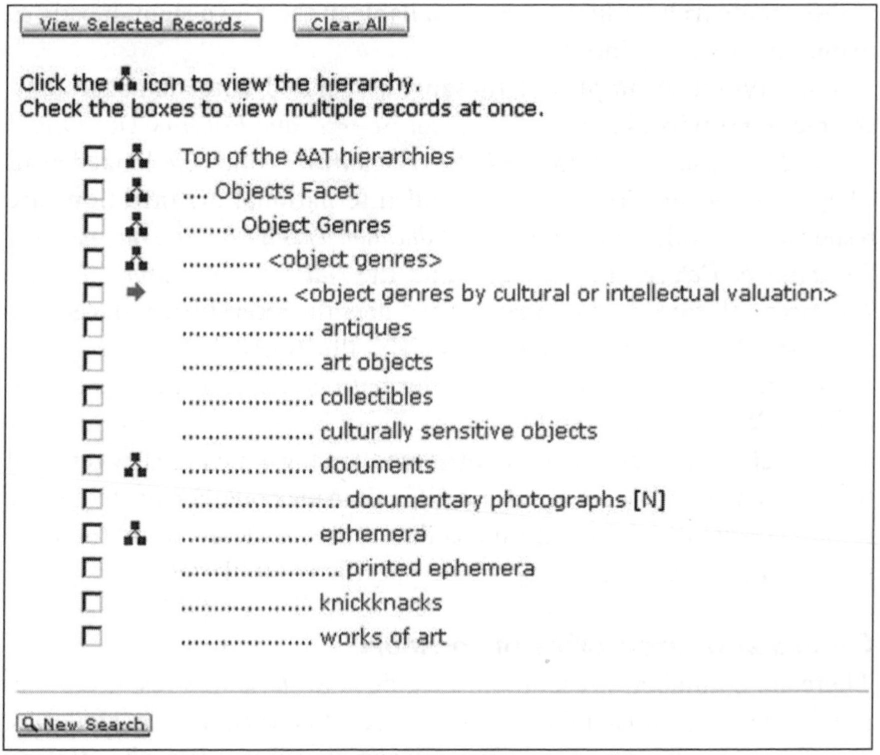

**Figure 6.2** Expansion of an array in *Art and Architecture Thesaurus®* (AAT)
© 2006 J. Paul Getty Trust

Data Archive, and based originally on the *UNESCO Thesaurus*, but maintained and expanded independently over the last twenty years. *HASSET* covers politics, sociology, economics, education, law, crime, demography, health, employment, and technology, but because its primary purpose is to index the datasets deposited with the Archive by various research and government bodies, its vocabulary is related to the subject content of those data. Nevertheless it is a good general purpose tool, and can be acquired at no cost by non-profit organizations.

## Subject specialist thesauri
Despite these broadly based tools, the majority of thesauri deal with much more specific subjects, often because they have been developed in conjunction with a subject specialist collection, or with a subject related publication or service, such as an abstracting or indexing service. Many

of these thesauri have now become available in their own right, mostly as a consequence of online access.

Some typical examples of thesauri associated with databases and abstracting services include the *Aquatic Sciences and Fisheries Thesaurus*,[11] the *NASA Thesaurus*,[12] and the *LISA Thesaurus*,[13] which we looked at in Chapter 4. Government agencies and international organizations are responsible for others; the *European Education Thesaurus*,[14] the *International Thesaurus of Refugee Terminology*,[15] and the *National Agricultural Library Thesaurus*[16] all come into this category, as does the recently introduced UK *Integrated Public Sector Vocabulary* (*IPSV*)[17] illustrated in Figure 6.3.

Locating electronic versions of information retrieval thesauri can be difficult. Web searches tend to return a very large number of results for general reference thesauri of the *Roget* type, among which the few retrieval thesauri can be widely scattered and difficult to pick out. Fortunately, some resources exist which identify and collate retrieval thesauri, and these are particularly useful for finding subject specific vocabularies.

## Guides and directories of thesauri

There are a number of useful online guides to thesaurus resources that provide a listing and a quick means of access to a variety of vocabularies. The Taxonomy Warehouse (www.taxonomywarehouse.com ) has already been mentioned as an excellent online database of terminology tools, and

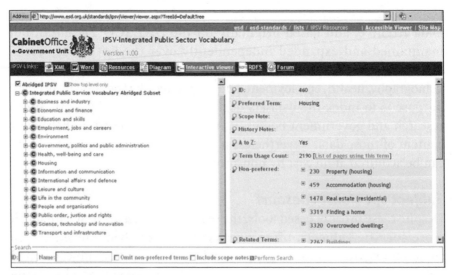

**Figure 6.3**  *Integrated Public Sector Vocabulary*

it is a good starting point for identifying thesauri. Although it fails to distinguish between different sorts of vocabulary, it does provide a basic subject breakdown and allows searching of multiple subject categories. It also gives a brief resumé of subject content attached to each title in the listing and a link to the resource itself. Taxonomy Warehouse is probably the most comprehensive collection of material, with the proviso that many so-called thesauri in its database are not in fact thesauri, and that some examination of individual resources is necessary to locate the legitimate examples.

The *High Level Thesaurus (HILT)* project[18] created a directory of resources which can be found at http://hilt.cdlr.strath.ac.uk/Sources/thesauri.html (*HILT Sources: Thesauri A–Z*). This is an alphabetical list with links to online thesauri and occasional brief notes on some titles. Some of these links are now out of date, but this is nevertheless a splendid collection of some 70 resources, including such gems as the *Access to Asian Vegetables Thesaurus* and *Australian Woman's Weekly Subject Thesaurus*.

Similar in nature, but broader in scope, because it also contains classifications and wordlists, is University of British Columbia's School of Library, Archival and Information Studies' *Indexing Resources on the World Wide Web* at www.slais.ubc.ca/resources/indexing/database1.htm#online. This is a substantial list, but consists only of links with no evaluations. One feature of this list is the number of thesauri of Australian origin that appear in it. The American Society of Indexers has a rather briefer list of online thesauri only at www.asindexing.org/site/thesonet.shtml.

## Thesauri for non-textual resources

It should be evident from several of the titles discussed above that a major application of the thesaurus is to non-text material. In some cases the thesaurus is used in conjunction with a conventional catalogue or database, but the thesaurus is particularly important here as a source of subject metadata. The retrieval of non-text items must require the use of metadata or subject descriptors of some sort since, to date, no search software has been developed which can scan images for content in the way that text can be machine-processed to identify matching character strings. Although there is currently some promising work in that area, for all practical purposes, metadata assigned by human indexers is vital to retrieval of these materials.

*The Art and Architecture Thesaurus* is probably the best known and most widely applied of these vocabularies, and is used for the description of texts, images and objects, for works about art and works of art. For example, the National Art Library uses *AAT* for subject headings for books, but also as a source of terms for physical description and provenance, and for genre. It is also used by a great number of museum libraries for object description as well as for the cataloguing of books, and is suitable for other formats, such as slides.

The *Thesaurus for Graphic Materials (TGM)*, produced by the Library of Congress for their own subject cataloguing of images, is another large vocabulary designed for visual formats. Intended specifically for the Library of Congress collection of prints and photographs, *TGM* is a very suitable extension of the *Library of Congress Subject Headings* for libraries that already use that system. The *TGM* descriptors tend to be simpler than *LCSH* and there is extensive provision for period specification.

A number of resources for the description specifically of objects have already been mentioned, notably the Museum Documentation Association's vocabularies. Regarding other unconventional information formats, *HASSET*'s application to datasets has been noted, and various thesauri have been developed for the indexing of archival and manuscript material, such as *UKAT*, the *United Kingdom Archival Thesaurus*.[19]

The description of works of art and other museum items often requires descriptors for the physical description of the item. As a consequence, thesauri may include non-subject terminology. *The Art and Architecture Thesaurus* contains vocabulary of this kind, as can be seen in the expanded hierarchy for physical condition of objects (Figure 6.4).

In fact, a great number of the descriptors in any thesaurus designed for the description of objects (as opposed to texts or

```
Check the boxes to view multiple records at once.

    □  ⚹   Top of the AAT hierarchies
    □  ⚹   .... Physical Attributes Facet
    □  ➜   ........ Conditions and Effects
    □  ⚹   ........... <conditions and effects>
    □          .............. accretion
    □          .............. blanching
    □          .............. blisters
    □          .............. blur
    □  ⚹   .............. bloom
    □          .............. cleavage
    □          .............. cockle
    □          .............. color shift
    □          .............. corrosion products
    □  ⚹   .............. cracks
    □          .............. creases
    □  ⚹   .............. damage
    □  ⚹   .............. dampness
    □          .............. defects
    □          .............. foxing
    □          .............. mildew
```

**Figure 6.4**   Physical condition descriptors in *Art and Architecture Thesaurus®* (www.getty.edu/vow/AATHierarchy ?find=&logic=AND&note=&subje ctid=300186269) © 2006 J. Paul Getty Trust

images) will be terms relating to physical attributes, such as colour, materials, size, and so on, rather than the subject content terms associated with most indexed items.

## Thesauri for local collections

Despite the current abundance of thesauri of all kinds and for all subjects, in some cases the needs of a local collection will require a far more detailed vocabulary than a broadly based thesaurus can provide. The student thesaurus for bereavement mentioned in Chapter 1 is a good instance of this kind of very specific subject domain where relatively few descriptors exist in a more general tool (the *UNESCO Thesaurus*, for example, contains the term 'death', but not 'bereavement' or 'loss').

In such a situation many indexers will choose (or be forced to choose) to create an in-house tool, tailored to local requirements, and an important function of this book is to meet the needs of information professionals in that situation.

## Summary
- Thesauri exist at different levels of detail and for different purposes
- Thesauri covering all or most subjects comprehensively are rare, although there are several large multi-disciplinary thesauri
- Most thesauri are designed for a specific subject field, and may be associated with bibliographic and current awareness services in that field
- There are a number of online directories of thesauri
- A major use of the thesaurus is for indexing non-text media such as images and museum objects
- Many in-house, unpublished thesauri exist for highly specialized subject-specific collections.

## Notes
1   Aitchison, J. (1977) *UNESCO Thesaurus: a structured list of descriptors for indexing and retrieving literature in the fields of education, science, social science, culture and communication*, Paris, Unesco.
2   BSI (1988) *ROOT Thesaurus*, 3rd edn, Milton Keynes, British Standards Institution, (2 vols).

3  CAB (1999) *CAB Thesaurus*, Wallingford, Oxon, CAB International, www.cabi-publishing.org/DatabaseSearchTools.asp?PID=277 (accessed December 2005).

4  Getty Vocabulary Program (1998–) *Art and Architecture Thesaurus (AAT)*, Los Angeles, J. Paul Getty Trust, Vocabulary Program, www.getty.edu/research/conducting_research/vocabularies/aat.

5  *Archaeological Objects Thesaurus*, www.mda.org.uk/archobj/archcon.htm (accessed December 2005).

6  *British Museum Materials Thesaurus*, www.mda.org.uk/bmmat/matintro.htm (accessed December 2005).

7  *British Museum Object Names Thesaurus*, www.mda.org.uk/bmobj/Objintro.htm (accessed December 2005).

8  Holm, S. (ed.) (2002) *Railway Object Name Thesaurus*, Museum Documentation Association. Railway terminology working group, Cambridge, MDA, www.mda.org.uk/railway/railrefs.htm (accessed December 2005).

9  *Inland Waterways Object Name Thesaurus*, www.mda.org.uk/waterw/intro.htm (accessed December 2005).

10  *HASSET Humanities and Social Science Electronic Thesaurus*, www.data-archive.ac.uk/search/hassetSearch.asp (accessed December 2005).

11  *Aquatic Sciences and Fisheries Thesaurus*, www4.fao.org/asfa/asfa.htm (accessed December 2005).

12  *NASA Thesaurus*, www.sti.nasa.gov/thesfrm1.htm (accessed December 2005).

13  *LISA Thesaurus*, http://md1.csa.com/ids70/thesaurus.php?SID=598423c3 6320bfbbcae930662bc27ddc&tab_collection_id=999 (accessed December 2005).

14  *European Education Thesaurus*, www.eurydice.org/TeeForm/frameset_en.HTM (accessed December 2005).

15  *International Thesaurus of Refugee Terminology*, www.refugeethesaurus.org/content.php/home?expand=2 (accessed December 2005).

16  *National Agricultural Library Thesaurus*, http://agclass.nal.usda.gov/ agt/search.htm (accessed December 2005).

17  *Integrated Public Sector Vocabulary*, www.esd.org.uk/standards/ipsv/ (accessed December 2005).

18  *High Level Thesaurus* project, http://hilt.cdlr.strath.ac.uk/ (accessed December 2005).

19  *United Kingdom Archival Thesaurus (UKAT)*, www.ukat.org.uk/ (accessed December 2005).

# 7 The format of a thesaurus

As we have already seen in the introduction and in the examples, a thesaurus can take a number of forms, from a simple keyword list to a fully integrated systematic and alphabetic display with all the detailed relationships between terms carefully worked out. Although the simple keyword list may still be sufficient for a very small document collection, in the majority of cases the needs of users are better served by having a properly constructed system, based on logical principles, since this is in the long run easier to update and maintain, and is more compatible with the machine management of the thesaurus.

In this chapter we shall consider the various parts of the thesaurus as it is laid out on the page or screen. You should remember that although there are various national and international standards for thesaurus construction, these differ in some respects, and in practice, individual thesauri may use a local style different from any format proposed in the standards.

Most modern thesauri consist of two elements: a systematic structure where the relationships between terms can be seen in a visual display; and the alphabetical display, where the terms are listed in A–Z order, each with cross-references to other terms related in some way.

## The systematic display

The systematic display is sometimes not given prominence in the published tool, and in older thesauri it may provide no more than a summarization of the topics covered. Nevertheless, it can play a vital part in designing the thesaurus and establishing relationships. A browsing tool of this sort can also be of great use to the indexer (and also to the end-users, although they are less likely to be aware of it) in providing a map of the subject. The capacity to scan the broad subject structure, to see which subjects are represented, and to select appropriate descriptors, can often be more easily achieved in a systematic display than in the distributed vocabulary of the A–Z list.

For example, in the section for dentistry in a hypothetical medical thesaurus, part of the systematic display might look like this:

```
AB              Teeth
                    (Parts of teeth)
AB2                 Crown
AB3                 Root
AB4                 Enamel
                (Kinds of teeth)
AB5                 Incisors
AB6                 Canines
AB7                 Molars


AC              Dental processes
AC1                 Growth
AC2                     Eruption
AC3                 Disease
AC4                     Decay
AC5                         Cavities


AD              Dental techniques
AD1                 Cleaning
AD2                 Filling. Repair
AD3                 Extraction
```

The systematic display brings together a number of terms which are widely scattered in the A–Z format (teeth, dental techniques, crown, extraction, etc.), and also gives a sense of the number and range of terms in the vocabulary which are available for indexing in this particular subject area.

## The alphabetic display

The alphabetic list of terms presents the same entry terms in an alternative format, and, because terms from the same subject area are necessarily dispersed, it relies on cross-referencing to identify them. Here is a part of the above systematic display shown in a typical A–Z format:

```
Canines      AB6
     BT    Teeth
     RT    Incisors
     RT    Molars

Cavities     AC5
     BT    Decay

Cleaning     AD1
     BT    Dental techniques
     RT    Extraction
     RT    Filling

Crown        AB2
     BT    Teeth
     RT    Enamel
     RT    Root

Decay        AC4
     BT    Disease
     NT    Cavities
```

You can probably see that for each entry only a few other terms in the same subject area are apparent through the cross-references. These are the ones most closely related to the entry term. The complete range of the vocabulary can only be established by a series of steps following the cross-references and subsequent cross-references, and so on. The relationships between a term and others more distantly related are not as clear as in the systematic display.

In online thesauri, it is often even more difficult to obtain an overview of the vocabulary from the alphabetic display, since the entry for only one term may be visible at a time. These examples from the *Finnish/English Agriforest Thesaurus*, maintained at the University of Helsinki, show how the sense of context can easily disappear in the A–Z display:

**trooppiset metsät**
eng (Agrovoc):
    tropical forests
eng:
    tropical forests

> tropical woodlands

Broader terms:

> metsät

See also:

> sademetsät

**vanhat metsät**

eng (Agrovoc):

> virgin forests

Broader terms:

> metsät

See also:

> aarnialueet
> aarnimetsät
> luonnonmetsät

**vajaatuottoiset metsät**

eng:

> low-yielding forests
> under-productive forests

## Interdependence of the systematic and alphabetic display

Although generally speaking the alphabetic display of the thesaurus is more dominant, the systematic display is vital to the construction of the system. The relationships between terms which are implicit in the A–Z format are explicit in the structural display, and it is from the latter that the relationships are most easily determined.

In early forms of the thesaurus, the systematic display did not always contain all the terms of the A–Z format. In effect, it was a brief overview of the subject content. However, in the modern thesaurus there is (or should be) a more exact correspondence between the terms in the two aspects of the vocabulary.

## Summary

- Most thesauri consists of two elements: a systematic display and an alphabetical display
- The systematic display shows the relationships between terms and can be used as a browsing tool for the vocabulary

- The alphabetical display lists the terms in A–Z order and uses cross-references to indicate related terms
- In a properly constructed thesaurus the alphabetical and systematic displays are closely related, and the former may be derived from the latter.

## Elements in the display

The standard thesaurus format uses a number of different conventions for the layout and display of the entry terms. These may vary in individual thesauri, and electronic thesauri in particular may not show all of these features. We will begin with the alphabetical display.

### Entry terms

The alphabetical display essentially consists of a number of terms, each accompanied by various notes and cross-references arranged in alphabetical order. A typical entry may look something like this:

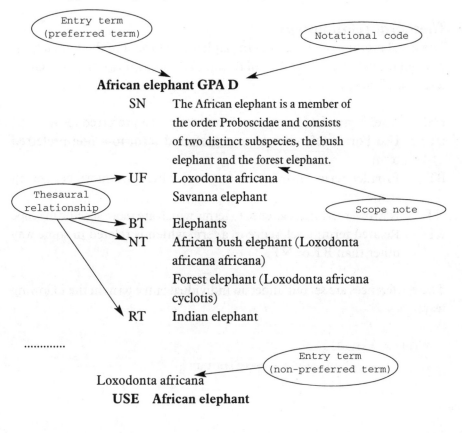

Although in a controlled vocabulary a restricted number of terms are being used for indexing, there will still be a number of non-valid or non-preferred terms retained because users will search for them. In the example above, a zoologist might search under Loxodonta africana, so one would want to keep that term in the list, despite it not being used in indexing. It is common to make some typographical distinction between the preferred terms and the non-preferred terms. The elephant example has the preferred term in bold, and there is a corresponding entry in non-bold type:

Loxodonta africana
    **USE**    **African elephant**

Other methods of doing this are quite common, and include using italics, upper and lower case, or an alternative font. In electronic thesauri, different colours are sometimes used. The object is to provide a quick visual guide to the preferred terms by making them stand out in some way.

## Thesaural relationships

The usual method of navigating the alphabetic format of the thesaurus is through the use of a standard set of thesaural relationships, or types of cross-reference. These are:

USE    A reference from a non-preferred term to a preferred term
UF     Use For: a reference from a preferred term to a non-preferred term
BT     Broader term: a reference to terms which are more general in scope
NT    Narrower term: a reference to terms which are more specific in scope
RT    Related term: a reference to a term which is related in some way other than BT or NT

These references are set out under an individual entry term in the following way:

```
Yellow armadillos
     UF     Euphractus sexcinctus
```

```
BT    Armadillos
RT    Great long-nosed armadillos
RT    Hairy armadillos
RT    Nine-banded armadillos
RT    South American armadillos
```

The thesaural relationships are always shown in the same order.

The first set of relationships (USE and UF) are concerned with vocabulary control, and the others (BT and NT and sometimes RT) refer to the hierarchical relationships in the thesaurus. RT is also used to accommodate other sorts of relationship. If there is more than one term in each category, they are listed individually, and in alphabetical order, as you can see in the list of RTs to the Yellow armadillos above. How the thesaural relationships are decided on, and the rules affecting their use, are discussed in more detail in Chapter 13.

## Scope notes

**Scope notes** may be added to a term when the meaning of the term is ambiguous or unclear, or there are potential problems with the way in which it may be applied. Sometimes it is no more than a definition of the term, but it may also include instructions or examples. The scope note is in some sense equivalent to the caption in a classification scheme. The *UNESCO Thesaurus* provides a nice example of a 'definition' type scope note:

```
Cultural property preservation
     SN   Refers to the conservation, preservation and
          restoration of cultural property, as well as
          its protection against vandalism, theft and
          removal from the country of origin.
```

## Notational codes

The terms in a thesaurus may have some sort of notation attached. This may be no more than an ordering device (to generate the systematic order if the vocabulary is maintained as a database), or it may be that the vocabulary is also used as a classification system.

In this example from the *DHSS Thesaurus*, the thesaurus is derived from the faceted BC2 classification of health sciences used to arrange the collection, and the classmarks are included in the A–Z display, as shown here:

**BRAIN INJURIES**
> HUY MX
> RT   Brain
> > Brain diseases


**BRAIN STEM**
> HVA T
> BT   Brain
> NT   Medulla oblongata

## Node labels

**Node labels** may appear in the systematic display of the thesaurus. They are not themselves terms but rather indicate the way in which terms have been organized. They are essentially structural signposts. In classification schemes they are usually called characteristics, or principles, of division, since they express those common characteristic of terms which have been used to group them. They are very typical of faceted structures, and are much more likely to be found in that kind of tool. Here is an example from the *The Art and Architecture Thesaurus*:

> Physical attributes facet
> > Color
> > > colors
> > > > <color types>
> > > > > complementary colors
> > > > > cool colors
> > > > > primary colors
> > > > > secondary colors
> > > > > tertiary colors
> > > > > warm colors

The entry <color types> is a node label and not a term proper. It should not be used in indexing, and is only there to show you the principle or characteristic on which the terms have been brought together. Its lack of status as an indexing term is shown by the angle brackets. Brackets are commonly used to indicate that a term should not be used, but they may be round or square instead.

## Summary

- The thesaurus uses a number of standard conventions for display
- Terms used for indexing are usually distinguished typographically from non-indexing terms; the use of upper and lower case, italics and bold text are all common
- A standard set of five thesaural relationships is common; these deal with vocabulary control and relationships to other terms
- Scope notes are used to define or explain terms, and to give instructions
- Some thesauri include a coding system for terms which controls the order of terms in the systematic display
- Node labels are used to indicate ways in which the systematic display has been structured; these are not to be used in indexing, and they are usually enclosed in brackets of some kind.

# 8  Building a thesaurus 1: vocabulary collection

Having decided that you need to build your own thesaurus, the first stage in the process is to gather the vocabulary. There are several ways in which you can do this, and which method you choose may depend on the use to which the thesaurus will be put. Further on in this chapter we will look at the factors that may affect this decision. You do need to keep in mind the fact that the thesaurus will be used for indexing, object description, or document management of some sort, and not for making a theoretical study of the subject itself. You should therefore always consider whether individual terms are useful for the purpose of information retrieval, and whether they correspond to the material to be organized.

There are a number of potential sources that can be mined for terms. They fall into two groups: sources of actual terms and sources of document titles. Collecting document titles is an essential part of assembling vocabulary, but some additional work will be required to derive terms from the titles.

## Existing vocabularies

The most obvious and most accessible source of terminology will be published vocabulary tools. These can be divided into two categories:

- vocabularies for indexing and information retrieval
- dictionaries, glossaries and word lists for study and reference.

The first category includes such things as classification schemes, subject heading lists, keyword lists, taxonomies and other thesauri – in fact, all the kinds of tools we considered in Chapter 3. These have the advantage that the terms in the vocabulary will be intended for document (or object) description, so that they will be of the kind and form that are required for a thesaurus. Vocabularies may also give a sense of the structure of the subject. The disadvantage, particularly for technical subjects, is that the meaning of terms may not be provided.

The second group embraces general and subject specialist encyclopaedias, and subject-specific dictionaries, glossaries and word lists intended for use in subject work. These tools have the advantage that the terms are accompanied by definitions which may be necessary at the stage of analysing and organizing the vocabulary. They can also be very helpful in establishing the structure of a subject and giving some indication of the relationship between terms. The disadvantage is that a proportion of the terms may be very theoretical or abstract in nature, and not represented in the literature, whereas others may be too specific to be the subject of documents. While the reference terminology gives you a very good overview and map of the *subject*, this may not correspond exactly to the literature itself.

For example, the *Concise Oxford Dictionary of Art and Artists*[1] contains terms such as:

Brush
Dipper
Emulsion
Linseed oil
Turpentine

While these terms need to be understood by students of art, they are not very likely to appear as the subjects of books or articles, and are therefore unlikely to be needed as indexing terms.

## Encyclopaedias and reference sources

If the work is in the form of a straightforward alphabetical list of terms this makes the process of extracting the terms, somewhat easier. Articles in an encyclopaedia or authoritative textbook will require more work in identifying the necessary terms where these are embedded in continuous text. Nevertheless, the general encyclopaedia (such as *Encyclopaedia Britannica*) is usually readily accessible, and is a good starting point for the investigation of a subject and its key concepts. Subject specialist encyclopaedias and reference works (including authoritative monographs) will normally provide a fuller and more detailed vocabulary. In a subject-specific work, the index can also be a useful source of important concepts. I would recommend that you use a reliable tool of this kind if you are dealing with a subject you know little about as it is invaluable in providing a map of the country.

## Dictionaries, glossaries and word lists

An alphabetical list of terms with brief definitions is one of the most useful sources of vocabulary and provides an uncomplicated method of collecting terms for a thesaurus. General dictionaries and thesauri are not particularly useful for the purpose, since the proportion of relevant terms will be small and there is no obvious easy means of extracting them from the text. On the other hand, a specialist dictionary or word list is an excellent source, and can also serve as a checklist for the vocabulary of the subject. In constructing a subject-specific thesaurus it is in any case essential to provide yourself with a good dictionary of the subject so that the precise meanings and relationships of terms can be checked against a reliable authority.

A one-volume dictionary (or concise encyclopaedia since often they are indistinguishable) is probably the single most useful item to have to hand when building any controlled vocabulary. There are several series of inexpensive subject dictionaries available (the Penguin dictionaries and the Oxford series are two excellent examples), and they cover most traditional academic disciplines and a number of more practical and general interest topics. Oxford and Penguin, for example, include such subjects as building, folklore, business, world religions, accounting, the theatre, and American political slang, as well the more usual subjects like art history, astronomy, biology, geology, mathematics, music and philosophy. Acquiring such a dictionary should be one of the first things you do, as it will prove invaluable as a source of terms, a provider of definitions, and a checklist for other authorities.

## Summary

- Published vocabularies provide a good starting point for building a thesaurus
- Indexing languages, such as classification schemes or other thesauri, are an easy way to locate terms in a subject, but they usually do not provide definitions
- Dictionaries and encyclopaedias are more useful, particularly in technical subjects, for the additional information they contain
- Care should be taken to distinguish between terms that are likely to be needed for indexing documents and those that are unlikely to occur as the subject of publications
- A good subject-specific dictionary or one-volume encyclopaedia is an essential tool in compiling a thesaurus.

## Published literature

The second, but perhaps more important, source of terms for a thesaurus is the literature itself. I've considered above the difference between the terms used to describe and to study a subject and those occurring in the literature, and it is vital to look at current publications to establish the terminology that is actually in use. Again, a number of sources are potentially helpful:

- published bibliographies, both general and subject-specific
- current awareness services
- journal indexes and abstracting services.

### Currency of terminology

Currency of terminology is a compelling reason for considering the literature. Authoritative works of reference may be some time in the creation, and in fast-moving fields the newest terminology may not be picked up for some time. This is less of a problem now that so many sources are online, but nothing will be more up to date in terms of potential indexing vocabulary than the latest issue of an abstracting or current awareness service.

### Level of detail

It is important to think too about the level of material for which the thesaurus will be used. If only monographs need to be indexed, then the journal literature might not need to be considered. A factor to take into account here is the increasing level of specificity of subjects. It is generally accepted that the level of subject specificity in monographs is only a few years behind that of the journal literature. In other words, the subjects of journal articles will be found to be the subjects of monographs some five to ten years later, depending on the subject. In areas where the rate of growth of knowledge is very rapid (e.g. in the physical sciences, or in communication technologies) this period can be even shorter. For a thesaurus of any technical or scientific subject it is really essential to analyse the topics represented in the relevant periodicals. Even if you are quite clear that you only want to index monographs, including the journal literature now will keep your thesaurus up to date for several years to come, and avoid the need for revision, at least in the short term.

## Where to look

A number of sources can be used to identify recent book publications in a subject:

- the *British National Bibliography* (or other appropriate national bibliography)
- online catalogues of copyright deposit libraries
- online catalogues of specialist collections in the subject
- publishers' catalogues
- subject specialist bibliographies.

When collecting book titles for the library and information thesaurus shown in Figure 2.2 (see p. 5) , I used the catalogues of the Library of Congress, COPAC (the merged catalogues of 24 British university and research libraries plus the British Library and national libraries of Scotland and Wales) and the catalogues of several specialist LIS publishers.

Locating relevant titles in a general resource such as COPAC is obviously more difficult than looking at a collection of items in a specialist publisher's catalogue. You will need some keywords with which to start searching and this can present problems in an unfamiliar field. Searching by classmarks, where this is possible, or by subject heading can be a useful way into the collection. Once you have found a few titles the keywords in those items can form the basis of further searches. In online catalogues you can often use hypertext to access, for example, all the records with a particular subject heading or from a particular publisher.

If you are lucky enough to have a relevant specialist collection to search, it can be much simpler to search by date of publication, bringing up just the most recent acquisitions. Of course it is not essential to be comprehensive in your searching; the idea is to get a representative sample of terms in the subject, and the gaps can be filled in at a later stage.

If you are building a thesaurus for a very specific subject (railway objects for example, or Asian vegetables), you will almost certainly have to look at journal articles to find the level of detail that you need, as books are most likely to deal with the subject generally rather than more detailed topics within it. The journal literature has its own sources, although many of these are not as accessible as those for book titles:

- citation indexes
- bibliographic databases
- specialist abstracting and indexing services

- comprehensive subject services
- electronic journals.

Most resources of this kind are subscription only, and are not available to everyone. Nevertheless, in a specialist resource you are more likely to have a subscription to a relevant service. If not, the UK academic community has access to Zetoc, the electronic contents database of the British Library, which gives citations only (no abstracts or annotations) for the contents of journals taken by the library. I find this an invaluable resource for gathering titles in all sorts of areas, and it has the great advantage that, being multi-disciplinary, it will deliver material from all kinds of publication that you might never have thought to look at. If your subject is cross-disciplinary, it is a huge time saver to be able to search a database of this kind.

If your organization subscribes to electronic journals, these are eminently searchable. Often the contents pages are available to non-subscribers through publishers' websites, and although working through these is a slower process than searching a database, they are another useful resource. Some publishers provide a free cross-journal search facility.

### Websites and other online material

If you are going to index general web resources (as opposed to academic material published commercially on the web), it is sensible to get a feel for the level and nature of websites as well. This is also one means of accessing journal and conference literature where this has been posted on to free access sites.

Using a search engine is not especially effective because of the millions of results that will be returned for any moderately general subject search. That said, they are improving, and a good engine will probably give you the best subject-related directories and portals on the first page or so. Google Scholar (www.scholar.google.com) is useful for finding books and articles on very specific topics, and can give results comparable with searching COPAC and Zetoc.

Making use of managed resources, such as those of the Resource Discovery Network (www.rdn.ac.uk), is a quick method of finding subject directories and portals which will offer up a variety of quality digital resources related to your subject. Contents of these collections of resources are often patchy in terms of the subject coverage but nonetheless useful for indicating what *is* to be found.

## Summary

- It is essential to consider the published literature as a source of subject terms
- The level of detail required can best be judged in this way, as can terminology in current use
- Specialist publishers' catalogues, bibliographies, databases, and online catalogues are all excellent resources for this
- Broad subject searches will provide entry into the literature
- Keywords from retrieved items can then be used as the basis of more specific searches
- If the subject of the thesaurus is very specific, the journal literature should form part of the search
- Websites should be used if the thesaurus is to be applied to digital resources
- Managed resources, such as portals and gateways, are often easier to use for this purpose than search engines.

## Other sources of vocabulary

To these two most important sources of vocabulary I should like to add two lesser but significant ones:

- expert opinion
- your own collection.

Expert opinion can be a useful supplement to published sources when the exact meaning of a term, its relationship to another term, or its possible interpretations need clarifying. Local expertise can also be invaluable when building a thesaurus for a very specific topic not well covered by published resources. Exercises such as the group building of concept maps can be very important, particularly if they involve both those who are going to organize the subject-related material and those who will use the collection. Knowledge of the terminology that occurs in the literature, the identification of sought terms, and the way in which the subject structure is perceived by end-users are important factors. There are situations where such a map has been used as the basis of a browsing tool for a local intranet, although I consider that creating a properly structured thesaurus for anything other than a very small vocabulary requires more formal and more rigorous methods. Nevertheless this is a very good means of collecting highly specialized vocabulary for unusual subjects.

Similarly, a collection of resources related to an unusual subject can itself provide terms that will not easily be found elsewhere. If the thesaurus is going to be used to index that collection, then extracting terms from the items in the collection itself is a highly efficient way to proceed.

If a thesaurus is being constructed for a collection of objects, say, for a museum, then a rather different approach to the collection of terms must be adopted. A more conceptual approach is necessary, since compilers must themselves determine the names and attributes of the objects that will be required in indexing, rather than deriving them from some external source. For example, if you want to create a thesaurus to describe a collection of jewellery then you will need descriptors relating to:

- metals and other materials
- gemstones
- beads
- shapes, including styles of gem cutting
- types of composite arrangement of components
- function of the piece (bracelet, cuff-links, etc.)
- terms relating to provenance (when created, and where)
- artistic style
- individual jewellers
- terms relating to physical condition
- contextual data (history of the piece, ownership, etc.).

You will probably not need terms relating to techniques, equipment, or activities such as mining of metals or gems, artificial gem manufacture, marketing, and so on.

Publication in the subject may not be of great help in this situation, although it can be used as far as physical objects and their description are reflected in the literature. Published vocabularies may be more useful, although they too are likely to exceed the range of terms required. The collection of terms is therefore a more abstract and a more contained exercise, and must to a great degree be based on the collection itself.

## Summary

- Personal knowledge of the subject (i.e. of those involved with it) can be an additional source of information

- Team exercises, such as the building of concept maps, can be a good way to manage this
- Documents in the collection that the thesaurus will be used with should be considered; in a small, specialist collection they may be the only source required
- If objects rather than documents are to be described, a careful conceptual analysis of their attributes must be carried out.

## Thesauri for local and general use

At this stage you may have collected terms from published vocabularies, classifications, thesauri, dictionaries and encyclopaedias, reference works, bibliographies, databases, search engines, portals, expert individuals, and your own collection. The number of terms is getting larger, and you begin to wonder how far this needs go. To what extent do you need to pursue this task with a view to comprehensive coverage?

This depends to a large extent on the expected use of the thesaurus. If it is meant only for your local collection, then it is perfectly possible to build a thesaurus using only those terms encountered in that set of resources. You can easily add new terms when they occur, and if the thesaurus is properly constructed this is a very straightforward process.

If the thesaurus is going to be used by other organizations, or for collections that you have not seen, it is more important that it is comprehensive in an absolute sense. You need to make an effort to represent the whole terminology of the subject in the thesaurus, and therefore to be more wide-ranging in the sources you search.

Having said that, it is not necessary to begin the process of constructing the thesaurus with the complete terminology to hand. In some respects it is easier to take a smaller list of terms (provided that it is representative) and, having established the general structure, to add extra terms as appropriate. For instance, if you notice that names of places often occur in the titles you are collecting, it is not necessary to search for these in the literature. There are plenty of lists of names of countries that you can use to expand that section of the thesaurus. The same would be true of names of plants and animals, diseases, parts of the body, chemical compounds, and so on.

A collection of between 100 and 500 terms is a good number from which to start building the thesaurus. Fewer than this may not ensure that all the aspects of the subject are covered. A great many more and the process of analysis is made more difficult since it is hard to keep the whole thing in mind at any one time. When the broad structure is in place, extra terms can be imported as needed.

## A model thesaurus

From this point on, I shall be using a model thesaurus to demonstrate the process of construction, and as a basis for discussion of the underlying theory. I use the term 'model' in the sense of a sample, rather than as an ideal of any sort. Thesaurus construction is not an exact science, and interpretations of the meanings of terms and their relationships with each other may vary from one person to another. There is also always some manual editing of the thesaurus to be done (because of the difficulty and complexity of language, rather than because the method is faulty) and the way this is carried out is also to some extent subjective. The model is therefore intended as a guide to the reader, rather than a study in perfection.

I have chosen the subject of animal welfare as the demonstration topic. It is quite difficult to decide on anything which is not, at least in part, atypical of the subjects that practitioners will tackle, but this topic has some features that are advantageous in a demonstration context:

- It is cross-disciplinary.
- It includes both scientific terminology and social scientific aspects.
- The greater part of the vocabulary is non-technical, and hence accessible to the non-specialist.
- The literature is international and reflects differences in culture and terminology in different places.
- There are problems of vocabulary control related to the use of names.
- There are sufficient difficulties in analysing and managing the terms to demonstrate commonly occurring problems.
- It is not so difficult that the reader will be discouraged.

Unfortunately, there is no single terminological resource (a dictionary or encyclopaedia) for animal welfare, so I was not able to use this as a starting point. When definitions and spellings need to be checked, a range of resources for animal science, zoology, veterinary medicine, and so on, will be used.

I therefore began by examining the literature itself. Collecting titles of current documents, whether these are books or journals, or in print or electronic format, is probably the most important way of assembling a vocabulary that is current, relevant, and representative of the material to be indexed. With the sorts of resource indicated above in mind, I began by searching some catalogues and databases, and other online resources for the titles of documents in the field. I searched for books, journals and websites, beginning with the following resources:

- COPAC (www.copac.ac.uk)
- the Library of Congress catalogue (www.loc.gov)
- the Royal Veterinary College catalogue (http://library.rvc.ac.uk/uhtbin/ cgisirsi.exe/E8csbmuzWG/0/57/49)
- Zetoc (http://zetoc.mimas.ac.uk/)
- Resource Discovery Network (www.rdn.ac.uk).

Although I found a number of book titles using the first two resources, they were of a very general nature and did not provide any very detailed or specific terms. The catalogue of the Royal Veterinary College provided more detailed terminology (although many of its titles were still very general) and report literature, and UK and European legislation were well represented here.

Zetoc allowed me to search the journal literature. Having run a general journal search using the subject heading 'Animal welfare', I identified three journals (*Animal Welfare, Animal Technology and Welfare* and *Animals and Society*), which I then searched systematically.

The Resource Discovery Network led me to the biomedicine gateway, Biome (www.biome.ac.uk/), and thence to Agrifor (http://agrifor.ac.uk/about/), a portal for resources in agriculture, food and forestry. Among its contents I found a bibliography of alternative farming from the Animal Welfare Institute of the USA (www.awionline.org) (itself an excellent source of information), which provided a number of websites.

In the end, I selected titles from among 200 journal articles, 100 book titles from the Royal Veterinary College, and from the online bibliography of websites. The material fell into six main groups:

- ethical and philosophical aspects of animal welfare
- welfare of farm animals
- welfare of laboratory animals
- welfare of animals in the wild
- welfare of zoo animals
- welfare of working animals.

As I worked through the titles I was looking for those rich in terminology with combinations of a variety of different concepts. I discarded items of a very general nature, and inevitably, as the list grew, I did not bother to include items that duplicated terms I already had. The list is intended to provide as broad a vocabulary as possible, and the selection of items is made with that in mind. The final list appears in the Appendix 1.

I should add a warning about the use of document titles in some subjects, particularly arts and humanities. When compared to the sciences and social sciences, titles of documents in these disciplines often do not accurately describe the subject contents. While the literature of the subject should still be examined, it may be necessary to pose the question 'what is this document about?' rather than 'what does the title say it's about?', and make some more detailed investigation of the contents.

At this stage I prefer to work in a text or word file that can be printed out so that the whole vocabulary can be seen and compared at the same time. Trying to analyse terms on screen can sometimes be very time-consuming and frustrating. Later on the whole thing can be input to a database but at this early stage, before the structure is decided, it is much more straightforward to look at the vocabulary as a whole.

## Deconstructing the vocabulary

The first stage in building the thesaurus is to list the terms that will appear in the thesaurus. Where vocabularies have been used as a source, the terms will already be in an appropriate form, but where titles have been harvested, there is a need to reduce the titles, phrases, compounds and so on, which you have extracted from your various sources, to a list of relatively simple concepts.

Before we start to do this with our selection of titles, it will useful to look at some of the general rules that affect the form and structure of thesaurus terms, and the next two chapters are concerned with this.

## Note

1 Chilvers, I. (ed.) (1996) *Concise Oxford Dictionary of Art and Artists*, 2nd edn, Oxford, Oxford University Press.

# 9 Vocabulary control I: selection of terms

In the preliminary stages in the construction of the thesaurus you have begun to assemble your vocabulary and you will have a number of terms. If you have followed the methods of vocabulary collection described, these have come from a number of different sources, and the style and form of the terms may vary quite a lot. The vocabulary is only at the first stage of being properly managed, and you should start to work towards a fuller level of standardization.

Creating a list of standard terms (that is, a vocabulary) for indexing requires the compiler to do several things:

- reduce the number of terms overall, by abandoning natural language in favour of a limited set of terms
- when terms are similar in meaning, decide on which of them should be used
- when terms have different spellings, decide on which should be used
- decide on the exact form of the entry term, for example whether it should be plural or singular, and how punctuation should be employed
- decide about the handling of compound terms, for example when and how words should be combined to make multi-word terms and phrases, and word order.

This process is even more important when any degree of automation is involved, since the search software will demand (nearly) exact matching between indexing and search terms if retrieval is to occur at all. Although the development of **fuzzy searching** systems allows some variation in terms (such as a mistyped letter), the form of terms still needs to be very close to the original to get a result.

All of the above actions together constitute what is known as **vocabulary control**. You will see that there are two main aspects of this process:

- the selection of terms
- deciding on the exact form of terms.

## The selection of terms
### Synonym control: preferred and non-preferred terms

**Synonymy**, that is the occurrence of a number of different words for the same idea, creates considerable problems for the online searcher. In a system such as a classification scheme, where notational codes are used to represent concepts, the existence of different names for the same idea doesn't present a problem, since the notation equates to as many words as necessary and acts as a kind of shorthand for the concept. However, where words themselves are used for indexing and retrieval, the many-to-one relationship of the words to the concept causes a difficulty.

For example, when searching in an uncontrolled environment, such as the world wide web, for the topic 'Religion', one must also make separate searches for terms such as 'religious systems', 'religious groups', 'religions', 'beliefs', 'belief systems', 'faiths', 'faith groups', 'minorities', as well as the names of individual groups. To further complicate the situation, as recently as July 2005 a new term 'communities' has entered the common word stock as a synonym for groups identified by religious or cultural beliefs.

In a managed environment, life is made much easier if we all agree to use only one term to represent the concept. Such an agreed term is called a **preferred term**. The terms that have been rejected as indexing terms are known as **non-preferred terms**. The relationship between these is sometimes referred to as an **equivalence relationship**. In the example above, we might decide on 'Religions' as our preferred term, and this will then be used as the descriptor for any document where terms such as religion, faiths, religious groups, religious minorities, and so on, are used.

This process of synonym control is absolutely vital in English language thesauri because English is a language particularly rich in synonyms, but it will be necessary in other natural languages as well.

### Near synonyms and quasi-synonyms

Sometimes, when words are not exact synonyms, but, to all intents and purposes, they are used interchangeably, the same control can be imposed on them. A good example of this occurs with the terms 'United Kingdom' and 'Great Britain' used to denote the United Kingdom of Great Britain and Northern Ireland. Although the definitions of United Kingdom, Britain, Great Britain and the British Isles all differ slightly, for general purposes one of them could be preferred for indexing purposes.

Whether a decision of this kind is valid can depend on the circumstances. For example, the *Library of Congress Subject Headings* at one time had a heading 'Theological education', which it treated as a synonym of 'Religious education'. In the British situation I think these two would not be regarded as synonymous, since 'Religious education' is the term used for that subject in school, whereas 'Theological education' suggests training for the church, and is very unlikely to be applied to a school situation. In the same way, the United Kingdom example would be acceptable in a general thesaurus, but not in one dealing with politics or law, where the differences between the terms are significant.

### Guidelines for selecting preferred terms

While they should not be regarded as absolutely binding, there are some general conventions in the choice of preferred terms. Some of these are based on the earliest work on subject indexing, Cutter's *Rules for a Dictionary Catalog*,[1] which formulated the early theory of subject description, and established an approach which is still used today in the catalogues of the Library of Congress, and many other important subject indexes.

You may not agree with all of Cutter's decisions, but the problems associated with the choice of headings that he identifies are all important, and it's necessary to give some thought to the options available. Cutter's rules stress the following:

- 'Everyday', non-technical, forms of words should be chosen
- Established use should provide a guide
- Bias in the terminology should be avoided
- Obsolete terms should not be used
- Foreign words (or **loan terms**) should not be used, except where there is no English equivalent.

Cutter was formulating his rules for the situation of the general (i.e. non-specialist) reader, so he had a strong tendency towards non-technical language, and towards the sorts of search term that would occur naturally to the average person. In a specialist organization the reverse might be the case; for example, a botanist might prefer the use of Latin names for plants, since that would be more accurate and avoid ambiguity. Similarly, one can envisage situations where obsolete terminology is inappropriate or dangerous (gender studies, race relations, brain surgery) and others where it is entirely suitable (mediaeval architecture, history of science). Nevertheless, these are useful principles to consider and a thesaurus needs to have a consistent policy on the style of terms chosen. For example:

## Technical terms

| | | |
|---|---|---|
| Robin | or | Erithacus Rubecula |
| Thigh bone | or | Femur |
| Aspirin | or | Acetylsalicylic acid |

## Outdated or historical terms

| | | |
|---|---|---|
| Black death | or | Bubonic plague |
| Alsatian dog | or | German shepherd dog |
| Burkina Faso | or | Upper Volta |
| Mercury | or | Quicksilver |

## National variations in words

| | | |
|---|---|---|
| Gasoline | or | Petroleum |
| Fenders | or | Bumpers |
| Hogs | or | Pigs |
| Byres | or | Barns |
| Brumbies | or | Wild horses |

## Foreign words

| | | |
|---|---|---|
| Angst | or | Anxiety |
| Glasnost | or | Openness |

Having a clear policy allows users to have certain expectations about which of possible alternative terms will be chosen. The use of a consistent pattern or style improves the **predictability** of the thesaurus, which in turn improves retrieval.

## Summary

* Synonyms must be controlled to improve the effectiveness of indexing and retrieval
* This is a particular problem for the English language

- For practical purposes words which are very similar in meaning (near synonyms) can be regarded as synonyms
- A choice should be made where there are, for example, scientific and everyday terms, or variants in different forms of English
- Decisions must also be made about the inclusion of foreign words, or historical and older terms
- These policies should be applied consistently.

## Names
### Personal names

You will probably have noticed that some of the examples above are names. What to do about variant forms of names is a particular problem for indexers. Personal names present fewer difficulties (unless titles are involved) since usually an individual has only one name. There are many accessible **name authorities** that can be referred to for guidance – the Library of Congress **authority** files (http://authorities.loc.gov/) are probably the best known, and are freely available if you need to check the correct form of a name. Nevertheless, in the event that someone is known by more than one name, a decision must be made as to the form to be used. For example:

| | | |
|---|---|---|
| Ouida | or | Louise de la Ramee |
| John Wayne | or | Marion Morrison |
| Elton John | or | Reginald Dwight |
| John Paul II | or | Karol Wojtyla |

All of these examples show people who are generally known by one name, even if it isn't the name they were born with. An interesting situation arose in a student thesaurus built for professional wrestling, where individuals might have several names used in different sorts of venue. Here the choice of a preferred term was often fairly arbitrary.

In the case of personal names, choices must also be made as to whether the form in the authority file (which probably uses a descriptive cataloguing standard such as *Anglo-American Cataloguing Rules*) is to be followed, or whether natural language word order is to be followed. Both forms are to be seen in thesauri, although I think the use of surname followed by forenames is more logical and more likely to be the way in which users will search.

## Names of places

Geographical names do present real difficulties, since there is frequently more than one legitimate form for a variety of reasons:

- names vary in different natural languages
- names are altered with changes of government and/or status
- boundaries change, affecting the definition of a name.

The following examples demonstrate these features:

```
Rome                or    Roma
Peking              or    Beijing
Suomi               or    Finland

Rhodesia            or    Zimbabwe
Leningrad           or    St. Petersburg
Thailand            or    Siam

Oakham (Rutland)    or    Oakham (Leicester)
```

As in the case of personal names, local conditions will often affect the decision. It is most usual to adopt the English form of a place in an English language thesaurus, but in one designed for international use, the vernacular form might be more acceptable to the majority of users. Most less important places do, of course, not have anything other than the vernacular name. Similarly, the use of historic names is inappropriate in a thesaurus for current government use, but helpful in one designed to deal with older or historical material.

Authorities exist for place names. The *Library of Congress Name Authorities* include geographical names, but they are not easy to search for, and you need to be familiar with the form of entry in the Library of Congress catalogues, since keyword searches do not work well on the authority files.

A better and more usable source for many purposes is the Getty Institute's *Getty Thesaurus of Geographic Names* (www.getty.edu/research/conducting_research/vocabularies/tgn/) (*TGN*),[2] which is truly a thesaurus (rather than an authority file) since it provides broader and narrower terms and a proper thesaural structure for each entry term. Figure 9.1 shows the thesaurus hierarchy for my home village.

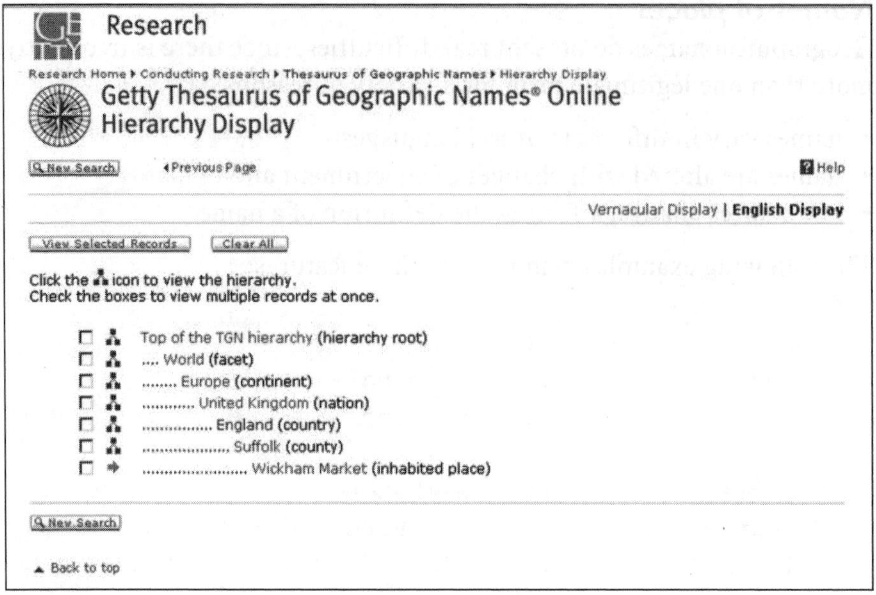

**Figure 9.1**   Hierarchy from *Getty Thesaurus of Geographic Names* (TGN)
© 2006 J. Paul Getty Trust

Needless to say, in a vocabulary which is used internationally, feelings can be strong about the forms of place names used, and regime and boundary changes often give rise to a demand for changes in the vocabulary. In such cases, appeal to an external authority is judicious. The *Universal Decimal Classification*, for instance, uses that form of a place name recognized by the United Nations.

## Summary

- Names can occur in different forms, and are a specialized case of synonymy
- Various authorities exist which can give guidance on the correct form of a personal name
- Geographic names often have vernacular and English (or other language) forms
- As with general synonyms it is important to have a clear policy about which is to be used
- Changes in place names also require decisions about which form should be adopted
- Geographic name authorities are useful and may be helpful in creating a neutral position.

## Disambiguation

So far we have looked at situations where there is a many-to-one relationship between a concept and the words used to describe it, that is, the proliferation of synonyms and **near synonyms,** or of quite disparate alternative names for the same person, place or thing.

A reciprocal situation exists where the many-to-one relationship is between the meaning and the word. Here the same form of the word may have different meanings, or the same name may be used for different people or places. A related problem occurs when a word is understood differently in different countries, traditions, or schools of thought.

The process of making the proper meaning clear, and removing ambiguity, is commonly known as **disambiguation.** There are two ways of doing this. First, if the word simply has two quite different meanings which cannot be known out of context, or if two people or places have the same name, an explanatory term, known as a **qualifier,** is added in brackets. Secondly, if the differences are those of understanding or interpretation, a longer definition or explanatory note may be added.

### *Qualifiers*

A written word with two or more common meanings is known as a **homograph** since the different concepts have the same written form to represent them. Homographs may have different pronunciations but this of course cannot distinguish them in the thesaurus, so the qualifier must be added:

```
Bows  (decorations)
Bows  (gestures)
Bows  (ships)
Bows  (weapons)

Moles  (animals)
Moles  (skin pigmentation)
Moles  (structures)
Moles  (tunnelling machines)
```

If the homographs all derive from the same linguistic source, they may be known as **polysemous** (from **polysemy** = having many meanings), but many homographs are completely accidental occurrences with no linguistic links at all.

Identical names are frequently found (particularly names of places) and are similarly qualified:

```
Woodbridge (California, U.S.A.)
Woodbridge (Connecticut, U.S.A.)
Woodbridge (New Jersey, U.S.A.)
Woodbridge (Ontario, Canada)
Woodbridge (Suffolk, England)
Woodbridge (Virginia, U.S.A.)
```

Names of persons may also be ambiguous, although, since people are less likely to be the subjects of documents than places, this is only a problem in the case of well known individuals. Two people with the same name may be distinguished by their dates of birth (as is common in cataloguing practice):

```
Francis Bacon (1561-1626)
Francis Bacon (1909-1992)
```

Alternatively, some subject qualifier may be used instead:

```
Francis Bacon (Painter)
Francis Bacon (Statesman and philosopher)

Eric Coates (Composer)
Eric Coates (Classification theorist)
```

You should be careful not to put words in brackets if they are not proper qualifiers. For example:

```
Frogs (amphibians)
Frogs (fastenings)
```

are correct because they represent quite different meanings of the word 'frog'. On the other hand:

```
Frogs (tree)
Frogs (marsh)
```

are incorrect, because in both these examples, the word 'frog' is being used in exactly the same way, and the bracketed words are different varieties of frog, not different meanings of frog. These terms should take the form:

```
Frogs, tree
Frogs, marsh
```

or better still:

```
Tree frogs
Marsh frogs
```

## Scope notes

When the meaning or interpretation of a term is open to doubt, a note containing a definition of the term as it is used in the thesaurus, or instructions about its application, should be added. Such a note is known as a **scope note**. Definitions will indicate the meaning of the term within the context of the thesaurus, and need not be formal or authoritative in any broader sense. This example from the *DH/DSS-Data Thesaurus* demonstrates this very clearly:

**BOUNDARY MANAGEMENT**
    IQR T

    *SN   Method of applying clearly defined limits to group work, so as to meet the needs of emotionally disturbed children.*

The definition evidently applies only to the subject domain of this thesaurus, and not, for example, to estate management, agriculture, or mathematics. It simply indicates the way in which the term is used in the local situation.

Other sorts of scope note include **instructions,** and **including notes,** which indicate the range and content of a term. Another example from the *DH/DSS-Data Thesaurus* is typical:

**BOYS**
    QLJ NT or QLR JNT

    *SN   Use class QLJ NT for boys as children and QLR JNT for boys as young people*

And from the *UNESCO Thesaurus*:

**Oceanographic research**
> SN   Use for works dealing with research Projects.
> For general scientific works, use 'oceanography'.

Notes of this kind guide the indexer in the application of the scheme and ensure consistency of practice. Even in a local environment more than one person may be using the thesaurus and such aids help to ensure it is systematically applied.

## Summary

- Words of different meanings but having the same form are known as homographs
- These must be distinguished in the thesaurus by adding a qualifier to indicate the specific meaning of the term
- Homographs are common in the area of geographic names and are normally qualified by country or administrative area
- Homographic personal names are more unusual, and may be qualified by the subject's occupation or dates of birth and death
- More detailed information about the intended meaning of a term can be provided by scope notes
- These can include specific instructions about a term's application, or indications of the range and coverage of a term.

## Notes

1   Cutter, C. A. (1876) *Rules for a Dictionary Catalog*, Washington, DC, Government Printing Office.
2   Getty Vocabulary Program (1988–) *Getty Thesaurus of Geographic Names* (*TGN*), Los Angeles, J. Paul Getty Trust, Vocabulary Program, www.getty.edu/research/conducting_research/vocabularies/tgn/.

# 10 Vocabulary control 2: form of entry

Choosing between **synonyms** or **near synonyms** usually involves choosing between two or more quite dissimilar words. When this has been done, decisions also have to be made about the precise form of a word as it will be entered in the thesaurus. Aspects of the exact form of an entry term cover a range of problems, including spelling, punctuation, and the linguistic form of the entry term. From the indexer's point of view, decisions made here do not have quite the same implications for searching as the selection of synonyms, but they are important for the sake of consistency and predictability in the design of the thesaurus. Much of what follows is accepted convention rather than a theoretically based system. Nevertheless there is a strong element of common sense involved, as well as awareness of user searching behaviour.

## Grammatical forms
### Nouns and noun phrases
The majority of terms used in thesauri (and in other sorts of subject tool) are nouns or noun phrases. In **noun phrases** the noun is qualified by an adjective or another noun, or more unusually a preposition links two nouns – very, very occasionally an adverb may occur:

    Female emancipation
    Black magic
    Professional wrestling
    Vegetarian cookery
    Medicinal herbs
    Atomic weight
    Penal colonies
    Boundary management

    Prisoners of war
    Rites of passage

```
Balance of trade
Payment in kind
Hunting with dogs

Highly charged ions
Very high energy phenomena
```

## Adjectives and adverbs

Except where they form part of an adjectival or adverbial phrase of this kind, adjectives and adverbs are not used as entry terms in the thesaurus, and they can never stand alone.

## Verbs

A great number of the terms in the thesaurus will be activities or actions of some sort. The verbs necessary to represent them can be used in a restricted way, that is in the form of **verbal nouns** and **gerunds**. The infinitive form of the verb (to organize, to manage, to operate, to cook) and the past and present participles (organized, organizing, managed, managing, operated, operating, cooked, cooking) are never used, except where participles are used adjectivally in phrases (Organized crime, Managed learning environment, Operating systems, Cooked meats).

Conversion to the appropriate noun form is necessary for inclusion in the thesaurus. Often this requires addition of '–ation', '–ment', or '–y' to the stem of the verb (information, arbitration, elimination, government, alignment, resentment, advocacy, prophesy, recovery), although these are by no means the only forms in English:

```
Organization
Management
Operation
Cookery
```

Confusion may arise because the gerund has the same form as the present participle, and there is often no alternative noun form of the type shown above. There are many examples of this in English:

```
Dancing
Horse racing
```

```
Advertising
Sailing
Indexing
```

In all of these (and countless other) examples, the '–ing' form is the noun equivalent of the verb and is perfectly acceptable in the thesaurus.

### The definite article

Generally speaking, the definite article should be omitted. Most software packages disregard the article for filing purposes, and users will not normally use it as a search term, so little purpose is served by keeping it in. So:

| | | |
|---|---|---|
| Arts | rather than | The arts |
| Ballet | rather than | The ballet |

Sometimes the article forms part of a proper name, and then a decision must be made whether to leave it in the lead position, or invert the word order.

```
Le Havre
El Alamein

Beatles, The
City of London, The
```

In an English thesaurus it is probably less acceptable to have 'the' as a lead word than its foreign language equivalents.

## Summary

- Certain conventions are used in the form of entry of terms which reflect user behaviour and expectations
- Nouns are the usual form of terms, or noun phrases consisting of nouns and qualifying adjectives
- Verbs should be converted to a noun form, and adjectives and adverbs should never be used alone
- Definite articles should not be used, except as part of a proper name.

## Spelling

Spelling is a factor in retrieval in the case of the English language, since British and American English do differ somewhat:

| | | |
|---|---|---|
| Aesthetics | or | Esthetics |
| Labor | or | Labour |
| Defence | or | Defense |

Fashion and the passage of time can also affect spelling:

| | | |
|---|---|---|
| Mediaeval | or | Medieval |
| Judgment | or | Judgement |
| Realisation | or | Realization |

As in the case of names, resorting to an external authority is the best solution. In the case of English language thesauri, those of American origin will probably use Webster's *Third New International Dictionary of the English Language,* and for British English some version of the *Oxford English Dictionary* is likely, although possibly the *Shorter* or the *Concise*, as the full dictionary itself contains so many variant spellings and archaic forms of English words. *Chambers' Dictionary* is another popular British spelling authority.

Spelling of technical terms of all kinds can benefit from the use of terminological reference works such as technical glossaries. In time, a well constructed and properly maintained thesaurus can itself become an authority.

Closely related to spelling is the matter of **transliteration** from one alphabet to another (or, more correctly, Romanization when the transliteration is into the Roman alphabet used in English and most western European languages):

```
Tchaikovsky
Tchaikovski
Chaikovsky
Tschaikowski
```

Again, a known standard should be adopted, but problems can arise when there is a familiar Romanized form that doesn't match the transliteration scheme. The switch from 'Peking' to 'Beijing' as the name of China's capital city accompanied a change in transliteration scheme from Wade–Giles to pinyin, which was official policy of the Chinese government. Where personal names are well established in one form, it is probably better to maintain the well recognized version:

`Mao Tse-Tung`   **rather than**   `Mao Zedong`

## Punctuation and other symbols

Akin to spelling is the question of what to do with punctuation marks and other symbols. The British and international standards for thesaurus construction do not give any rules on how to handle them, although the American standard does. Generally speaking, it is best to avoid these characters wherever possible because of the problems they create in filing and searching. Different software packages may deal very differently with the filing status of the hyphen, for example, regarding it as having no value, the value of a space, a value less than a letter, or a value greater than a letter. This can create quite different sequences for the same set of words and phrases containing hyphens.

Established good practice suggests that hyphens should be retained in the case of:

• terms which would not make sense without it (`X-rays`, `Blue-green algae`)
• where the hyphen indicates a relationship between the terms (`Left-right symmetry`, `Mother-daughter bonding`).

Otherwise the elements on either side of a hyphen should be run together where one is not a complete word, or separated by a space when both parts can stand alone:

| | | |
|---|---|---|
| `Anti-matter` | becomes | `Antimatter` |
| `Post-partum` | becomes | `Postpartum` |
| `Multi-media` | becomes | `Multimedia` |
| `Organo-metallic` | becomes | `Organometallic` |
| `Nineteenth-century` | becomes | `Nineteenth century` |
| `Fruit-growers` | becomes | `Fruit growers` |
| `Mangel-wurzels` | becomes | `Mangel wurzels` |

Numbers have a recognized **filing value** (usually preceding letters) and do not cause the same problems as other non-letter symbols. Except where they form part of a word (Uranium-231), numbers are usually spelt out:

```
Three colour printing
Four horsemen of the Apocalypse
Hundred years' war
```

As you can see from the last example, apostrophes are usually reproduced:

```
Men's magazines
War of Jenkins' ear
```

In many older thesauri capital letters were very liberally used, either for the whole vocabulary, or for entry terms, with cross-references in lower case. Nowadays this is less likely to occur, and some thesauri use all lower case letters, although it is still more usual to capitalize the first letter of the term (see also Chapter 7 on display). Otherwise capitals will mainly be used for proper names, initials and acronyms, and where they occur in names of organizations or in trade names:

```
Lake Placid
Vitamin C
PVC
GMT
OPACs
InfoTrac
```

If you're in any doubt about whether abbreviations and acronyms will be recognized, it is better to expand them to the full form:

```
Polyvinyl chloride
Greenwich Mean Time
Online public access catalogues
```

## Summary

- Spelling should be consistent and ideally should be based on a published authority
- Where names originally in non-roman scripts are transliterated, this also should use a known and established method
- Hyphens and other punctuation marks should generally be avoided
- Numbers should be spelled out in full
- Acronyms and abbreviations should be expanded to the full form.

## Plural and singular

Conventions about the use of plural and singular form tend to vary with the language used. Here we shall only consider what happens in the English language thesaurus.

In the first instance we can draw a useful distinction between concrete entities – things that are part of the material world – and abstract concepts, which include abstract ideas proper (knowledge, freedom, chance) as well as phenomena (lightning, magnetism), properties (beauty, sustainability), actions (cataloguing, singing, cricket) and disciplines (chemistry, palaeontology).

### Concrete entities

Let's consider the more straightforward case of the concrete entities first. In general, anything that can be counted (**count nouns**) is put into the plural, and anything that cannot (**non-count nouns**) has a singular form. Therefore:

```
Rabbits
Deep fat fryers
Balloons
Pen knives
Policemen
Bluebells

Cheese
Chewing gum
Interstellar matter
Titanium dioxide
```

You will notice that the first list consists of objects and living things, whereas the second group is composed of substances or materials. This division often provides a good indication of whether to pluralize or not, although I think the count/non-count status is more immediately obvious and reliable. A theoretical basis for choosing the plural form can be found by looking at the class membership of entities and this can be very helpful where there is doubt about the correct form. The classes of rabbits or bluebells, for instance, have many members and therefore rabbits and bluebells are plural. The class of interstellar matter, on the other hand, does not have numerous members so it should be singular. A concept like cheese has a hybrid status. Sometimes it is just the substance cheese and takes the singular form. If the thesaurus contains terms for different types of cheese (Wensleydale, Stilton, Roquefort), then cheese could be said to be a class with many members and the entry 'Cheeses' would be more appropriate.

A nice exception to the count/non-count noun rule occurs in medical and veterinary vocabularies, where plural or singular forms for parts of the body are based on the number that individual humans or animals possess. For example:

```
Legs
Ears
Brain cells

Digestive tract
Pelvis
Aorta
```

Where scientific names are used for a specific organism (as opposed to rabbits or bluebells as a general class), these are normally put in the singular. The convention is the same for both Latin and English forms:

```
Lepanthes Caritensis
Carite babyboot orchid
Chaetophractus vellerosus
Screaming hairy armadillo
```

## Abstract terms

Whereas, with these exceptions, the majority of concrete entities take the plural form, most abstract concepts are singular. If the same criteria for class membership and countability are applied to the abstract terms, their singularity is logical, and indeed it seems unlikely that, on an intuitive basis, any searcher would ever look for 'Magnetisms' or 'Singings'. Therefore:

```
Intuition
Slavery
Coastal erosion
Piezoelectricity
Disease resistance
Classification
Clog dancing
Fretwork
Archaeology
Epistemology
```

If a discipline or activity normally is pluralized or ends with an –s, this should be reproduced:

```
Physics
Gymnastics
Biblical hermeneutics
Media studies
```

Occasionally an abstract concept can be judged to be countable or to have more than one member of the class, in which case it satisfies the usual criteria for the plural form:

```
Virtues
Diophantine equations
Research methodologies
```

## Summary
• Concrete nouns which are countable should normally be entered in the plural form

- Non-count nouns, such as substances and materials, usually take the singular form
- In scientific vocabularies parts of the body which are singular take that form, as do names of species
- Abstract terms are put into the singular except where they are clearly countable.

## Compound terms

In the discussion of how the thesaurus evolved in Chapter 2, we considered how the general intention of the thesaurus compiler was to use relatively simple terms for indexing, and to avoid the pre-coordination of terms that was very common in book cataloguing and indexing tools. Nevertheless, very many of the terms to be found in thesauri (as you may already have noticed) do not look very simple at first glance, usually because they are **multi-word terms,** or phrases:

```
Horse racing
Solar heating
Brain surgery
Civil disobedience
Ancient Greek language
Information and communication technology
Low carbohydrate diets
Single lens reflex cameras
Brass band music
```

Nearly all of these subjects could be alternatively expressed as combinations of their constituent parts, for example:

```
Racing + Horses
Surgery + Brain
Languages + Ancient Greek
```

You might ask whether it would be easier and more straightforward always to break down the **compound terms** and only use the 'simpler' concepts as indexing terms. The extent to which one can or should replace compound terms with simpler ones is an important factor in deciding on the preferred terms in the thesaurus.

## Factoring

This process of breaking down compounds into simpler concepts is known as **factoring** or **splitting**. You will notice that the terms in a compound usually consist of a 'key' subject or concept (called the **focus**), which is the most important part of the compound, and a 'qualifying' concept (called the **difference** or **modifier**). The addition of the difference to the focus often creates a sub-class of the focus. Hence:

| | | |
|---|---|---|
| Music | sub-class | Brass band [music] |
| Racing | sub-class | Horse [racing] |
| Diets | sub-class | Low carbohydrate [diets] |

The relationship between the focus and the difference or modifier will prove to be an important one in deciding when and how to break down a compound. You therefore need to be clear about which is the focus and which is the modifier in a compound. More often than not, the lead word is the modifier rather than the focus. In the example of Brass band music, the subject is *music* and not more generally brass bands. Similarly, the compound Knitting wool is about a kind of wool, not a kind of knitting, and Horse racing is about a type of racing, not a type of horse. Compare these with British-style brass bands, Fair Isle knitting or Police horses, and you will see the difference. Interestingly, the focus term has now moved out of the lead position, although you should not assume that this invariably happens.

## When not to factor

Theoretically, it should (almost) always be possible to break down compounds, but the results are not always particularly useful, and some level of pre-coordination inevitably occurs in any thesaurus. Sometimes this is because a compound term, although multi-word, is essentially a single concept, as in the case of Civil disobedience above. To make this into a two-part heading, or to use two keywords, would make a nonsense of it, as well as rendering it unfindable by searchers.

In other cases, the compound could be otherwise expressed but the factored version may not be very useful, either because it doesn't really equate to the original term, or because the end-user is not very likely to look for the concept in that form. Some examples of these are given in the section on semantic factoring below. You should keep a term in compound form in the following situations:

- When the compound form is very well established as a topic, either in the specialist area of the thesaurus or more generally:

    ```
    Information retrieval
    Greyhound racing
    Trades unions
    ```

- Where there may be confusion as to the meaning of the constituent words when recombined:

    `Bridge girders` (a component for bridge building)
    `Girder bridges` (a kind of bridge)

    (The classic example used in my student days was that of 'Blind Venetians' and 'Venetian blinds', but in practice the rules for entering nouns and adjectives would prevent the use of 'Blind' as an entry term other than in its noun sense; 'Blindness' would have to be used for vision impairment, and there would be no ambiguity.)

- If one or more of the constituent words doesn't make sense on its own, or is very general in nature:

    ```
    Central heating
    Extreme ironing
    ```

- If one or more of the constituent words is used other than in its dictionary sense, e.g. metaphorically:

    ```
    Blue movies
    One-armed bandits
    Cats' eyes
    Crab nebula
    ```

- When additional terms would need to be added to make the meaning clear:

    `Adventure holidays`
    (`Holidays` for `Young people` with `High risk` activities)

- For proper names or compounds which contain proper names:

```
Mothering Sunday
London Transport
Brownian motion
Wolf-Rayet stars
```

For compounds not in these categories you should consider whether the term is better factored. Two types of factoring can be used: **semantic factoring** and **syntactic factoring.** Of the two, semantic factoring is less satisfactory from a retrieval point of view.

## Summary
- Compound terms are very common in thesauri, and the compiler must consider whether to retain them or enter the components as separate terms
- Compounds consist of a focus term and a difference or modifier which can help in coming to a decision
- Compounds should not be broken down when:
  — the compound term is very well established
  — the components could be re-combined in different ways
  — one or more components would not make sense on its own
  — components are used in a metaphorical rather than literal sense
  — the compound contains a proper name.

### Semantic factoring
Although now both British and American standards use the term 'splitting' rather than 'factoring', I have retained the older term because it embraces both syntactic and semantic aspects.

Semantic factoring occurs when a precise conceptual analysis of the compound term takes place. This process is very common when using analytico-synthetic classification schemes, where it helps to determine the correct synthesized notation for a **compound concept**. In the thesaural environment, however, this can result in the use of different words from those in the compound term. For example:

```
Renal dialysis becomes
Kidney + Function + Artificial

Impressionism becomes
Art + Movements + Europe + Nineteenth century
```

In many instances, a term which is a complex concept might be only a single word. This phenomenon is particularly widespread in medicine. For example:

```
Arthritis      =     Joints + Inflammation
Gastrectomy    =     Stomach + Removal
Piriformis     =     Thigh + Muscle
```

While factoring such terms has some advantages for retrieval, in that it allows general searches for, say, muscles, or types of inflammatory disorder, the loss of sought terms, particularly in a specialist situation, is a far greater disadvantage. Semantic factoring is therefore generally to be discouraged. You can see that very often semantic factoring involves the breaking down of terms which do not appear to the eye to be compound, and it may be for that reason that the standards no longer address it in detail. However, the conceptual make-up of terms is extremely relevant to facet analysis since it helps to guide the compiler in the correct location of such terms in the systematic structure.

### Syntactical factoring

Syntactical factoring occurs where the compound is more obviously a combination of two ideas, and these can be separated and used as independent indexing terms without loss of meaning. Here, the more recent term 'splitting' describes accurately what occurs:

```
Limestone quarrying    →     Limestone + Quarrying
Teacher training       →     Teachers + Training
Railway passengers     →     Railways + Passengers
Payroll stationery     →     Payroll + Stationery
```

### Rules for factoring

Established thesaurus practice, as well as the published standards, provide us with some guidelines for when to factor. While it should be made clear that these rules are not binding on thesaurus compilers, they do represent good practice and produce entry terms that are natural and intuitive to the end-user. The rules may be briefly stated as follows:

- If the relationship between the difference (i.e. the qualifying word) and the focus (i.e. the key word) is that of an entity and a component or part of the entity, then the constituents of the compound can be separated:

```
Aircraft engines        →        Aircraft + Engines
School canteens         →        Schools + Canteens
```

- The same applies when the focus is a property which is possessed by the difference:

```
Joint flexibility       →        Joints + Flexibility
Textile flammability    →        Textiles + Flammability
Bone density            →        Bones + Density
```

- Factoring should also occur when the compound consists of an action as the focus, plus the person or thing on which the action is performed:

```
Potato harvesting       →        Potatoes + Harvesting
Infant immunization     →        Infants + Immunization
Dog training            →        Dogs + Training
```

- Factoring also applies in the case of an action where the person or thing which performs the action is part of the compound:

```
Student volunteering    →        Students + Volunteering
Machine vibration       →        Machines + Vibration
Artery narrowing        →        Arteries + Narrowing
```

Exceptions to the rules may be made when the difference or modifier creates a specific type of the focus:

```
Flammable textiles
Trained dogs
Narrowed arteries
```

It's clear that in such cases it is the object or person which is now the focus, and not the part, property or action as in the examples above. The parts, properties and actions are now the modifiers, and are being used adjectivally as part of a noun phrase.

A rather complicated situation exists when there is more than one modifier. Usually a compound of this sort should be broken down as follows:

```
Polyester knitting yarn        →     Polyester yarn
                                     Knitting yarn

Women music teachers           →     Women teachers
                                     Music teachers
```

In both of these cases the focus is modified equally by both differences; the yarn is both polyester and knitting yarn, the teachers are both women and teachers of music.

In a situation where one difference modifies the other, the breakdown is only partial:

Toughened glass furniture **needs a factored term**

Glass furniture

but **NOT**   Toughened furniture

because it is the *glass* that is the object of the toughening, not the furniture. In such a case the full compound will also be included as an entry term.

## Summary
- Factoring may be semantic or syntactical in nature
- Semantic factoring requires a conceptual analysis of the term and may result in the loss of the original term
- It should for that reason be avoided

- Syntactical factoring involves the separation of terms in compounds where those terms can be used as meaningful terms in their own right
- A compound can be syntactically factored when:
  — the focus is a component or a property of the difference
  — the compound consists of an action and the recipient or agent of the action
- Where there is more than one difference or modifier the factoring must reflect whether the differences all modify the focus.

## Word order

In manual systems, such as card indexes, it used to be common practice to use an **inverted order** of terms in a compound where this was necessary to bring the most important word (the focus) to the front:

```
Art, Modern       rather than   Modern art
Peas, Frozen      rather than   Frozen peas
Crime, Juvenile   rather than   Juvenile crime
```

This ensured that the searcher would find the compounds associated with a particular subject gathered together in the alphabetical sequence:

```
Archaeology, Classical
Archaeology, Industrial
Archaeology, Roman
Archaeology, Underwater
```

In automated retrieval systems this isn't a requirement, since the search software will find words wherever they happen to be. Natural **word order** is therefore preferred to inversion:

```
Domestic pets       rather than   Pets, Domestic
Football boots      rather than   Boots, Football
Chinese takeaways   rather than   Takeaways, Chinese
```

The rules for form of entry, particularly those for dealing with compound terms, are quite complicated. Although overall they represent good practice, not every rule discussed here is contained in all of the published standards, and some large published thesauri (notably *The Art and Architecture*

*Thesaurus*) have their own rules for dealing with compound terms. It also happens that thesauri intended for indexing documents may have different criteria for the form of entry from those intended for indexing objects.

In a local thesaurus it may well not be necessary to consider these things in such great detail, particularly if the vocabulary is relatively small. What is important to remember, and which these guidelines implicitly state, is that the form of entry should be:

- consistent: similar types of term should be treated in the same way
- meaningful: meanings of terms should always be clear and unambiguous
- logical: the form of an entry as it is likely to be perceived by both indexers and end-users should take precedence over inverted, factored or otherwise modified forms.

With these constraints in mind, a local policy with a simpler set of rules may well serve. What is important is that there should be guidelines in place so that consistency in indexing is observed and the efficiency of retrieval is maintained.

During the process of constructing the thesaurus it may be easier to deal with the vocabulary control at the editing stage. While it is sensible to keep these aspects of the vocabulary in mind, some of the problems of synonym control and the management of compound terms will be dealt with naturally as the structure of the thesaurus develops, so that it isn't necessary to address them before beginning on the analysis and sorting of terms.

# 11 Building a thesaurus 2: term extraction from document titles

Following the systematic searches on catalogues and databases, we now have about 150 titles which will form the basis of the working vocabulary. Because these were selected carefully to avoid duplication of terms where possible, this should provide us with about 400–500 terms. This is really as big a vocabulary as one can comfortably manage in the initial stages, and there are quite enough terms to establish a sound and reliable structure for the thesaurus. There will probably be gaps in the terminology, but it is more efficient to fill these in at a later stage if necessary. In the majority of cases, far fewer terms than this can provide a reasonable structure for the thesaurus, so if you are dealing with a small, specialist vocabulary you can manage with around 100 terms as a starting point.

The titles must now be analysed to identify relevant terms. I find it easiest to do this in a rather rough and ready way, using a list of the titles, and cutting and pasting the relevant terms into another document. Some level of vocabulary control can be imposed as you go along and, at the end, the extracted terms are easily sorted using the A–Z sort facility of a word processing package.

## Identification of significant terms

Let's start by picking out the key concepts in each title. We will look at some examples of titles from our list, starting with a very straightforward one:

```
Cat overpopulation in the United States
```

Here there are three important terms:

```
cat - overpopulation - United States
```

A similar straightforward example is:

```
Preference of domestic rabbits for grass or coarse mix
feeds
Domestic rabbits - grass - coarse mix feeds
```

You will notice that I did not select 'preference' as a term to be used. Vague or general terms of this kind are not generally used in indexing, and the purpose of the exercise is to identify significant terms. If you find it hard to decide on what is significant or not, you may think about the kinds of terms that an end-user is likely to search for. A useful tip is to look for nouns or noun phrases first, and then for any significant verbs. You will remember from the previous chapter that most thesaurus terms fall into these two categories. Adjectives (except where they are attached to a noun) and adverbs can be ignored, as well as all the prepositions, conjunctions and articles. If you are in doubt, include the term – it can always be discarded later, but you will not necessarily remember it if you dispose of it now.

Most titles will include some irrelevant or unhelpful terms. For example, in the titles:

```
Grass-based dairies hold promise for southern Iowa
producers
Assessing pain in animals: putting research into practice
```

only the terms 'grass-based', 'dairies' and 'southern Iowa' in the first title, and 'assessing', 'pain' and 'animals' in the second, have meaning for indexing and retrieval purposes. Subtitles, as in the second example, frequently do not add anything to the core subject of the document, as is confirmed by these titles:

```
Boredom with zoo animals - a matter of animal welfare?
Dog training methods: their use, effectiveness and
interaction with behaviour and welfare
```

Nevertheless, sometimes the situation is reversed, and a subtitle can explain an unhelpful title, as in this example where the important terms are in the second half of the title:

```
Rattling the cage: towards legal rights for animals
```

Sometimes terms are significant in a general sense, but redundant in the specific context. A large number of these titles contain terms such as 'welfare' or 'animal welfare'. We do not need to keep recording these since that can be understood as the context. Hence, from the title:

```
Animal welfare and contraception of zoo and wild animals
```

we only need to select 'contraception', 'zoo' and 'wild animals'. Similarly, as terms recur, it's not necessary to list them over and over again (although undoubtedly some slip through and your list will contain duplicates to be weeded out).

**Exercise 11.1**

Identify the significant terms in the following titles:

- Free-range poultry production and marketing
- Infections in laboratory animals
- Review of the welfare of horses and ponies at markets
- Effects of road traffic accidents on domestic cats and their owners
- Housing of breeding ostriches in Germany and aspects of animal welfare.

## Simple vocabulary control

As the key terms are identified and added to the list you will probably find yourself almost automatically adjusting the form of a term to fit the normal thesaural conventions, or to conform with other occurrences of the term already in the list.

## *Word forms and punctuation*

For example, we know that concrete nouns should be put into the plural form, and it's easy to alter the 'cat' in 'Cat overpopulation in the United States' to the more usual 'cats'. If you were not sure about this, the cats affected by road accidents might make you think about whether the singular or plural is necessary.

There are several instances of this kind of formatting problem in the list of titles: we have 'human animal interactions', but 'human-livestock interactions', and 'human-cat relationships'. Hyphens indicating relationships are normally retained, and in this particular case, a hyphen would make·

it clear that we are concerned with interactions between humans and animals, and not with the human animal (as opposed to non-human animals).

Verbs in participle or other forms can also quickly be converted to the gerund or noun form ('managing' to 'management' for instance, or 'measuring' to 'measurement').

Some examples for you to identify yourself are given in Exercise 11.2, below:

### Exercise 11.2
Identify and correct terms *not* in the conventional thesaural form:

- Handbook of primate husbandry and welfare
- Assessing pain in animals – putting research into practice
- Catching animals who have escaped from their primary enclosure
- Consistency of piglet crushing in sows
- Enriching the lives of zoo animals and their welfare
- Health and welfare of rehabilitated juvenile hedgehogs
- Importance of straw for pig and cattle welfare
- Managing manure in harmony with the environment and society.

## Homographs and qualifiers
Occasionally you may encounter a homograph, or a word with more than one meaning. It is sensible to deal with these at the time you discover them so that they are not subsequently forgotten and the alternative meaning(s) are lost.

A nice example in our list is 'food', which occurs in the sense of food for animals and also of animals as food. You should attach qualifiers to these two terms to remind yourself of the different uses. These need not be considered at length, and they do not need to be very elegant, as you can polish up the terminology at a later stage. The important thing is to record the dual meaning. So

```
Food (for animals)
Food (animals as)
```

is quite sufficient to keep this in mind.

## Compound terms

As you work through a list you will obviously come across a number of compound terms and wonder whether these should be factored or not, according to the rules in Chapter 10. As we go through the process of constructing the thesaurus, we shall look at the placing of individual compound terms and that is probably a better point at which to make a decision about whether to factor or not. Nevertheless you will need quickly to decide how far to break down the terms as you process them. For example, you may wonder how to deal with:

```
Boredom with zoo animals - a matter of animal welfare
```

Should 'zoo animals' be one term, or two, 'zoo' and 'animals'? I would be inclined to keep it as a compound, but also to add the component terms to the list for the sake of completeness. The rules for factoring generally discourage semantic factoring, and it is better not to lose your compound term at this stage, if ultimately it should be kept. Similarly, in these examples:

```
Effects of road traffic accidents on domestic cats and
their owners
Welfare of feral cats
Livestock guard dogs reduce predation on domestic sheep
in Colorado
Free-range poultry, production and marketing
Veterinary, behavioural and welfare implications of
bear farming in Asia
```

I would retain 'road traffic accidents', 'domestic cats', 'feral cats', 'guard dogs', 'domestic sheep', 'free-range poultry', and 'bear farming'.

## Adding compound terms

You should also be vigilant for compound terms that need adding, because they are implicit rather than explicit. A lovely example occurs here:

```
Livestock guard dogs, llamas and donkeys
```

You should add the compound terms 'guard llamas' and 'guard donkeys' to the explicit 'guard dogs', otherwise the potential guarding function of the llamas and donkeys may be lost from the vocabulary. Similarly,

```
Manual of the care and treatment of children's and exotic
pets
```

tells us that, as well as recording the term 'exotic pets', you need to create and record the term 'children's pets'.

As with the example of homographs above, the purpose is to preserve the meaning of the original term, when removing it from its context. This is a central problem for indexing and retrieval. Systematic tools, such as classifications, invest a term with meaning on the basis of its context, or location, in the system. If the term 'dog' appears as a subdivision of a class for 'police personnel and agents', we can infer that the dog is a police dog. In a language-based tool such as a thesaurus, no such context exists, and we must be explicit and make the term 'police dog'.

### Other aspects of vocabulary control

Some aspects of vocabulary control are more conveniently dealt with at various stages during the construction of the thesaurus. Identification of synonyms is much simpler to do when the vocabulary is organized than when it is totally unstructured. Related matters, such as the management of names and the use of scientific terms, are also much easier to address a little further along the line.

At present we are attempting no more than to produce a tidy list of terms, in acceptable thesaural format, with obvious anomalies and inconsistencies removed. The steps in this process can be summarized as follows:

- collect terms from a variety of sources, including published literature
- from titles in the subject extract relevant terms
- identify significant terms and record these
- discard vague or very broad terms, and terms unlikely to be sought
- look particularly for nouns, noun phrases, and verbs
- pluralize concrete nouns
- convert verbs to noun equivalents
- standardize use of punctuation
- add qualifiers to homographs and terms with variable meanings

- preserve compound terms, and add their components as single terms
- add implicit compound terms.

The collection of terms can now be alphabetized using the A–Z sort facility from the Table menu in Word or its equivalent. It is not absolutely essential to do this, but it makes for a methodical approach, and it has two obvious advantages. First, it identifies duplicate entries and slight variants of entries, allowing these to be eliminated and adjusted. Secondly, it enables you, when working with the vocabulary, to locate any particular term quickly and easily (or to discover that a particular term is missing).

I have worked through my list of 170 titles, and have extracted approximately 500 terms from them. The resulting list (in alphabetical order) is to be found in Appendix 2.

## Answers to exercises

### Exercise 11.1
Identify the significant terms in the following titles:

- Free-range poultry production and marketing
    = free-range, poultry, production, marketing
- Infections in laboratory animals
    = infections, laboratory animals
- Review of the welfare of horses and ponies at markets
    = horses, ponies, markets
    'review' is unlikely to be a sought term and probably means no more than 'an article about...'
    'welfare' is also unnecessary since this is a thesaurus about welfare
- Effects of road traffic accidents on domestic cats and their owners
    = road traffic accidents, domestic cats, owners
    'effects' is another not very useful word. It's hard to imagine an article about road accidents and cats that doesn't include discussion of the effects of the one on the other, and the term isn't likely to be used when searching
- Housing of breeding ostriches in Germany and aspects of animal welfare
    = housing, breeding ostriches, Germany

### Exercise 11.2
Identify and correct terms *not* in the conventional thesaural form:

- Handbook of primate husbandry and welfare
  - = primate → primates
- Assessing pain in animals – putting research into practice
  - = assessing → assessment
- Catching animals who have escaped from their primary enclosure
  - = escaped → escape
- Consistency of piglet crushing in sows
  - = piglet → piglets
- Enriching the lives of zoo animals and their welfare
  - = enriching → enrichment
- Health and welfare of rehabilitated juvenile hedgehogs
  - = rehabilitated → rehabilitation
- Importance of straw for pig and cattle welfare
  - = pig → pigs
- Managing manure in harmony with the environment and society
  - = managing → management

# 12 Building a thesaurus 3: vocabulary analysis

As we have seen in Chapter 7, a thesaurus consists of a systematic display and an alphabetical display, the two being interdependent. In the systematic display the relationships between terms are shown visually by the indentation of terms, so that subordinate and coordinate status are evident from the page layout. In the alphabetical display these relationships between terms are obscured, so must be identified by a system of cross-references, that is the thesaural relations.

It is easiest to establish the correct relationships by constructing the systematic display, so this is done as a first stage. It is then converted to an alphabetical format when the structure of the vocabulary has been determined.

We shall do this for our model thesaurus by a method known as **facet analysis**. It should be emphasized that this is not the only method of constructing a thesaurus, but it is a well established and reliable method, underpinned by a rational, scientific theory.

## Facet analysis

The idea of facet analysis was conceived by S. R. Ranganathan in the 1920s and 1930s, and was implemented in a library classification scheme, the Colon Classification. The established library classifications of the time tended to be lists of topics likely to occur as the subjects of books, arrived at on a pragmatic basis, and including large numbers of compound classes (such as 'the pineapple canning industry in Hawaii', or 'science and religious belief in 17th century England'). The central notion of facet analysis is that vocabulary tools for subject fields can be better organized by identifying the individual constituent concepts of the subject (and combining them as and when needed), than by detailing all the possible combinations of concepts in a long list of pre-coordinated classes.

The faceted type of vocabulary tool tends to be briefer, more logical, and more flexible than a pre-combined enumeration of compound subjects. It is also closer to the culture of post-coordinate indexing, with the use of relatively simple keywords or descriptors. Although Ranganathan's methods were initially used to create a library classification for the physical arrangement of documents, the economical structure of the faceted classification makes it very easily turned into a thesaurus.

## Fundamental categories

Facet analysis works by applying broad principles of division to the concepts in the subject field to achieve a separation of these into **facets**, or aspects, of the subject. In a practical sense, this means that terms in the subject are sorted into a series of **categories**. A set of generally applicable categories has been arrived at, originally based on Ranganathan's five **fundamental categories,** but extended by the work of the UK Classification Research Group (CRG) to a group of 13. For some subjects, additional categories, special to that subject, are required, and these may be created on the basis of need.

Even before the formal realization of faceted classification by Ranganathan, indexers and classifiers were aware that some elements of compound subjects occurred very frequently, and in all subjects. Place and time were the first to be identified, in topics such as 'coal mining in Brazil', 'North American birds', 'British 19th century foreign policy', and so on. Even in the early 20th century, some systems for classification or indexing located these kinds of concept in generally applicable tables, thus saving the constant enumeration of combinations of subject with particular countries or periods. The rudimentary indexing theory then developing also began to propose the existence of general categories of concepts, such as the 'concretes' and 'processes' used by Kaiser in his 1911 work on subject indexing.[1]

Ranganathan theorized that there were five fundamental categories: the 'space' (or place) and 'time' categories that had already been recognized; concepts that expressed actions or activities, which he called the 'energy' category; concepts that were physical substances, which he called 'matter'; and a category of concepts that were central to the nature of a subject, which he called 'personality'. This latter category often consisted of concrete entities (such as plants, animals, geographical features, astronomical objects, and so on). These five categories generate a basic facet formula, Personality – Matter – Energy – Space – Time, or PMEST, reflecting the order in which they are normally combined when dealing with compound subjects.

The CRG categories are more numerous, and they allow for a more detailed analysis of concepts than that which Ranganathan's categories supported. They form a parallel set to the PMEST categories, but expand some of them. Table 12.1 shows the correspondence between the two.

**Table 12.1**   Fundamental categories of Ranganathan and CRG

| CRG categories | Ranganathan's categories |
| --- | --- |
| Thing | Personality |
| Kind | |
| Part | |
| Property | |
| Material | Matter |
| Process | Energy |
| Operation | |
| Patient | |
| Product | |
| By-product | |
| Agent | |
| Space | Space |
| Time | Time |

You can probably see that the **personality** category has been split to provide for not only the kinds of an **entity** or **thing**, but also its **parts** and **properties**, and that **energy** has two sub-categories, **processes** (actions which happen by themselves) and **operations** (actions which are carried out by an external agent of some sort). **Matter** (or **material**), **space** and **time** are the same, but there is an additional group of categories which are related to Operations. These are the object of the operation (the **patient**), **products** and **by-products** of the operation, and the means by which the operation is carried out (the **agent**, which can be a person or a piece of equipment). This group of categories is particularly important in technology and manufacturing, an area in which much of the early work of the CRG was conducted.

These categories have been found to work well for the majority of subjects, but they are not all applicable to every subject. The group as a whole is particularly appropriate to the sciences and technology, but some of the categories are not relevant to the social sciences and humanities (the patient, product, by-product group, for example). Occasionally I find that students will try too hard to make the terms in a subject match the whole range of categories, when in some cases it just isn't possible.

On the other hand, some subjects contain terms that don't fit the existing categories, and some impromptu categories must be created to accommodate them. Well known examples are 'genre' in literature and art, and 'movements' in the fine arts, neither of which really match any of the 13 possibilities. If you can identify a grouping of terms which have some common characteristic like this, it is always permissible to introduce a new label for them.

## The universality of categories

It should be understood that the idea of categories is essentially a practical one. It provides a very useful way of organizing the concepts in a subject domain to produce a reliable and logical vocabulary tool. There is a well developed theory of how and why this works (some of which we shall examine further on), and what are the limits of the methodology. It is not, however, a universal truth that holds in all contexts and all subjects, and it can be modified to suit the needs of the situation.

## Categories versus clustering

An important aspect of categorization that must be understood for it to work properly is that the categories are functional in nature, and that they do not work by grouping concepts that are related to each other in a general way. Take this group of concepts, for example:

| | | |
|---|---|---|
| cage | kennel | saddle |
| collar | leg-ring | stable |
| dog | nose-ring | sty |
| flying | parrot | tracking |
| horse | pig | |
| jumping | rooting | |

Your instinctive thought might be to group them in the manner shown in Figure 12.1.

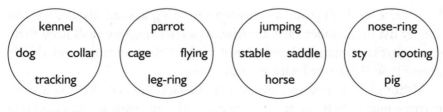

**Figure 12.1** Grouping terms

Here, the various concepts associated with a particular animal have been brought together, so that the animal acts as a focal point in its own little universe. This is the sort of arrangement that is often used in drawing concept maps, and also in ontologies, where the relationships between concepts might also be specified. See Figure 12.2, for example.

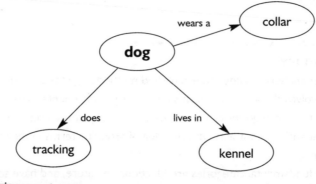

**Figure 12.2** Simple concept map

This is not the same as categorization of the facet analytical variety, which groups the concepts by their function, as in Figure 12.3.

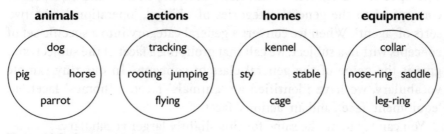

**Figure 12.3** Concepts grouped in categories

In practice we don't group our concepts in this graphical display, but can simply list them under each heading. At a later stage we shall need to do some further organization and ordering of the concepts, and this is perfectly well managed within a linear sequence.

Although it is not an explicit part of facet theory, there is a close correspondence between the general categories and parts of speech, so that the roles of the categories can be interpreted in a linguistic way. For example, most 'things' are nouns (as are their kinds and parts), and their 'properties' are adjectives. 'Operations' are transitive verbs (those in which there is an object of the action) and 'processes' are intransitive verbs (those in which there is no object). In English language vocabularies, 'agents' are nouns (although in some languages which inflect more than English they would be distinguished from other nouns when they act as agents).

## Summary

- Facet analysis provides an established methodology for constructing a thesaurus
- It involves the analysis of terms into a set of fundamental categories
- Additional categories can be created if the subject requires them
- Facet analysis contrasts with the idea of grouping terms in the same subject area
- The fundamental categories are functional in nature, and have some correspondence with grammatical forms.

## Categories and facets

The specific categories of animals, actions, homes and equipment correspond to the general categories of 'things', 'operations', and two sorts of 'agent'. When we convert a general category into a specific set of concepts within a subject, we call that grouping a facet of the subject, and give it the name of the general class of concepts. In our tiny sample vocabulary, we have identified an 'animals' facet, a 'homes' facet, an 'equipment' facet, and an 'actions' facet.

You can try to do the same for this slightly larger vocabulary.

## Exercise 12.1

Organize the following terms into categories. Say which general categories they correspond to and give a name to each facet.

| | | |
|---|---|---|
| bricks | floors | stone |
| bricklaying | glass | tiling |
| castles | hods | timber |
| cathedrals | hospitals | towers |
| chimneys | palaces | trowels |
| cleaning | plastering | walls |
| cottages | restoration | wheelbarrows |
| doors | roofs | windows |
| farmhouses | spades | |

## The stage 1 facet

The use of the fundamental categories is primarily to guide us towards appropriate grouping of concepts. It can be helpful to examine the vocabulary specifically for the presence of operations, or agents, or properties and so on, since that can help to ensure that all the possibilities are covered. Often, however, particular groupings are quite evident without the need to validate them by matching them against the basic categories.

In our animal welfare vocabulary, for example, the existence of a category for different kinds of animal is immediately apparent. This is likely to correspond to the 'thing' category, but we don't need to know that in order to spot the presence of a lot of animal names in the vocabulary, and to group them into an animals facet. I've extracted all the terms that refer to animals, and put them into a single group which you can see in Figure 12.4.

At this stage of the analysis there is still a great deal of work to be done in organizing the terms. Although we can label the set of terms 'animals facet', it is very rudimentary as a structure, and lacks most of the elements that are needed to establish the complex interrelationships in the finished thesaurus.

You will notice that there are a number of different sorts of terms for animals gathered here. Some are just the normal names for animals, such as pig, emu or llama. There are also some Latin names (pongo pygmaeus, or giraffa camelopardalis). Other terms refer to the role or function of animals (pets, zoo animals, farm animals), or how they are managed (free-range poultry, caged rabbits). Others still describe the condition of the animals or relate to their age or gender (chicks, piglets, sows, pregnant

| | | |
|---|---|---|
| African elephants | free-living wild animals | pets |
| animals used in education | free-range poultry | piglets |
| baboons | giraffa camelopardalis | pigs |
| badgers | giraffe | pongo pygmaeus |
| bears | goats | ponies |
| blue foxes | gorillas | poultry |
| breeding ostriches | grey parrots | pregnant mares |
| broiler breeders | grey squirrels | pregnant sows |
| broilers | growing pigs | primates |
| caged hens | guard animals | rabbits |
| caged rabbits | guard dogs | rainbow trout |
| calves | guard donkeys | ratites |
| captive animals | guard llamas | rats |
| captive chimpanzees | guinea pigs | rearing pigs |
| captive tigers | hedgehogs | rheas |
| capuchin monkeys | hens | rhesus macaques |
| cats | hogs | rodents |
| cattle | horses | Scottish blackface sheep |
| chickens | inbred strains | sheep |
| chicks | intensively farmed animals | Siberian hamster |
| children's pets | Japanese quail | sows |
| chimpanzees | kennelled dogs | sport horses |
| coyotes | laboratory animals | squirrels |
| dairy cows | laying hens | swine |
| dogs | livestock | tigers |
| domestic cats | llamas | trotting horses |
| domestic rabbits | loxodonta africana | tufted capuchin monkeys |
| domestic sheep | lutra lutra | turkey poults |
| donkeys | males | turkeys |
| ducklings | mares | veal calves |
| ducks | meat goats | vertebrate pests |
| emus | mice | vertebrates |
| equids | mink | western lowland gorillas |
| Eurasian otters | monkeys | wild animals |
| exotic pets | mules | wild conspecifics |
| farm[ed] animals | non-human animals | wild-caught animals |
| farmed fish | orangutans | working equids |
| farmed mink | ostriches | working horses |
| feeder pigs | otters | zoo animals |
| feral cats | outdoor sows | zoo housed animals |
| fish | pastured cows | zoo housed gorillas |

**Figure 12.4** Rudimentary 'animals' facet at stage 1 of organization

mares). During the next stage of analysis, we shall have to organize these different kinds of animal terms into appropriate groups.

The list is, for convenience, in alphabetical order. This doesn't show any relationships between different species, so another task will be to structure the vocabulary to reflect taxonomic (and other) groupings. We shall also have to decide whether any of these terms are essentially the same concept (imposing vocabulary control) and to look for relationships of hierarchy between terms.

However, the rest of the vocabulary must also be organized into its constituent facets. You may like to take the original vocabulary listed in Appendix 2, and see if you can identify which terms belong to each of the general categories discussed above. Remember that not all of the categories might appear. A complete set of these 'stage 1' facets is included in Appendix 3. Each facet is preceded by some brief notes about the nature of the facet, and any particular problems associated with the subject and its terminology in that area.

## Note

1    Kaiser, J. (1911) *Systematic Indexing*, London, Pitman.

## Answers to exercises

### Exercise 12.1

Organize the following terms into categories. Say which general categories they correspond to and give a name to each facet.

| | | |
|---|---|---|
| bricks | floors | stone |
| bricklaying | glass | tiling |
| castles | hods | timber |
| cathedrals | hospitals | towers |
| chimneys | palaces | trowels |
| cleaning | plastering | walls |
| cottages | restoration | wheelbarrows |
| doors | roofs | windows |
| farmhouses | spades | |

| (things) | (parts) | (operations) | (materials) | (agents) |
|---|---|---|---|---|
| **buildings** | **parts** | **techniques** | **building materials** | **tools and equipment** |
| castles | chimneys | bricklaying | bricks | hods |
| cathedrals | doors | cleaning | glass | spades |
| cottages | floors | plastering | stone | trowels |
| farmhouses | roofs | restoration | timber | wheelbarrows |
| hospitals | walls | tiling | | |
| palaces | windows | | | |
| towers | | | | |

You would undoubtedly want to sort these lists out rather better, not leaving them in alphabetical order, but trying to show some relationships between the concepts. You may have chosen other names for your facets – these are only suggestions.

# 13 The thesaural relationships

The next stage in managing the controlled vocabulary is to introduce some internal structure into each facet. Among other things, it's necessary to identify synonyms and near synonyms in the vocabulary, and to establish relationships of hierarchy. It's therefore useful to take a more detailed look at the **thesaural relationships** and how they are used to express these in the alphabetical display.

## The principal thesaural relationships

The form of cross-referencing in thesauri is now formalized in a standard manner, and the great majority of thesauri use five abbreviated codes to indicate the different kinds of relationship between an **entry term** and other terms in the vocabulary. These are:

USE    a reference from a non-preferred term to a preferred term
UF     Use For: a reference from a preferred term to a non-preferred term
BT     broader term: a reference to terms which are more general in scope
NT     narrower term: a reference to terms which are more specific in scope
RT     related term: a reference to a term which is related in some way other than BT or NT

## Other codes

In addition, the code SN (**scope note**) is used when it is necessary to explain or define a term or otherwise indicate how and where it should be used. The word 'scope' is used in the sense of the range of meaning of the term, and any limitations on that meaning. Scope notes can take the form of definitions, explanations, or instructions on the application of a term. They may also include examples of how a term should be used.

There are other examples of codes besides those used to express inter-term relationships. Both the new British Standard and the American

Standard include HN (history note) for information about when terms were added or amended and other editorial details of that kind. Some thesauri employ a formal code for notations, such as CC (classification code). The British Standard also includes DEF (definition) for thesauri which explicitly distinguish these from other aspects of the scope note.

## *Top term*

The relationship TT (or **top term**) may be encountered in a multi-disciplinary thesaurus, indicating the general subject area in which a term occurs. It can be useful in establishing the general context of a term, and, where a term can have slightly different meanings, it can help to clarify the way in which it should be used.

In the *UNESCO Thesaurus* the relationship MT, which stands for MicroThesaurus, is used instead of top term to denote a specific subject area within the vocabulary. It has the same meaning as TT:

```
Voodoo
    MT    3.20    Religion

Vocal music
    MT    3.55    Performing arts
```

## Summary

- A standard set of thesaural relationships are used in most thesauri
- These allow users to navigate the thesaurus and to locate other relevant terms in the vocabulary
- The relationships deal in the main with:
  - — synonym control and the identification of preferred and non-preferred terms
  - — hierarchical relationships and the identification of more general and more specific terms
- Other thesaural codes include scope notes and top terms.

## USE and UF relationships: equivalence relationships and synonym control

We have already considered the need to control vocabulary in the thesaurus, and how synonyms and near synonyms must be evaluated to decide on a preferred term for indexing. The USE and UF relationships make it explicit which are the terms actually to be used in indexing. However, because the thesaurus should be as rich as possible in terms of the overall vocabulary, and give the largest possible number of **access points** to the vocabulary, it should contain as many terms as are likely to be sought by the user. It is therefore normal practice to retain all the non-preferred forms of terms in the vocabulary, cross-referencing them to the preferred forms.

USE and UF always come in pairs, since for every reference one way, there will be a corresponding 'reverse' or **reciprocal reference**. For example, in the *UNESCO Thesaurus* we find:

**Aquaculture**
    UF    *Fish farming*

*Fish farming*
    USE   **Aquaculture**

Note here also the use of italics to distinguish between preferred and non-preferred terms. It goes without saying that UF and USE can never occur together, since any term is either the preferred form, or it is not.

Of course, it is sometimes the case that there are more than two variant forms of a term, because of multiple synonymy or combinations of synonymy, alternative spellings, existence of technical terms, and so on. Where there are a group of alternatives and more than one non-preferred term, the references are made only between the preferred term and each non-preferred term. No thesaural relationships exist between the non-preferred terms. For example:

**Rosa spinosissima**
    UF    Scotch rose
    UF    Burnett rose

Burnett rose
    USE   **Rosa spinosissima**

Scotch rose
    USE   **Rosa spinosissima**

No cross-reference can be made between 'Burnett rose' and 'Scotch rose' because both are non-preferred terms.

## Summary

- USE and UF relationships indicate which terms are preferred in indexing
- Non-preferred terms are always retained to provide as many entry points to the vocabulary as possible
- USE and UF relationships always occur in reciprocal pairs
- UF relationships may have multiple references to non-preferred terms
- Non-preferred terms can only ever refer back to the preferred term.

## Broader and narrower terms: relationships of hierarchy

When we consider the conceptual structure of the vocabulary, the major relationships are those of hierarchy. These relationships are expressed in the thesaurus by the codes BT (broader term) and NT (narrower term). Occasionally RT (related term) can also be used, although the RT is mainly used for other kinds of relationship.

### The concept of hierarchy

Many of the terms in a thesaurus can be organized into hierarchical structures; the terms 'brass instruments', 'cellos', 'French horns', 'musical instruments', 'oboes', 'stringed instruments', 'trombones', 'trumpets', 'violins', 'wind instruments' and 'woodwind instruments' can be displayed together as a visual hierarchy:

> Musical instruments
>> Stringed instruments
>>> Violins
>>> Cellos
>> Wind instruments
>>> Brass instruments
>>>> Trumpets
>>>> French horns
>>> Woodwind instruments
>>>> Oboes

Indentation of terms is used to show that one term is wholly contained by another. This could be represented in a graphical manner using logical diagrams (otherwise known as Venn diagrams), as in Figure 13.1.

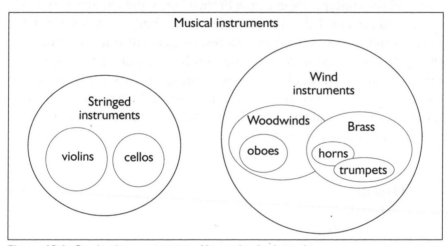

**Figure 13.1**  Graphical representation of hierarchical relationships

You can see in Figure 13.1 the idea of inclusion of one concept by another. In classifications these relationships are said to be those of subordination and superordination. 'Wind instruments' are said to be subordinate to 'musical instruments' and superordinate to 'oboes'. Concepts that are at the same level in the hierarchy, such as 'French horns' and 'trumpets', are said to be coordinate. These relationships correspond directly to the broader term and narrower term of the thesaurus, and one of the roles of the related term is that of the coordinate relationships (Table 13.1). Taxonomists often name the same set of relationships as 'parent', 'child' and 'sibling'.

**Table 13.1**  Relationship names in different vocabulary tools

| Thesaurus | Classification | Taxonomy |
|---|---|---|
| Broader term | Superordinate | Parent |
| Narrower term | Subordinate | Child |
| Related term | Coordinate | Sibling |

### *Varieties of hierarchical relationships*

The hierarchy of musical instruments shown above lists a number of different concepts and their subordinate concepts which are 'kinds' or 'types' of the concept; for example French horns and trumpets are kinds of brass instrument. This relationship between a thing and its kinds or types is also referred to as a genus/species, or **generic relationship**. The thing/kind relationship is one important hierarchical relationship. The other is the relationship between a thing and its constituents or components. This is known as a whole/part, or **partitive relationship**. This hierarchy of botanical terms relating to the parts of a flower demonstrates this second category of relationship:

Flowers
   Perianth
      Corolla
         Petals
      Calyx
         Sepals
   Androecium
      Stamens
         Filament
         Anther
   Gynoecium
      Carpel. Pistil
         Stigma
         Style
         Ovaries
         Ovule
   Receptacle
      Thalamus
      Peduncle

This hierarchy can also be represented as a series of ever decreasing circles in a logical diagram. It should be emphasized that the whole/part relationship must be of this kind, that is the part must be completely subordinate to the whole. A component or constituent which can be part of another entity is not a true whole/part relationship. For example:

```
Heart
    NT Ventricle ✓
```

is a correct example, because the ventricle is peculiar to the heart, but

```
Shirts
    NT Sleeves ✕
```

is incorrect because, although sleeves are parts of shirts, they are parts of other sorts of clothes as well. Such as relationship is RT (see below). Correct hierarchical relationships are sometimes referred to as **semantic relationships** or **paradigmatic relationships**.

## Summary
- Relationships of hierarchy are the most common in any vocabulary tool
- They are usually expressed visually by successive indentation of text in the systematic display
- They indicate whether one concept contains or is contained by another, or whether both are members of the same containing class
- These relationships may be described variously as:
    — superordinate, subordinate and coordinate classes
    — broader, narrower and related terms
    — parent, child and sibling terms
- The hierarchical relationship may be that of a thing and its kind or types (generic relationship), or that of a whole and its parts (partitive relationship).

## Broader terms
Another way of describing the broader term relationship is that it directs the user to terms which are more general in nature than the entry term, or 'higher up' in the hierarchy. For that reason, BTs are also referred to as **upward references**. For example:

```
Violins
    BT  Stringed instruments
```

```
Crocodiles
    BT  Reptiles
```

```
Cosmic radiation
    BT   Radiation

Oboists
    BT   Musicians

Semantics
    BT   Linguistics
```

Generally speaking, a broader term should represent only one step upwards in a hierarchy, so that progression towards the top levels of the hierarchy is achieved in a series of steps through the thesaurus. For example:

```
Sculpture
    BT   Plastic arts

Plastic arts
    BT   Visual arts

Visual arts
    BT   Arts
```

This avoids the need to reproduce the whole of the preceding hierarchy under each entry term. Some thesauri may include references to different levels of hierarchy, as in the following example from the *UNESCO Thesaurus*, but this is fairly uncommon. In most cases navigation through the thesaurus proceeds one step at a time.

```
Seismometers
    BT1   Measuring instruments
    BT2   Scientific equipment
```

### Narrower terms

Just as the USE and UF relationships connect pairs of terms, so broader terms are paired with narrower terms in reciprocal relationships. As the BT deals with upward, superordinate or parent relationships, the narrower term indicates downward, subordinate or child relationships. For the musical instruments hierarchy we can identify NTs such as:

```
Brass instruments
    NT   Trumpets
```

```
Wind instruments
     NT   Woodwind instruments
```

These correspond to the upward references:

```
Trumpets
     BT   Brass instruments
```

```
Woodwind instruments
     BT   Wind instruments
```

As with the upward references, the **downward references** too are normally restricted to a single step down the hierarchy.

It is quite common for an entry term to have more than one narrower term, so that the reciprocal entries may be many-to-one:

```
Hospitals
     NT   Cottage hospitals
     NT   Isolation hospitals
     NT   Teaching hospitals

Cottage hospitals
     BT   Hospitals

Isolation hospitals
     BT   Hospitals

Teaching hospitals
     BT   Hospitals
```

Some thesauri make a distinction between thing/kind and whole/part relationships, and identify narrower terms which are kinds of the containing class and those which are parts. These may be encoded as NTG (**narrower term generic**) and NTP (**narrower term partitive**):

```
Corolla
     NTP  Petals
```

```
Woodwind instruments
     NTG  Oboes
```

Both sorts of NT can be encountered together. For example:

```
Birds
     NTG   Chiffchaffs
     NTG   Oystercatchers
     NTG   Yellowhammers

     NTP   Beaks
     NTP   Feathers
```

A special category of the NTG is the **narrower term instantive** (otherwise called the **instantive** or **instantial relationship**), where the NTG is an individual example of the broader term. For example:

```
Wizards
     NTI   Harry Potter

Animated characters
     NTI   Gromit
```

These are not further distinguished in the thesaurus, and for all practical purposes they are treated in the same way as general classes of narrower terms.

If the relationships NTG, NTP and NTI are used in the thesaurus, their corresponding BTs will take the form BTG, BTP and BTI.

Terms in a hierarchy must be of the same general type for any of these relationships to hold good. Our examples show types of musical instrument, bird, tool, discipline, parts of a flower, and hospital. Where the terms are not of the same type, it is likely the relationships are not BT/NT, but some other relationship (RT). In this imperfectly constructed hierarchy, the terms are a mixture of categories:

Railway engines. Locomotives
   Steam engines
    Fuel supply
   Diesel locomotives
   Shunting locomotives

   The Flying Scotsman

Fireboxes
Buffers

Running trials
Signalling

The terms 'steam engines', 'diesel locomotives' and 'shunting locomotives' (which are all kinds of locomotive) and 'fireboxes' and 'buffers' (which are parts of locomotives) are legitimate NTs of 'locomotives', as is the Flying Scotsman, which is a specific instance of a locomotive. On the other hand, 'running trials', 'signalling' and 'fuel supply' are not kinds, parts or instances of locomotives, and cannot be NTs. They are RTs of 'locomotives', or **non-hierarchical relationships**.

## *Polyhierarchy*
Although it is unusual, it is possible for a term to have more than one BT. This occurs when a term represents the combination of two concepts. The phenomenon is known as **polyhierarchy** since the term can be located in more than one hierarchy:

```
Deaf children
     BT   Deaf persons
     BT   Children

Children
     NT   Deaf children

Deaf persons
     NT   Deaf children

Brain cancer
     BT   Brain diseases
     BT   Cancer

Brain diseases
     NT   Brain cancer

Cancer
     NT   Brain cancer
```

It is essential to be quite certain that the relationships to the BTs are both strictly hierarchical (i.e. that the terms are of the same general type) before deciding that polyhierarchy exists. In the examples above the terms are, respectively, all kinds of person, and all kinds of disease. We shall look at this in more detail in the chapters on thesaurus construction.

In most of the examples in the preceding section the terms have been entities (or 'things' in facet analytical terminology). Hierarchies can equally well occur in other facets, such as 'action' terms, or place or time.

> Photography
>> Processing techniques
>>> Developing
>>> Toning
>>> Fixing
>> Finishing
>>> Retouching
>> Conservation
>
>> Digital photography
>> Portrait photography

In this hierarchy of photographic techniques, all the subdivisions are types or parts of the broader term.

The important criterion for establishing true hierarchical (BT/NT) relationship is that the narrower term is either a type, or a part, of the broader term. If this principle is kept in mind, then you can't go very far wrong.

## Summary

- In the thesaurus, references to a broader term are sometimes called upward references
- Reference is made only to terms one step upward in the hierarchy
- Narrower terms, or downward references, should also be made only for terms one step downward
- Broader and narrower terms must occur as reciprocal pairs, but any particular broader term may have many narrower terms
- In some thesauri, narrower terms are identified as being generic, partitive or instantive

- For the BT/NT relationship to be valid, the terms must be of the same type (i.e. in the same category or facet)
- Occasionally terms may have more than one broader term; this phenomenon is known as polyhierarchy.

## Related terms and associative terms

Terms that are linked in some way other than the strictly hierarchical are known as related terms (RT), or **associative terms**. RT is used to accommodate any relationship between terms that does not fall within the USE/UF and BT/NT categories.

Within a hierarchy, RT may be used to express the relationship between terms that are on the same level, that is coordinate terms or siblings:

```
Butterflies
    NT   Common blue
    NT   Holly blue

Common blue
    RT   Holly blue

Holly blue
    RT   Common blue
```

For the most part, related terms do not derive from the same hierarchy, and therefore tend not to be of the same general type, although they will be in the same subject area and may have linguistic similarities. A relationship between terms from two different hierarchies, or two different facets, is almost by definition a related term. Relationships between terms from different facets are sometimes called **syntactic relationships:**

```
Honey
    RT   Bees

Dosage
    RT   Drugs

Gymnastics
    RT   Gymnasia
```

```
Magnets
    RT  Magnetism
```

Relationships of this sort are not controlled by any specific rules and are usually identified by a more *ad hoc* approach than those derived from hierarchies. Manual editing of the thesaurus will often make compilers aware of these associations as they read through the complete vocabulary.

Current thesaural conventions do not distinguish between different kinds of related term. This makes the RT a very useful category for accommodating any relationship not otherwise covered, but there is no doubt that it lacks precision, and this is one area where tools such as the topic map and ontology are seen as having an advantage over the thesaurus. The working party for the new British Standard is currently attempting to identify some distinctive types of RT, and the facet analytical approach is useful because it provides such a range of categories. Examples of potential subdivisions of the RT might be an action and the equipment used to perform it (ploughing and ploughs), an activity and the person who carries it out (teaching and teachers) or a process and its outcome (disease and symptoms).

## Summary

* Relationships not in the BT/NT category are covered by the related (or associative) term relationship
* These may be:
  — terms at the same level of the hierarchy (i.e. coordinate terms)
  — terms related in some other way
  — relationships between terms in different facets
* Current thesaural conventions do not distinguish between different types of related term.

# 14 Building a thesaurus 4: introducing internal structure

In Appendix 3 you can find the animal welfare vocabulary very roughly sorted into a selection of standard categories which form some crude facets of the subject. I hope you were able to attempt some analysis yourself and found it not too difficult. In this chapter we shall look at how the terms are organized into a more helpful order, so that the precise relationships between terms begin to emerge. The facet of animals will be used to show how this is done, but I shall include some examples from other facets so that you can see that the method can be applied to all categories of terms.

## Vocabulary control

At this stage it is not necessary to bring the full range of vocabulary control techniques into play, but we do need to identify synonyms so that we avoid the possibility of having the same concept in different places under different names.

The animals facet contains a number of examples of two kinds of synonym: the first is the existence of common names for animals alongside their Latin equivalents; the second is the presence of different common names in UK and US English. There are four Latin names in our facet, given here with their English equivalents:

giraffa camelopardalis = giraffe
loxodonta africana = African elephant
lutra lutra = Eurasian otter
pongo pygmaeus = orangutan

There are also three synonyms for one animal, 'hogs', 'pigs' and 'swine', and two for another, 'chickens' and 'hens'.

As a preliminary to making any decision about the preferred terms, we can bring these synonyms together so that the concepts they represent are not in two or more places in the list. This also ensures that the preferred and non-preferred terms are kept together so that when a choice is made the USE and UF relations can be assigned speedily.

Synonyms are easily grouped by putting them in a row in the alphabetical sequence. At this stage we don't have to decide on the preferred term, as long as they all sit together.

A section of our amended list would now look like this:

guinea pigs
hedgehogs
hens. chickens
hogs. pigs. swine
horses
Japanese quail
kennelled dogs
laying hens
llamas
loxodonta africana. African elephants
lutra lutra. Eurasian otters
males
mares

Having identified the synonyms, we shall need to make some decisions about which alternatives to adopt. (You should understand that these choices only hold for this thesaurus, and different ones might well be more appropriate for another subject field.)

My own inclination is to choose the popular names over the Latin ones in the context of animal welfare. The cross-disciplinary nature of the subject means that many users are likely to be non-scientists, and for them the popular names come more readily to mind and are more likely to be selected as search terms. In other environments one might prefer the Latin names where these are more natural to the users, as would be the case in an academic zoology library. Choosing the Latin names would of course avoid the problem of there being various different common names for animals (a major reason for the existence of scientific names). Had we chosen the Latin names, we should now need to find a suitable dictionary or other authority, and look up the scientific names for all the other species in the list.

As I'm writing this in the United Kingdom I shall choose British English over American English, and make 'pigs' my preferred term in the

could be organized more effectively within a medicine classification by introducing some additional arrays:

Medical buildings and facilities
    (by duration of stay)
        Emergency hospitals
        Sanatoriums

    (by stage of disease)
        Convalescent homes
        Hospices

    (by medical specialization)
        Clinics
        Maternity hospitals

## Exercise 14.1

Organize the following terms from the 'people' facet of a sociology classification into appropriate arrays:

adult, baby, blue-collar worker, child, divorced, female, home-owner, homeless, male, married, old person, poor, professional, single, teenager, tenant, unemployed, wealthy, white-collar worker, widowed

## *Order within array*

There are no broadly applicable principles for deciding on the order of terms within an array. Some intuitive and general ordering principles can be applied, and often there is an evident natural order of the terms. In the exercise above, the group of terms relating to age would be most sensibly arranged beginning with the baby and finishing with the old person.

Some common ordering rules for arrays can be summarized as follows:

* chronological order
* developmental order, or order of complexity
* sequential order (when terms represent stages in a process)
* physical or geographical proximity.

Alphabetical order should be resisted as far as possible since it does not produce any useful groupings or associations of concepts, and will be of no particular help when generating the thesaurus.

## Order between arrays

The order of arrays within a facet involves deciding on an order of precedence among the different principles of division. This can often be decided by applying two well established classificatory principles:

- the principle of **general-before-special**
- the principle of **increasing concreteness**.

The notion of general-before-special is axiomatic in classification, and seems to be intuitive to users. It governs all sorts of ordering in systematic structures, including the idea that a containing class should precede its members (or a broader term its narrower terms). General-before-special is a driving principle in the organization of hierarchies. So, for example, the sequences:

> Furniture – Chairs – Armchairs

and

> Games – Board games – Scrabble

proceeding from the broader to the narrower, the general to the special, is considered to be more logical and natural than any alternative combination.

The principle of increasing concreteness delivers fairly similar results, except that here the emphasis is on the progression from abstract to concrete. This is rather more helpful in deciding on priorities between arrays, since clearly a concept such as age or gender is more abstract than the concept of a cow.

Nevertheless, in many cases there is little to choose between two arrays, and the compiler must make an arbitrary decision (as is frequently the case in imposing vocabulary control).

In organizing the arrays in the animals facet, I've decided on an order of gender – age – physiological condition – living conditions – function – species. This seems fairly well to observe increasing concreteness, and complies with general-before-special in terms of 'population size'. That is to say, sets such as female animals, young animals, wild animals, working animals, horses, are sets with increasingly specific characteristics and correspondingly fewer members in each subsequent set. This cannot be regarded as a universal principle, but it is the sort of pragmatic approach that works very adequately in a specific situation.

## Summary

- Within a facet there needs to be further organization of terms into sub-facets or arrays
- All the members of an array should share some common property
- This property is called the principle, or characteristic, of division, or the node label
- There are no particular rules for the order of terms within an array
- Any useful and appropriate means of ordering the terms can be used
- Order between arrays can be decided by using the principles of general-before-special and increasing concreteness.

The effects of applying these principles to our basic animal facet can be seen in Figure 14.2 (overleaf).

Although the grouping of terms is now rather better, the order within each array still lacks coherence. One example of a very muddled array is that for 'animals by age or gender', where two principles have been applied simultaneously:

(animals by age or gender)
calves
chicks
ducklings
males
mares
piglets
sows
turkey poults

While all these terms contain some aspect of gender or age implicit in the term, these aspects are far from explicit, and need to be made so. We can do this by analysing these terms to give the following:

young [cows]
young [birds]
young [ducks]
males
female [horses]
young [pigs]
female [sows]
young [turkeys]

**(animals by age or gender)**
calves
chicks
ducklings
males
mares
piglets
sows
turkey poults

**(animals by physiological condition)**
inbred strains
pregnant
 pregnant mares
 pregnant sows

**(animals by living conditions)**
caged
 caged hens
 caged rabbits
captive animals
 captive chimpanzees
 captive tigers
domestic animals
 domestic cats
 domestic rabbits
 domestic sheep
farm animals. livestock
 farmed fish
 farmed mink
feral cats
free-living wild animals
free-range
 free-range poultry
intensively farmed animals
kennelled
 kennelled dogs
outdoor
 outdoor sows
pastured
 pastured cows
wild animals
wild conspecifics
wild-caught animals
zoo animals. zoo housed
 animals
 zoo-housed gorillas

**(animals by function)**
animals used in
 education
breeding
 breeding ostriches
broilers
children's pets
dairy
 dairy cows
 dairy herds
exotic pets
feeders
 feeder pigs
growing
 growing pigs
guard animals
 guard dogs
 guard donkeys
 guard llamas
laboratory animals
laying
 laying hens
meat
 meat goats
pests
 vertebrate pests
pets
rearing
 rearing pigs
sport
 sport horses
trotting
 trotting horses
veal
 veal calves
working
 working equids
 working horses

**(animals by species)**
African elephants.
 loxodonta africana
baboons
badgers
bears
blue foxes
capuchin monkeys
cats
cattle
chickens. hens

chimpanzees
coyotes
dogs
donkeys
ducks
emus
equids
Eurasian otters. lutra lutra
fish
giraffe. giraffa
 camelopardalis
goats
gorillas
grey parrots
grey squirrels
guinea pigs
hedgehogs
horses
Japanese quail
llamas
mice
mink
monkeys
mules
non-human animals
orangutans. pongo pygmaeus
ostriches
otters
pigs. hogs. swine
ponies
poultry
primates
rabbits
rainbow trout
ratites
rats
rheas
rhesus macaques
rodents
Scottish blackface sheep
sheep
Siberian hamster
squirrels
tigers
tufted capuchin monkeys
turkeys
vertebrates
western lowland gorillas

**Figure 14.2** Animals facet concepts roughly sorted into arrays

There are obviously three concepts here relating to age or gender which can be stated explicitly. At the same time the two principles of age and gender can be separated:

(animals by age)
   young

(animals by gender)
   males
   females

(For the time being the compound terms have been retained in their original positions in the facet until subsequent stages of analysis determine their final location.)

The separation of principles of division is important, since the concepts in an array should be **mutually exclusive**. In other words, two terms from the same array should not be applicable to the same subject (as would be the case if indexing an item about young male pigs, for example). This is sometimes alternatively expressed by stating that the concepts (in a single array) should consist of different 'values' within the same range.

This may seem a trivial thing, but it contributes to the whole picture of accuracy in the vocabulary analysis, and it makes the resulting structure conceptually more consistent, and thus more reliable. Such rigour in constructing systems is particularly important when they are to be used in mechanized environments.

### Exhausting the principle of division

These arrays need to be expanded further to make them complete. This listing of all the possibilities in an array is called **exhausting the principle of division**. For these two arrays (bearing in mind the likely categories of farmed animals), we might arrive at:

(animals by age)
   newborn
   young
   growing
   mature
   aged

(animals by gender)
   males
   neutered males
   females
   neutered females

Because of the limitations on space in a book of this sort, I don't wish to follow this through for every area of the vocabulary, and in any event it isn't always necessary to represent every possibility. We do not, for instance, need to include every known kind of animal, since they will not be represented in the literature on animal welfare. However, very obvious gaps in coverage can, and should, easily be addressed by completing arrays in this manner, and this compensates for the possibility that the initial selection of vocabulary may not have been comprehensive.

Figure 14.3 shows the animal vocabulary with the arrays made more explicit, and with some sense of order imposed upon them. Compound terms are retained, and at the locations to which they were originally assigned. They will be assigned to their proper places (if these are different) when the analysis is complete.

| (animals by gender) | (animals by physiological | feral |
|---|---|---|
| males |   condition) |   feral cats |
| neutered males | inbred strains | domestic animals |
| females | pregnant |   domestic cats |
|   mares |   pregnant mares |   domestic rabbits |
|   sows |   pregnant sows |   domestic sheep |
| neutered females | | |
| | (animals by living | farm animals. livestock |
| (animals by age) |   conditions) |   farmed fish |
| newborn | indoors |   farmed mink |
| young | outdoors |   intensively farmed |
|   calves |   outdoor sows |     animals |
|   chicks | wild animals | caged |
|   ducklings | wild conspecifics |   caged hens |
|   piglets | free-living wild animals |   caged rabbits |
|   turkey poults | wild-caught animals | kennelled |
| growing | captive animals |   kennelled dogs |
| mature |   captive chimpanzees | pastured |
| aged |   captive tigers |   pastured cows |
| | zoo animals. zoo | free-range |
| |   housed animals |   free range poultry |
| |   zoo housed gorillas | |

*Continued on next page*

**Figure 14.3** Animals facet arrays with ordering of concepts

| | | |
|---|---|---|
| **(animals by function)** | sport | guinea pigs |
| pets | sport horses | hedgehogs |
| children's pets | trotting | horses |
| exotic pets | trotting horses | Japanese quail |
| animals used in | | llamas |
| education | pests | mice |
| breeding | vertebrate pests | mink |
| breeding ostriches | | monkeys |
| rearing | **(animals by species)** | mules |
| rearing pigs | African elephants. | non-human animals |
| laboratory animals | loxodonta africana | orangutans. pongo |
| | baboons | pygmaeus |
| (food production) | badgers | ostriches |
| dairy | bears | otters |
| dairy cows | blue foxes | pigs. hogs. swine |
| dairy herds | capuchin monkeys | ponies |
| laying | cats | poultry |
| laying hens | cattle | primates |
| meat | chickens. hens | rabbits |
| meat goats | chimpanzees | rainbow trout |
| veal | coyotes | ratites |
| veal calves | dogs | rats |
| broilers | donkeys | rheas |
| feeders | ducks | rhesus macaques |
| feeder pigs | emus | rodents |
| growers | equids | Scottish blackface sheep |
| grower pigs | Eurasian otters. lutra | sheep |
| | lutra | Siberian hamster |
| working | fish | squirrels |
| working equids | giraffe. giraffa | tigers |
| working horses | camelopardalis | tufted capuchin monkeys |
| guard animals | goats | turkeys |
| guard dogs | gorillas | vertebrates |
| guard donkeys | grey parrots | western lowland gorillas |
| guard llamas | grey squirrels | |

**Figure 14.3** *Continued*

# Summary

- There may need to be further organization of large arrays
- Principles of division should be determined and arrays divided where more than one principle is in operation
- Each principle of division should be 'exhausted', so that the array contains all the possible values for that principle of division
- It is not essential to list every possible class in large facets or arrays where these will not be needed in practice

• Where compound terms have been retained, the concept that is being used for analysis should be clearly identified.

## Answers to exercises

### Exercise 14.1

Organize the following terms from the 'people' facet of a sociology classification into appropriate arrays:

> adult, baby, blue-collar worker, child, divorced, female, home-owner, homeless, male, married, old person, poor, professional, single, teenager, tenant, unemployed, wealthy, white-collar worker, widowed

### Persons

| (by age) | (by gender) | (by marital status) | (by income) | (by accommodation) | (by occupational status) |
|---|---|---|---|---|---|
| baby | male | single | poor | homeless | blue-collar |
| child | female | married | wealthy | tenant | white-collar |
| teenager | | divorced | | home-owner | professional |
| adult | | widowed | | | unemployed |
| old person | | | | | |

# 15 Building a thesaurus 5: imposing hierarchy

An obvious way in which the structure of arrays can be improved is by displaying any hierarchical relationships between concepts. We have already looked at the nature of the broader/narrower term relationship in some detail in Chapter 13, together with a large number of examples of different kinds of relationship. Consideration of the **hierarchy** in this chapter is mainly of the particular needs of the animals facet, so, although some general principles are discussed, this is mainly a demonstration of putting the theory into practice in a specific situation.

## Hierarchical structure

Compared with an enumerative, pre-coordinated system, a faceted structure is usually a rather flat structure, with limited levels of hierarchy. This is because it doesn't contain many complicated compounds. Nevertheless some degree of hierarchy will exist and should be represented in the systematic structure. Concepts that exist in a superordinate/subordinate or broader/narrower term relationship need to be brought together in the linear order so that these relationships can be properly displayed.

The recognition of these broader/narrower term relationships seems to be intuitive, and even novice thesaurus compilers experience little difficulty with this part of the process. This is particularly so when the terminology can be easily understood by a lay person, although in the case of a technical subject, some help may be required from a dictionary or encyclopaedia. Our animal terms are relatively straightforward to interpret, to some extent because of the decision to use vernacular names. Despite that, there are a few challenging terms (because no vernacular equivalents exist) and I needed the aid of a dictionary to discover that 'ratites' is the containing class for emus, ostriches and rheas.

### *Representation of hierarchy*

We normally represent hierarchy in the systematic display by indenting a subordinate concept to its containing class, as follows:

> Primates
> > Gorillas
> > > Western lowland gorillas

This visual representation of subordinate classes will enable us to identify the broader and narrower terms very easily when we come to convert the taxonomic structure to thesaurus format. Because all the terms in a facet are of the same general kind (i.e. all entities, or processes, or products) there will not usually be any problem in establishing whether the relationships are genuine hierarchical relationships, of a thing/kind or whole/part nature, since they cannot really be otherwise. In the hierarchy

> Primates
> > Monkeys
> > > Capuchin monkeys
> > > > Tufted capuchin monkeys

because all the terms in the facet are animals (and, by definition, 'things' or 'entities'), there is no possibility of a relationship occurring between these entity terms and others from different fundamental categories, such as operations or products. Separating the categories and organizing them individually means that this situation will always hold good.

At the same time, it can still be helpful to ask the 'thing/kind/whole/part' question in respect of the relationship between a particular pair of terms. For example, enquiring whether a western lowland gorilla is a kind of gorilla would receive a positive answer:

> BT   Gorillas
> NT     Western lowland gorillas  ✓

whereas there is obviously no broader term/narrower term relationship between pigs and guinea pigs:

BT    Pigs
NT        Guinea pigs        ×

## Completing the hierarchy

Because initially we were selective in gathering the vocabulary, just as there are gaps in the application of principles of division, so there are also gaps in the hierarchy. We can't possibly (and don't need to) include every known animal, but we may need to introduce some extra terms to allow proper grouping of concepts and to make sure that the hierarchical structure is even and consistent. For instance, although we have many terms that refer to particular species, and the very general term 'vertebrates', there is no provision for intermediate groups such as mammals or birds. These need to be put in, as do the containing genera 'foxes' (for blue foxes), 'macaques' (for rhesus macaques) and 'hamsters' (for Siberian hamster). Like so many other aspects of the hierarchical structure, this is much more readily achieved within the systematic display.

## Classification authorities

The animals facet provides us with a slightly unusual situation in that the classification of animals is a well established field of scientific study and research in its own right and there are a number of authoritative zoological classifications to be found. The consequences of this are twofold:

- there is little point in spending time on the development of a classification when good ones already exist
- there is a danger of conflict with accepted structures if vocabulary compilers go their own way.

The latter could certainly cause difficulties if the thesaurus is to be used in a scientific environment where assumptions may be made about the order and relationships within animal nomenclature. For that reason it is sensible to follow an established authority when one exists. Animals and plants are probably the best known examples of such classifications, but you can also find classifications for chemical elements, rocks and minerals, stars, micro-organisms, diseases, and so on. In the social sciences they abound, albeit on a smaller scale, and even in the humanities there are instances of classifications for musical instruments, languages and religions. An internet search for 'classification of' throws up many interesting, and sometimes amusing, examples, and although most of these are not authoritative, they can nevertheless be an excellent guide to accepted conventions in a field.

## Modification of authorities

As it would be inappropriate to reproduce the whole formal structure of a zoological taxonomy, I have just used the 'classes' (mammals, birds, fishes), together with 'genera' (cats, equines), and species (tigers, horses). Where particular varieties or breeds are named, these have been included as a further subdivision. Hence, instead of

    Animalia
      Chordata
        Mammalia
          Carnivora
            Canidae
              Canis
                Canis familiaris

we shall have only a limited number of levels:

    Mammals
      Dogs
        Domestic dogs

Although this structure would not be sufficient for a scientific zoological thesaurus, it will avoid a number of difficulties in a non-technical area. Non-scientists will probably not be familiar with the names of the various orders, families and tribes to which species belong – few of these have any English equivalents, and the thesaural cross-references generated from such a sophisticated structure might be less than helpful. The formal taxonomy is therefore used primarily to provide an outline structure, and an acceptable and conventional order of species. The thesaurus taxonomy conforms in a general sense to the authority and additional species can be added fairly easily by reference to it.

Because of the cross-disciplinary nature of animal welfare, the classification of animals is more complicated than it might otherwise be. The standard zoological classifications are very suitable for wild species (including those in zoos), but less so for domestic animals. These cover a much smaller range of species, but have many varieties and breeds. In addition, the groupings of species in zoological taxonomies are not always appropriate for domestic and farm animals, where behaviour and function, rather than anatomy, may be the basis of grouping (e.g. dairy animals). Most documentary classification schemes provide alternative taxonomies for biological sciences and agriculture, and I have decided to adopt a compromise solution, using a taxonomic approach for the species of wild origin, and a more pragmatic arrangement for domestic animals.

## Hierarchy in different facets

Spotting the hierarchical relationships is relatively simple in an entities facet, such as that of animals, where taxonomic relationships are well established. Doing the same thing for more abstract concepts, such as processes, may not be so intuitive, but will come with a little practice. Here are some examples from the other basic animal welfare facets:

From the Agents facet:

    Foods
        Coarse mix feeds
        Grass
            Grass-based foods
        Monkey chow

From the Operations facet:

    Veterinary procedures
        Anaesthesia
        Dosing techniques
        Euthanasia

From the Processes facet:

    Animal behaviour
        Maternal behaviour
            Nest building
            Milk production

As in the case of the animals facet, there is normally no confusion over the validity of the hierarchical relationship since all the terms fall into the same category. For the most part relationships are of the thing/kind variety, and whole/part relationships are relatively rare. One example of the latter occurs in the operations facet

    Transporting
      Loading

where loading is a part of the more general operation of transporting animals.

## Summary

- The hierarchical relationships in the facet should be identified and displayed
- These are represented by indentation of a concept under its containing class
- The resulting taxonomic structure will allow easy generation of the broader and narrower terms in the thesaurus
- Because all concepts have the same categorical status the relationships are automatically of the BT/NT variety
- Some gaps in the hierarchy may need to be filled to create a consistent structure
- Existing classifications and taxonomies can be used as authorities to establish relationships
- Some modification of a scientific classification may be required to meet the practical needs of the thesaurus
- Hierarchical relationships can be found in all facets
- In the more abstract facets thing/kind relationships are commoner than whole/part relationships.

We have now covered all the techniques that are necessary to create a properly structured set of facets for our subject. Taking the animals facet in Figure 14.2, where synonym control and basic organization into arrays had already been carried out, we can now impose the display of hierarchical structure. This generates the nearly completed facet as shown in Figure 15.1.

Appendix 4 shows the other facets after internal structuring. To remind you, here are all the processes of facet organization in the order in which they have been applied above:

(animals by gender)
males
neutered males
females
  mares
  sows
neutered females

(animals by age)
newborn
young
  calves
  chicks
  ducklings
  piglets
  turkey poults
growing
mature
aged

(animals by physiological condition)
inbred strains
pregnant
  pregnant mares
  pregnant sows

(animals by living conditions)
indoors
outdoors
  outdoor sows

wild animals
  free-living wild animals
  wild-caught animals
  captive animals
    captive chimpanzees
    captive tigers
    zoo animals. zoo
      housed animals
      zoo housed gorillas
feral
  feral cats

domestic animals. domesticated animals
  domestic cats
  domestic rabbits
  domestic sheep

farm(ed) animals. livestock
  farmed fish

farmed mink
intensively farmed animals

(indoor). housed animals
  caged
    caged hens
    caged rabbits
  kennelled
    kennelled dogs
(outdoor)
  pastured
    pastured cows
  free-range
    free-range poultry

(animals by function)
pets
  children's pets
  exotic pets
animals used in education
breeding
  breeding ostriches
  rearing pigs
laboratory animals

(food production)
  dairy
    dairy cows
  laying
    laying hens
  meat
    meat goats
    veal calves
    broilers
    feeder pigs
    growing pigs

working
  working equids
    working horses
  guard animals
    guard dogs
    guard donkeys
    guard llamas
sport
  sport horses
  trotting
    trotting horses

*Continued on next page*

**Figure 15.1** Animals facet arrays with ordering of concepts and hierarchical relationships

pests
  vertebrate pests

**(animals by species)**
non-human animals
wild animals (usually assumed)
vertebrates

  fish
    rainbow trout
  birds
    anatidae. ducks
    ratites
      ostriches
      rheas
      emus
    gallinaceae. gamebirds
      domestic fowls. chickens. poultry
      turkeys
      quail
        Japanese quail
    psittacidae. parrots
      grey parrots

  mammals
    rodents
      squirrels
        grey squirrels
      rats
      mice
      hamsters
        Siberian hamster
      guinea pigs. cavies
    lagomorphs
      rabbits

  insectivora
    hedgehogs
  elephants. proboscids
    African elephant. loxodonta Africana

  hoofed animals. perissodactyla
    equids. equidae
      horses
      ponies
      donkeys. asses
      mules

    even toed ungulates. artiodactyla
      pigs. hogs. swine
      camels

      llamas
    ruminants
    giraffe. giraffa camelopardalis
    bovines
      cattle
    caprines
      sheep
        Scottish blackface sheep
      goats

carnivores. carnivora
  canidae
    foxes
      blue foxes
    coyotes
    domestic dogs
  ursidae. bears
  mustelidae
    mink
    badgers
    otters
      Eurasian otter.
        lutra lutra
  felidae. cats
    tigers
    domestic cats

simiae. apes and monkeys. primates
  monkeys
    capuchin monkeys
      tufted capuchin monkeys
    macaques
      rhesus macaques
    baboons
  apes. anthropoid apes
    chimpanzees
    orangutans. pongo pygmaeus
    gorillas
      western lowland gorillas

domestic animals. domesticated animals

poultry
  chickens
  ducks
  turkeys
  (turkeys)
  quail
    Japanese quail

*Continued on next page*

**Figure 15.1** *Continued*

| | |
|---|---|
| equids | Scottish blackface sheep |
|   horses | goats |
|   ponies | llamas |
|   asses. donkeys | |
|   mules | fur-bearing animals |
| |   mink |
| cattle |   rabbits |
|   beef cattle | |
|   dairy cattle | domestic pets |
|   dual-purpose breeds |   cats |
| |   dogs |
| pigs. hogs. swine |   rabbits |
| |   small rodents |
| sheep | |

**Figure 15.1** *Continued*

1 Identify and collocate any synonyms.
2 Make any necessary general policy decisions about preferred terminology.
3 Organize the terms into arrays and label the principles of division used.
4 Order the terms in array in whatever seems a useful sequence.
5 Identify hierarchical relationships, and display them through indentation.
6 Consult any necessary authorities to confirm your hierarchy.

This seems to me a natural and logical order in which to address the various tasks of synonym control and organization of concepts within a facet, but it is not absolutely binding on you. You won't create any particular difficulties if you sort out the hierarchical relationships before organization into arrays, although you will obviously be dealing with larger sets of concepts if you attack the problem this way round. In practice, when you become more adept, you can probably deal with different aspects of the organization simultaneously as you spot the various synonyms, subordinate concepts and principles of division.

# 16 Building a thesaurus 6: compound subjects and citation order

Having assigned concepts to fundamental categories, imposed some more detailed arrangement into arrays, and identified hierarchies, we now have a set of completed facets for the field of animal welfare. It would be quite possible to generate the thesaurus from the vocabulary in its current state, since most of the thesaural relationships are determined by the immediate context of a term in the systematic structure. Equivalence relationships and those of hierarchy are already evident, and many associative relationships can be derived from the facet internal structure without considering how the different facets relate to each other.

Nevertheless, there are some considerable advantages in bringing the systematic display to a more finished state:

- the systematic display can then be used as a taxonomy or classification in its own right
- considering the relationships between facets allows us to establish a policy for the correct location of compound concepts
- this in turn clarifies the nature of thesaural relationships, particularly the distinction between the broader and related terms of compounds.

Nowadays, when many taxonomies and other vocabulary tools only exist online, it is reasonable to ask whether the idea of order has any relevance. If the animal welfare vocabulary were to be managed digitally, it might be possible never to think about the overall order and structure of the vocabulary. The facets could sit independently in the digital space, indexing terms could be chosen and assigned without thinking about the order of combination, and retrieval would operate on the same basis, that is post-coordinately. The individual items indexed are dealt with both at the indexing and retrieval stage in isolation from each other, and this is perfectly adequate for a high proportion of information-seeking tasks. A number of retrieval systems using faceted techniques in a graphical interface make use of this approach, notably commercial retail sites which allow the customer to select and combine aspects of a product without having to refer to an overall list.

However, most of the 'terms' in such systems are very simple and don't involve anything in the way of overlap between concepts. In the area of documentation, the majority of items are complex, and the concepts dealt with can be compound both in the verbal form of a term and in its conceptual constitution. Having some rules helps us to sort out this complexity and manage the frequent combinations of concepts.

Rules for ordering also support the browsing function of tools, since order is an essential part of that activity. In many ways a faceted structure is like a multi-dimensional map, with compound topic descriptions corresponding to map references. A correct sequence of elements in a compound allows it to be located precisely, and hence retrieved efficiently. Systems in which any combination order is possible can 'locate' items in, and retrieve them from, a number of different positions, but such a system doesn't function as a map, and gives no clear overview of a subject field.

Lastly, a system of linear ordering is helpful in any situation where more than one item is to be displayed simultaneously. This might occur in a browsing context, where resources need to be presented in some organized manner, or in the listing of results of a search. Needless to say, if the taxonomy is being used to arrange items physically, either on shelves, in physical files, or in published lists, reliable rules for locating compound subjects are vital.

## Order of facets

There are two aspects to be considered in deciding on the order of facets in a systematic display, classification or taxonomy:

- the order in which the facets are listed in the vocabulary itself
- the order in which terms from different facets are combined when indexing, or when placing compound terms.

## Order of display of facets (filing order)

The order in which the facets are listed within the vocabulary itself is known as the filing order, or **schedule order**. This is very closely related to the order of combination between facets, which we shall consider shortly. The classification principles of general-before-special and increasing concreteness help to establish the optimum order in which the different facets should appear. In the case of faceted tools, the optimum filing order of facets is now well established.

In most situations the fundamental categories are arranged in the order:

Time – space – agent – product – patient – operation – process – material – property – part – kind – thing

This ensures that the more general (and more abstract) concepts, such as periods of time, come at the beginning of the sequence. The more specific and more concrete concepts (in the case of animal welfare, the animals themselves) appear at the end of the list. This kind of arrangement seems to be intuitive to most users; they expect very general items to file first, and more complicated and precise topics to be further down the list.

If we apply this generally accepted order to our facets in the animal welfare vocabulary, the resulting filing or schedule order should look like this:

Periods
Places
Agents
Products
Operations
Processes
Properties
Parts
Animals

In addition to the fundamental categories, we have two additional group-ings: form subdivisions and abstract concepts. Although these are not directly addressed by the theory of facet analysis, in practice they are conventionally placed at the beginning of any structured classification (because of their generality and level of abstraction). Adding these to the list, we can now construct a broad outline of the systematic order, as shown in Figure 16.1.

Animal welfare
    Common subdivisions of form
    Theory and philosophy of animal welfare
    History of animal welfare. Time periods
    Geography of animal welfare. Animal welfare in specific places
    Agents and equipment
        Persons in animal welfare
        Equipment
        Buildings and the environment
        Organizations
    Animal products
        Food
        Fur and wool
    Operations on animals. Management and husbandry of animals
        Animal abuse
        Veterinary care
        Farming. Agriculture

    Processes. Animal physiology
        Pathology. Animal health
        Animal psychology
        Animal behaviour
    Parts. Animal anatomy

    Animals
        Wild animals
            Zoo animals

        Domesticated animals
            Farm animals. Livestock
            Pets
            Working animals
                Animals used in sport

        Animals by species

**Figure 16.1** Outline of the finished systematic display

## Summary

- Facets are usually arranged in an order progressing from the most general or abstract to the most specific or concrete
- This order is known as filing or schedule order
- The default order of standard facet analysis is: time – space – agent – product – patient – operation – process – material – property – part – kind – thing.

## Order of combination of terms (citation order)

Having established the sequence or filing order of facets, we can now consider how to handle the location of compound terms, that is terms that are a combination of concepts from more than one facet or array.

Up to this point I have placed compound terms in the model thesaurus on a rather *ad hoc* basis, without much consideration of whether they are 'correctly' located, or of what the alternatives might be. The main concern with respect to compound terms has been to keep them intact, and to put them in an acceptable location, with a view to examining them more closely at this more advanced stage. Now we need to think about a proper policy for the placing of these compounds, and here facet analysis gives us some very clear guidelines.

### Citation order

In controlled indexing languages, the idea of a **citation order**, or **combination order**, is very common. Citation order means the order in which the elements in a compound subject are combined in any index description of that subject. For example, a bibliography of clog dancing in Wales might be indexed in six different ways as:

Clog dancing – Wales – Bibliography
Clog dancing – Bibliography – Wales
Wales – Clog dancing – Bibliography
Wales – Bibliography – Clog dancing
Bibliography – Clog dancing – Wales
Bibliography – Wales – Clog dancing

While it is theoretically feasible to include all these permutations, in practice it is better to have a single preferred order of combination (or citation order). In a pre-coordinate system such as a library classification used for arranging documents, or a system of subject headings used in a catalogue or database, the citation order chosen affects the order in which items (either documents or records) occur, that is the filing order. In such a situation it is vital to have a rule that determines the order in which the parts of a compound should be combined, since the item can have only one location. The rule will ensure that the combination of concepts is done on a consistent basis, and that the handling and location of compounds is predictable. This affects retrieval, which is easier and more efficient if the rules of the system are known and adhered to. The rules of combination for compounds, and devices that support them, are sometimes referred to as the system **syntax**.

It is also helpful to apply a citation order in a vocabulary tool in order to place compound terms. We could of course place a compound in all its possible locations in the vocabulary, although this would create a high level of duplication of material. In terms of arranging items, however, clearly only one location can be used for the document. It is possible to envisage a situation where a thesaurus is created, managed and applied digitally to digital objects, and where there is limited browsing or display. In such a case it would be possible to have multiple 'locations' for individual compounds, both in the thesaurus and in the collection. Even here, however, there would need to be some underlying structural principles.

The consistent and logical placing of compounds also allows us to be clear about the different hierarchies in which the compound could be found, and hence to be sure about the nature of relationships, and whether they are hierarchical or associative.

### Standard citation order

The established facet analytical method we have been using employs a default order, known as **standard citation order**, as follows:

Thing – kind – part – property – material – process – operation – patient – product – agent – space – time

You will notice that this is the reverse of the filing order. A systematic schedule which inverts the order of filing and citation in this way is known as an inverted schedule.

## Summary

- The order in which concepts or terms are combined in a compound subject is called the citation order
- The choice of citation order will affect the arrangement and filing order of items in a physical collection or listing
- The citation order must be clear and consistently applied, so that the location of compounds is predictable

- Facet analysis uses a standard citation order of facets
- This order is reversed, or inverted, in the filing order of facets.

## Combining and locating terms

The application of citation order in an inverted schedule ensures that compounds file in a logical position. Let's look at some examples:

| | | |
|---|---|---|
| 'Boredom in zoo animals' | = | 'Zoo animals (thing) – Boredom (process)' |
| 'Social organization of monkeys' | = | 'Monkeys (thing) – Social organization (process)' |
| 'Training of dogs' | = | 'Dogs (thing) – Training (operation)' |
| 'Farming in Sweden' | = | 'Farming (operation) – Sweden (place)' |

In each case the compound concept will be located under the most specific (i.e. the later filing) element. You can think of this another way, by stating that more specific (and later filing) concepts are qualified, or subdivided, by more general (or earlier filing) concepts. Any concept can be qualified by any concept that precedes it in the filing order. In a taxonomy or classification, this allows the building of compound classes in a systematic way. In the animal welfare vocabulary, we could build up a more detailed classification structure under, for example, a specific kind of animal, in the following manner:

Horses
    (Agents)
        Grooms. Stable workers
          Riders
    (Equipment)
        Saddlery. Harness
    (Buildings/environment)
        Stables
          Flooring
        Paddocks

> (Operations)
>> Training of horses
>> Horse management. Horse husbandry
>>> Pasture management
>>> Horse breeding
>>>> (Buildings/organization)
>>>>> Stud farms
> (Processes)
>> Equine physiology
>>> Diseases of the horse
> (Parts)
>> Locomotor system
>>> (Processes)
>>>> Diseases of the locomotor system
>>>> Bony enlargements. Spavin
>>>>> (Operation)
>>>>>> Veterinary treatment
>>>>>>> (Agents)
>>>>>>>> Drugs. Chemicals. Blisters
> (Kinds of horse)
>> (by function)
>>> Working horses
>>> Racehorses
>> (by breed)
>>> Welsh cob
>>> Arab. Arabian
>>> Thoroughbred

(Note that, for the purposes of demonstration, I've added a number of compound terms not in the original vocabulary.)

The consistent application of the rules means that no compound concept precedes any of its constituent parts, and thus it observes the rule of general-before-special. It also ensures that the handling of compounds is predictable.

The taxonomy that has been developed for this thesaurus uses the standard citation order, but it is important to know that citation order can be varied according to the needs of the subject field. For example, a thesaurus for history would probably need places to be the first cited (and last filing) facet, in order to keep all the terms relating to a country together. What you must remember is that the filing order of facets should be the opposite of the citation order.

Any number of elements in a compound can be managed in this way, since combination is not restricted. All you need to remember is that the citation order should be strictly observed. Here are some examples taken from the original list of document titles:

'Cat overpopulation in the United States'
 = Cats – overpopulation – United States

'Housing of breeding ostriches in Germany'
 = Ostriches – breeding – housing – Germany

'Changes in ear-pinna temperature as a measure of stress in sheep'
 = Sheep – ear pinnae – temperature – stress – measurement

'Effect of blindfolding horses on heart-rate and behaviour during handling and loading on to transport vehicles'
 = Horses – heart-rate – behaviour – blindfolding – loading – transport vehicles

Of course, these very complicated combinations usually occur only when indexing documents. The placing of compound terms in the vocabulary itself normally involves just two elements, or occasionally three. This is very much the case with thesauri, since one is usually trying to limit the complexity of entry terms rather than the reverse. Nevertheless, these examples do illustrate the capacity of a faceted structure to accommodate complicated subjects logically and consistently. If the taxonomy is to be used as the basis of a browsing tool which will be populated with actual resources, a very complex and sophisticated structure can be generated by the application of the citation rules.

## Summary

- Citation order should be applied to determine the sequence of concepts or terms in a compound subject
- Compounds are located under the concept coming latest in the filing order

- A concept can be qualified by any concept appearing earlier in the order
- Complex classificatory or taxonomic structures can be built up by this method
- A non-standard citation order can be used if it is more appropriate to the subject
- In that case the filing order of facets must also be altered so that it is the reverse of the citation order.

## The nature of compound terms

The sort of compound terms which we encounter in a thesaurus fall into two categories: those which are verbally compound, and those which are conceptually compound.

### Verbal compounds

Verbal compounds are terms consisting of more than one word, mainly nouns qualified by an adjective, or noun phrases. We have already looked at a large number of examples of verbal compounds in the chapters on vocabulary control, primarily to decide whether to retain them as compounds or to factor them into their constituent parts. If we examine the animal welfare vocabulary, we can spot a number of these:

```
Children's pets
Zoo housed gorillas
Pasture management
Tooth clipping
Bear farming
```

Verbal compounds are usually the combination of two concepts, and in these examples we can apply the factoring rules to decide whether to keep them or not. There is not much doubt that the last three examples can be factored without loss of meaning. Hence:

```
Pastures + Management
Teeth + Clipping
Bears + Farming
```

In the first two examples the combination of terms creates a kind or variety of the focus term, so they should be retained.

Sometimes a compound term represents a single concept:

```
Grey squirrels
Case studies
Zoological gardens
Adrenal glands
```

These compounds should always be retained.

## Conceptual compounds

Conceptual compounds are terms, which, although consisting of a single word, embody two or more different concepts. There are a number of these, noticeably in the animals facet, but also elsewhere:

```
Mares                 =    Horses + Females
Ducklings             =    Ducks + Young
Beef                  =    Cattle + Meat
Farrowing             =    Pigs + Parturition
Veterinary surgeons   =    Veterinary procedures +
                           Agent
```

The breaking down of these terms is semantic factoring. This is generally agreed to be undesirable, mainly because the entry term may not be related linguistically to its conceptual parts and would be lost if factored. Compounds of this kind must be preserved, and their correct location carefully considered.

Following our rules for citation order, these compounds will file under the last of their components to appear in the schedule of facets. 'Mares' will file under 'horses', 'ducklings' under 'ducks', 'beef' under 'cattle', 'farrowing' under 'pigs', and 'veterinarians' under 'veterinary procedures'. Figure 16.2 (on page 167) shows the animals facet with its compound terms in the correct location. The other facets, similarly treated, appear in Appendix 5.

## Summary

- Compound terms may be verbal compounds or conceptual compounds
- Verbal compounds are usually also conceptual combinations, and should be factored according to the rules for vocabulary control
- Some verbal compounds represent single concepts and should be retained

- Conceptual compounds that are single terms should be retained and not semantically factored

## Keeping things in order: notation

When the finished order has been established you will need to provide some means of denoting what the order is, so that if, for example, records for each entry are kept in a database, the sequence can be generated from it. This is achieved by assigning a notational code to each term.

Notation is an area of study in its own right, and there is insufficient space here to investigate all the pros and cons of various systems and character sets fully. Nevertheless, we can state some purposes of notational codes fairly briefly:

- The notational code can, as a minimum, act as a control number for the term.
- It can control the systematic order of terms, and generate that order from a non-ordered storage system such as a database.
- It will provide reference points, so that the alphabetical display of the thesaurus can act as an index to the systematic structure.
- It can represent the term in a 'neutral' way, for example in a multilingual environment, or to facilitate mapping from one vocabulary to another.
- It can be used for subject searching (if the catalogue or database software permits it) and, in the case of a controlled vocabulary, can allow simultaneous searching of synonyms.
- Notation for compounds can reflect the compound structure of the subject.
- If used in a pre-coordinate way for the physical arrangement of items, it controls the sequence and allows physical retrieval.

For the purpose of notating the display in a thesaurus, the codes can be very simple, since they are needed only to keep the terms in the required order. For example, we could notate the following section of the animals facet with a hypothetical notation as follows:

| 522 | even toed ungulates. artiodactyla |
| 523 |   pigs. hogs. swine |
| 524 |   camels |
| 525 |     llamas |
| 526 |   ruminants |

| 527 | giraffe. giraffa camelopardalis |
|-----|--------------------------------|
| 528 | bovines |
| 529 | cattle |
| 532 | caprines |
| 533 | sheep |
| 534 | Scottish blackface sheep |
| 535 | goats |

Here the codes do no more than keep the terms in the right order. They don't reflect any relationships of hierarchy, a feature which is often expected by users. A **hierarchically expressive notation** would need to look something like this:

| 522 | even toed ungulates. artiodactyla |
|-----|-----------------------------------|
| 522.1 | pigs. hogs. swine |
| 522.2 | camels |
| 522.23 | llamas |
| 522.3 | ruminants |
| 522.34 | giraffe. giraffa camelopardalis |
| 522.35 | bovines |
| 522.356 | cattle |
| 522.36 | caprines |
| 522.367 | sheep |
| 522.367.8 | Scottish blackface sheep |
| 522.368 | goats |

I've put some decimal points into the notation, simply to make it easier to read, but the same effect can be achieved without the points, or indeed, using letters rather than numbers. This kind of subdivision of notation is usually referred to as decimal filing, since the numbers are regarded as decimal fractions for filing purposes, as opposed to ordinal filing, where numbers file in order of their numerical value. Note that letters can equally well be used 'decimally', as in this example:

| GBF | caprines |
|-----|----------|
| GBFH | sheep |
| GBFHR | Scottish blackface sheep |
| GBFJ | goats |

Letters serve as well as numbers, although many people appear to find numbers easier to file and to retrieve. Although you might think that alphabetical order is extremely familiar, sorting and filing groups of letters that are not words seems much harder, and for that reason numbers might be preferred. Because there are fewer numbers than letters, codes using numbers will be correspondingly longer. Avoid using symbols other than numbers and letters – these have no natural filing order and may confuse users at all levels.

If the notation reflects the hierarchy, it is slightly more difficult to add new terms when they occur; not only must they go in the correct place in the sequence, but the notation must also represent their position relative to 'surrounding' terms. A simple sequence of running numbers can always be divided decimally if all the notational space is allocated:

| | | | | |
|---|---|---|---|---|
| 41 | Alien beings | | 41 | Alien beings |
| 42 | Babel fish | | 42 | Babel fish |
| 43 | The Borg | | 43 | The Borg |
| 44 | Ferengi | | 43.2 | Cybermen |
| 45 | Klingons | | 43 | Daleks |
| 46 | Vulcans | | 43.3 | Ferengi |
| 47 | Romulans | | 45 | Klingons |
| 48 | Vogons | | 45.2 | Martians |
| 49 | Horta | | 46 | Vulcans |
| 51 | Magratheans | | 47 | Romulans |
| | | | 48 | Vogons |
| | | | 49 | Horta |
| | | | 49.3 | Time Lords |
| | | | 51 | Magratheans |

On the other hand, it would clearly be very difficult to insert the extra terms in the second list if the hierarchical structure of the notation had to be maintained.

## Notation for compound terms

Ideally, the notation for compound terms should be constructed by combining the notation for the different parts of the compound. The simplest method of doing this is to use a linking symbol such as an oblique stroke, comma, colon, hyphen, or some other character not otherwise part of the notation. This makes it very clear when two notations are being combined, and avoids the need for more complicated systems. These examples from the animals facet show how this works:

```
Dairy cows        WD/RN
Piglets           WF/RCD
Guard dogs        WJD/RWG
```

More sophisticated synthetic notations do exist, but they require some considerable level of expertise in drafting notation to ensure that all the codes for simple and combined concepts are unique and do not conflict in any way.

The linking device can also function as a **facet indicator**. This need be no more than a single symbol, as described above, which simply indicates the addition of another facet. In other cases, different symbols are used for different facets so that the facet 'status' of a notation can be easily identified. Such systems are very useful in machine retrieval, especially if some degree of automatic indexing is attempted, but they are not at all necessary for our purposes.

A simple notation has been attached to the animals facet shown in Figure 16.2. You will notice that notational space has been left for the other facets to precede the animals facet in the filing order. You will also see that the characteristics and principles of division are not notated (because they are not entry terms). I have used a letter notation simply because it provides shorter codes. In this version an alternative sequence is provided for domesticated animals; other animals are listed in a broadly zoological taxonomic way.

The compound terms have been assigned to their correct positions and the compound notation has been synthesized for these. I have generally preferred the location for domestic animals where this is available. As the other facets are brought to the same level, additional compounds are added to the animals facet.

|       | (animals by gender)                              |
|-------|--------------------------------------------------|
| RBB   | males                                            |
| RBD   | neutered males                                   |
| RBF   | females                                          |
|       | mares → WCH/RBD                                   |
|       | sows → WF/RBD                                     |
| RBG   | neutered females                                 |

|       | (animals by age)                                 |
|-------|--------------------------------------------------|
| RCB   | newborn                                          |
| RCD   | young                                            |
|       | calves → WD/RCD                                   |
|       | chicks → WBC/RCD                                  |
|       | ducklings → WBD/RCD                               |
|       | piglets → WF/RCD                                  |
|       | turkey poults → WBK/RCD                           |
| RCG   | growing                                          |
| RCM   | mature                                           |
| RCW   | aged                                             |

|       | (animals by physiological condition)             |
|-------|--------------------------------------------------|
| RDB   | inbred strains                                   |
| RDP   | pregnant                                         |
|       | pregnant mares → WCH/RDP                          |
|       | pregnant sows → WF/RDP                            |

|       | (animals by living conditions)                   |
|-------|--------------------------------------------------|
| RED   | indoors                                          |
| REP   | outdoors                                         |
|       | outdoor sows → WF/REP                             |
| RFB   | wild animals                                     |
| RFF   | free-living wild animals                         |
| RFG   | wild-caught animals                              |
| RFM   | captive animals                                  |
|       | captive chimpanzees → VR/RFM                     |
|       | captive tigers → TR/RFM                           |
| RFP   | zoo animals. zoo housed animals                  |
|       | zoo housed gorillas → VT/RFP                      |
| RFS   | feral                                            |
|       | feral cats → TS/RFS                               |
| RG    | domestic animals. domesticated animals           |
|       | * Where the notion of domestication is inherent in the animal, this concept need not be added. |
|       | domestic cats → WJC                              |
|       | domestic rabbits → WHR                           |
|       | domestic sheep → WG                              |

| RHB   | farm(ed) animals. livestock                      |
|-------|--------------------------------------------------|
|       | farmed fish → SE/RH                               |
|       | farmed mink → WHM/RH                              |
| RHC   | intensively farmed animals                       |
| RHED  | (indoor). housed animals                         |
| RHEF  | caged                                            |
|       | caged hens → WBC/RHEF                             |
|       | caged rabbits → WHR/RHEF                          |
| RHEK  | kennelled                                        |
|       | kennelled dogs → WJD/RHEK                         |
| RHEP  | (outdoor)                                        |
| RHER  | pastured                                         |
|       | pastured cows → WD/RHER                           |
| RHES  | free-range                                       |
|       | free-range poultry → WB/RHES                      |

|       | (animals by function)                            |
|-------|--------------------------------------------------|
| RJ    | pets                                             |
| RJ/?  | children's pets                                  |
| RJX   | exotic pets                                      |
| RJY   | animals used in education                        |
| RK    | breeding                                         |
|       | breeding ostriches → SFF/RK                       |
|       | rearing pigs → WF/RK                              |
| RL    | laboratory animals                               |
| RM    | (food production)                                |
| RN    | dairy                                            |
|       | dairy cows → WD/RN                                |
| RP    | egg production. laying                           |
|       | laying hens → WBC/RP                              |
| RS    | meat                                             |
|       | meat goats → WGG/RS                               |
|       | veal calves → WD/RS/RCD                           |
|       | broilers → WBC/RS                                |
|       | feeder pigs → WF/RS                               |
|       | growing pigs → WF/RS                              |
| RW    | working                                          |
|       | working equids → WC/RW                            |
|       | working horses → WCH/RW                           |
| RWG   | guard animals                                    |
|       | guard dogs → WJD/RWG                              |
|       | guard donkeys → WCR/RWG                           |
|       | guard llamas → WGL/RWG                            |
| RWS   | sport                                            |
|       | sport horses → WCH/RWS                            |

*Continued on next page*

**Figure 16.2** Completed animals facet with notation

| | | | | | |
|---|---|---|---|---|---|
| RWT | | trotting | SM | hoofed animals. perissodactyla | |
| | | trotting horses → | SMB | equids. equidae | |
| | | WCH/RWT | SMC | horses | |
| | | | SMD | ponies | |
| RV | pests | | SMF | donkeys. asses | |
| | | vertebrate pests → SD/RV | SMM | mules | |
| | | | | | |
| | **(animals by species)** | | SP | even toed ungulates. artiodactyla | |
| SB | non-human animals (usually assumed) | | SPP | pigs. hogs. swine | |
| SC | wild animals | | SPQ | camels | |
| SD | vertebrates | | SPS | llamas | |
| SD/RV | vertebrate pests | | SR | ruminants | |
| | | | SRB | giraffe. giraffa camelopardalis | |
| SE | fish | | SRC | bovines | |
| SE/RH | farmed fish | | SS | cattle | |
| SER | rainbow trout | | SSC | caprines | |
| SF | birds | | ST | sheep | |
| SFD | ducks. anatidae | | STB | Scottish blackface sheep | |
| SFE | ratites | | SW | goats | |
| SFF | ostriches | | | | |
| SFF/RK | breeding ostriches | | T | carnivores. carnivora | |
| SFFH | rheas | | TC | canidae | |
| SFFM | emus | | TCF | foxes | |
| SFG | gamebirds. gallinaceae. | | TCG | blue foxes | |
| SFH | chickens. domestic fowls. | | TCH | coyotes | |
| | poultry | | TG | domestic dogs | |
| SFK | turkeys | | TL | ursidae. bears | |
| SFL | quail | | TM | mustelidae | |
| SFM | Japanese quail | | TMM | mink | |
| SFP | parrots. psittacidae | | TMN | badgers | |
| SFR | grey parrots | | TMO | otters | |
| | | | TMP | Eurasian otter. lutra lutra | |
| SG | mammals | | TP | felidae. cats | |
| SH | rodents | | TR | tigers | |
| SHB | squirrels | | TR/RFM | captive tigers | |
| SHC | grey squirrels | | TS | domestic cats | |
| SHG | rats | | | | |
| SHM | mice | | V | simiae. apes and monkeys. primates | |
| SHN | hamsters | | VC | monkeys | |
| SHO | Siberian hamster | | VE | capuchin monkeys | |
| SHP | guinea pigs. cavies | | VF | tufted capuchin monkeys | |
| SHQ | lagomorphs | | VG | macaques | |
| SHR | rabbits | | VL | rhesus macaques | |
| | | | VM | baboons | |
| SJ | insectivora | | VP | apes. anthropoid apes | |
| SK | hedgehogs | | VR | chimpanzees | |
| | | | VR/RFM | captive chimpanzees | |
| SL | elephants. proboscids | | VS | orangutans. pongo pygmaeus | |
| SLL | African elephant. loxodonta | | VT | gorillas | |
| | Africana | | | | |

**Figure 16.2** *Continued*

| | | | | |
|---|---|---|---|---|
| | *Continued on next page* | | WD/RHER | pastured cows |
| VT/RFP | zoo-housed gorillas | | WD/RN | dairy cattle |
| VW | western lowland gorillas | | WD/RS | beef cattle |
| | | | WD/RS/RCD | veal calves |
| W | domestic animals. domesticated animals | | WD/RS/RN | dual-purpose breeds |
| | | | | |
| WB | poultry | | WF | pigs. hogs. swine |
| WBC | chickens | | WF/RBD | sows |
| WBC/RCD | chicks | | WF/RBD/REP | outdoor sows |
| WBC/RHEF | caged hens | | WF/RDP | pregnant sows |
| WBC/RHES | free-range poultry | | WF/RCD | piglets |
| WBC/RP | laying hens | | WF/RK | rearing pigs |
| WBC/RS | broilers | | WF/RS | feeder pigs |
| WBD | ducks | | WF/RS | growing pigs |
| WBD/RCD | ducklings | | | |
| WBK | turkeys | | WG | sheep |
| WBK/RCD | turkey poults | | WGD | Scottish blackface sheep |
| WBQ | quail | | WGG | goats |
| WBR | Japanese quail | | WGG/RS | meat goats |
| | | | WGL | llamas |
| WC | equids | | WGL/RWG | guard llamas |
| WC/RW | working equids | | | |
| WCH | horses | | WH | fur-bearing animals |
| WCH/RBD | mares | | WHM | mink |
| WCH/RDP | pregnant mares | | WHM/RH | farmed mink |
| WCH/RW | working horses | | WHR | rabbits |
| WCH/RWS | sport horses | | WHR/RHEF | caged rabbits |
| WCH/RWT | trotting horses | | | |
| WCP | ponies | | WJ | pets. animals in the home |
| WCR | donkeys. asses | | WJC | cats |
| WCR/RW | working donkeys | | WJD | dogs |
| WCR/RWG | guard donkeys | | WJD/RHEK | kennelled dogs |
| WCS | mules | | WJD/RWG | guard dogs |
| | | | WJR | rabbits |
| WD | cattle | | WJS | small rodents |
| WD/RCD | calves | | | |

**Figure 16.2** *Continued*

## Summary

- The order of concepts can most easily be maintained by using a simple notation of numbers or letters
- Symbols without natural filing order should be avoided
- Notation can reflect the hierarchical relationships of terms, but such a notation is more difficult to assign and to maintain
- Some arbitrary symbols can be utilized to show when codes are being added together in a compound concept.

# 17 Building a thesaurus 7: conversion of the taxonomy to alphabetical format

With the taxonomy complete, the process of conversion to the alphabetical format can begin. The systematic structure contains all the information that is needed to generate the thesaural relations for each term, and the process is, for the most part, very straightforward.

### Editing the schedule for conversion

The first stage in converting the taxonomy to a thesaurus involves marking up the text with some of the thesaural relations. I shall use a section of the animals facet to show how this is done:

| | |
|---|---|
| SM | hoofed animals. perissodactyla |
| SMB | equids. equidae |
| SMC | horses |
| SMD | ponies |
| SMF | donkeys. asses |
| SMM | mules |
| | |
| SP | even toed ungulates. artiodactyla |
| SPP | pigs. hogs. swine |
| SPQ | camels |
| SPS | llamas |
| SR | ruminants |
| SRB | giraffe. giraffa camelopardalis |
| SRC | bovines |
| SS | cattle |
| SSC | caprines |
| ST | sheep |
| STB | Scottish blackface sheep |

## Selecting the preferred terms

The first step is to deal with any synonyms and equivalence relationships. You might have thought about the preferred terms in synonym pairs or sets earlier on, but otherwise the decision must now be made, as must any final policy decisions about spelling and other aspects of the form of entry.

I had already chosen to use vernacular rather than scientific names, and to use British terms rather than American. The preferred term should now be brought to the lead position, and the thesaural relation UF (Use For) appended to it in the following way:

| | |
|---|---|
| SM | hoofed animals UF perissodactyla |
| SMB | equids UF equidae |
| SMC | horses |
| SMD | ponies |
| SMF | donkeys UF asses |
| SMM | mules |
| | |
| SP | even toed ungulates UF artiodactyla |
| SPP | pigs UF hogs. swine |
| SPQ | camels |
| SPS | llamas |
| SR | ruminants |
| SRB | giraffe UF giraffa camelopardalis |

Every term following a UF reference will require a USE reference. In this hierarchy we can see:

```
perissodactyla           USE       hoofed animals
equidae                  USE       equids
asses                    USE       donkeys
artiodactyla             USE       even toed ungulates
hogs                     USE       pigs
swine                    USE       pigs
giraffa camelopardalis   USE       giraffe
```

If you can think of more synonyms, you can add them to the vocabulary. Even if they are non-preferred terms, they will help to increase the richness of the vocabulary, and provide additional points of entry to the thesaurus. It's important to ensure that as many terms as possible are included in the vocabulary even though a reduced number will be used in indexing. It's very hard to predict what search terms a user will choose and the greater the number of terms overall, the better the chance of matching that choice.

This is also a suitable point at which to add any explanatory notes or definitions, if they are needed. I shall add an explanation to the term 'equids', since this is not a very commonly encountered word. I want to retain it because it provides a very useful containing class for the horses and their relatives, but, while its meaning is clear from its context in the systematic display, this won't be the case when the terms are presented alphabetically. Therefore a SN (scope note) can be inserted thus:

| | |
|---|---|
| SM | hoofed animals UF perissodactyla |
| SMB | equids UF equidae |
| | SN A term for all the members of the class equidae including horses, ponies, donkeys and mules |
| SMC | horses |
| SMD | ponies |
| SMF | donkeys UF asses |
| SMM | mules |

I have put the note in a smaller font to distinguish it from the terms themselves, but this is purely a matter of personal taste.

## Summary
- Marking up the schedule is a preliminary to conversion to alphabetical format
- Equivalence relationships should be dealt with first
- Make a final decision about the preferred term in any synonym group and add UF between that term and the others
- Add any additional synonyms you can think of which might be used by searchers
- Add any necessary definitions or explanations in the form of scope notes (SN).

**Exercise 17.1**

Edit the following sections of schedule for synonyms and scope notes. You need not write the scope notes, but simply indicate where they might be required:

1.

| | | |
|---|---|---|
| V | simiae. apes and monkeys. primates | |
| VC | monkeys | |
| VE | capuchin monkeys | |
| VF | tufted capuchin monkeys | |
| VG | macaques | |
| VL | rhesus macaques | |
| VM | baboons | |
| VP | apes. anthropoid apes | |
| VR | chimpanzees | |
| VR/RFM | captive chimpanzees | |
| VS | orangutans. pongo pygmaeus | |
| VT | gorillas | |

2.

| | | |
|---|---|---|
| EL | the world. international place | |
| EM | Europe | |
| EMB | Great Britain. United Kingdom. UK | |
| EME | England | |
| EMF | France | |
| EMG | Germany | |
| EMS | Sweden | |
| EN | Asia | |
| EO | North America | |
| EP | United States. USA | |
| EPB | Massachusetts | |

Because the equivalence relationships come in reciprocal pairs, selecting the preferred terms automatically identifies the non-preferred terms as well. The USE relation has been implicitly stated when the UF is made explicit.

## Identifying hierarchical relationships

The next stage in editing is to mark up the broader and narrower terms. Since, like the USE and UF relations, these always come in pairs, identifying one half of the pair is enough. We shall mark the narrower terms since these are usually obvious from the schedule.  Taking each term in turn, scan the schedule which follows it for any narrower terms and mark these NT. Taking our original piece of schedule:

| | |
|---|---|
| SM | hoofed animals UF perissodactyla |
| SMB | equids UF equidae |
| | SN A term for all the members of the class |
| | equidae including horses, ponies, donkeys and mules |
| SMC | horses |
| SMD | ponies |
| SMF | donkeys UF asses |
| SMM | mules |
| | |
| SP | even toed ungulates UF artiodactyla |
| SPP | pigs UF hogs. swine |
| SPQ | camels |
| SPS | llamas |
| SR | ruminants |
| SRB | giraffe UF giraffa camelopardalis |
| SRC | bovines |
| SS | cattle |
| SSC | caprines |
| ST | sheep |
| STB | Scottish blackface sheep |

We can produce the following edited version:

| | |
|---|---|
| SM | hoofed animals UF perissodactyla |
| SMB | NT equids UF equidae |
| | SN A term for all the members of the class |
| | equidae including horses, ponies, donkeys and mules |
| SMC | NT horses |
| SMD | NT ponies |
| SMF | NT donkeys UF asses |
| SMM | NT mules |
| | |
| SP | even toed ungulates UF  artiodactyla |
| SPP | NT pigs UF hogs. swine |

| SPQ | NT camels |
| --- | --- |
| SPS | NT llamas |
| SR | NT ruminants |
| SRB | NT giraffe UF giraffa camelopardalis |
| SRC | NT bovines |
| SS | NT cattle |
| SSC | NT caprines |
| ST | NT sheep |
| STB | NT Scottish blackface sheep |

Because the animals facet is also a 'scientific' taxonomy, there are rather a lot more narrower terms than might be the case in most schedules.

Just as the UF relation for preferred terms generated its reciprocal USE for non-preferred terms, the NT will always be accompanied by its reciprocal BT. Having identified all the terms that have NT status, we don't need to mark the BTs as such because they can be inferred from the NT. In fact it would be confusing, as well as unnecessary, to add BTs because the result would overcrowd the schedule. Every term marked NT will have a BT one step up in the hierarchy. Hence, for the first few terms we could write:

```
equids    BT    hoofed animals
horses    BT    equids
ponies    BT    equids
donkeys   BT    equids
mules     BT    equids
pigs      BT    even toed ungulates
camels    BT    even toed ungulates
llamas    BT    camels
```

## Summary

- Stage two is the identification of hierarchical relationships
- Every term that is a narrower term should be marked NT
- This will allow you to identify the reciprocal BT references at a later stage.

## Exercise 17.2

Identify and mark up the narrower terms in the following sections of schedule:

1.
| | | |
|---|---|---|
| V | primates UF simiae. apes and monkeys | |
| VC | monkeys | |
| VE | capuchin monkeys | |
| VF | tufted capuchin monkeys | |
| VG | macaques | |
| VL | rhesus macaques | |
| VM | baboons | |
| VP | apes UF anthropoid apes | |
| VR | chimpanzees | |
| VR/RFM | captive chimpanzees | |
| VS | orangutans UF pongo pygmaeus | |
| VT | gorillas | |

2.
| | |
|---|---|
| EL | world UF international place |
| EM | Europe |
| EMB | Great Britain UF United Kingdom. UK |
| | SN For the purposes of this thesaurus, Great Britain and the United Kingdom can be regarded as synonymous, as the two terms are likely to be used interchangeably in the literature |
| EME | England |
| EMF | France |
| EMG | Germany |
| EMS | Sweden |
| EN | Asia |
| EO | North America |
| EP | United States UF USA |
| EPB | Massachusetts |

In the sample schedule used for the exercises, the taxonomic structure ensures that the NTs are very dense and form a complicated taxonomy. In a more typical schedule you may need to take greater care in identifying the NTs of a particular term since they may be more widely separated than they are here.

We have now effectively dealt with four of our five thesaural relations, the equivalence pair USE and UF, and the hierarchical pair BT and NT. It only remains to address the slightly knottier problem of the related terms.

## Related terms

Because the related term (RT) category embraces a whole range of relationships between terms, it is not so readily identified as the other relations we have looked at. Deriving the thesaurus from a systematic structure makes it rather easier to determine some of the commoner types of RT which are apparent from the hierarchy. These can be divided into three types: terms in the same array; terms coordinate in the hierarchy; compound terms not in a BT/NT relationship.

Terms which fall into these categories are not automatically RT in the way that the other relations have been, so it will be necessary to examine each potential cross-reference for its usefulness to the indexer.

### Terms in the same array

Terms in the same array (often called sibling terms) are usually in an RT relationship with each other because, by definition, they all share some common attribute. For example, in this section of schedule

| | |
|---|---|
| SM | hoofed animals UF perissodactyla |
| SMB | equids UF equidae |
| | SN A term for all the members of the class equidae including horses, ponies, donkeys and mules |
| SMC | horses |
| SMD | ponies |
| SMF | donkeys UF asses |
| SMM | mules |
| SP | even toed ungulates UF artiodactyla |
| SPP | pigs UF hogs. swine |
| SPQ | camels |
| SPS | llamas |
| SR | ruminants |

'horses', 'ponies', 'donkeys' and 'mules' are all members of the same array (sibling terms) and it would be sensible to make them all RTs of each other. When the record for each term is created there will be four sets of inter-related references:

```
horses            ponies            donkeys           mules
   RT ponies         RT horses         RT horses         RT horses
   RT donkeys        RT donkeys        RT ponies         RT ponies
   RT mules          RT mules          RT mules          RT donkeys
```

## Coordinate terms

Terms in the same array are also hierarchically coordinate, that is, they are not subordinate or superordinate, but all have equal status. If, as is usual, indentation is used to show hierarchical relationships, coordinate terms will be aligned.

Other pairs or groups of terms which are coordinate may also be useful RTs even if they are not in the same array. For example, in the section of schedule above, it would be sensible to make a reference between the hoofed animals and the ungulates, thus:

```
hoofed animals
   RT even toed ungulates

even toed ungulates
   RT hoofed animals
```

It might also be useful to relate the terms below ungulates in the hierarchy:

```
pigs              camels            ruminants
   RT camels         RT pigs           RT pigs
   RT ruminants      RT ruminants      RT camels
```

although some of these references look less helpful than the previous examples. References between other aligned terms, for example 'equids' and 'pigs', would clearly not be particularly useful.

The coordinate RT therefore has to be judged on its individual merits, as do many other RTs. Coordinate status is simply a good guide for the compiler to terms which might be RT but are not necessarily so.

## Compound terms not in a BT/NT relationship

The finished animals facet contains a number of compound terms, mostly built by combining concepts. These may on the surface appear simply to be NTs of the term under which they file:

| | |
|---|---|
| WJD | dogs |
| WJD/JY | dog training |
| WJD/PJD/PFH | hip bones |
| WJD/PJD/PFH/LQD | canine hip dysplasia |
| WJD/RHEK | kennelled dogs |
| WJD/RWG | guard dogs |

In fact, the situation is rather more complicated than this, and the solution depends on where the constituent parts of the compound have come from. In the case of the term 'guard dogs', two concepts have been combined: 'guard animals' and 'dogs'. Both these concepts come from the same facet, the animals facet, so both come into the category of 'kinds of animal'. If we apply the acid test for hierarchical relations (i.e. the question of whether the NT is a kind or a part of the BT), we find that this is the case for both of the constituent concepts. 'Guard dogs' are a kind of 'guard animal' and also a kind of 'dog'. As a result we can say:

```
guard animals
    NT guard dogs

dogs
    NT guard dogs

guard dogs
    BT dogs
    BT guard animals
```

This is a true case of polyhierarchy. The same conditions will hold for combinations of terms in the same facet whatever that facet is. Although it is much more likely to be an entity facet of some sort, you can see from this example of combination in a place facet that it is not exclusively so:

(place by land use)
EJG     gardens
EJH     urban areas
EJL     suburbs
EJL/EJG     suburban gardens
EJM     countryside

> gardens
>> NT suburban gardens

> suburbs
>> NT suburban gardens

> suburban gardens
>> BT gardens
>> BT suburbs

although in the case of 'suburbs' the relationship is a whole–part rather than thing–kind one.

Now let us look at another term from the dog hierarchy above, 'dog training'. Here the combination is of 'dogs' from the animals facet, and 'training' from the operations facet. If we apply the 'kind-or-part' criterion for hierarchical relationship, we see that, although 'dog training' is a kind of training, it is not a kind of dog. Therefore the correct relationships are:

```
training
    NT dog training

dogs
    RT dog training

dog training
    BT training
    RT dogs
```

A combination of terms from two different facets generates one BT/NT relationship to the compound term, and one RT relationship. The kind-or-part test will tell you which one is which.

You may have noticed that there is a link here with the focus and difference in the compound term; the BT/NT relationship will be with the focus, and the RT with the difference.

## Summary

- Related terms are harder to identify and cannot easily be marked up
- Terms in the same array are usually all RTs of each other
- Other examples of terms which are coordinate in the hierarchy may also be RTs
- You need to exercise judgement to decide whether the RT is useful or not
- Compound terms may stand in either a BT/NT or RT relationship with their constituent terms
- Combinations of terms from the same facet are usually polyhierarchical with a BT reference required to each of the constituent terms
- Combinations of terms from different facets usually require one BT and one RT reference to the constituent terms
- The 'kind-or-part' test can be applied to establish which is which.

### Exercise 17.3

Name the BTs and NTs for the compound terms in the following hierarchy:

| | |
|---|---|
| WC | equids |
| WC/LD | equine welfare |
| WC/RW | working equids |
| WCH | horses |
| WCH/JPM | horse maiming |
| WCH/RBD | mares |
| WCH/RDP | pregnant mares |
| WCH/RW | working horses |

## *Other types of related term*

Other RTs occur as a result of linguistic links between terms, or other less easily categorized but evident associations. These cannot be extracted by any methodical process but simply have to be spotted during manual editing. Some typical examples from the animal welfare thesaurus include the following (I've only listed one of each reciprocal pair):

```
toys
   RT play

monkey chow
   RT monkeys
```

```
slaughter
  RT death
```

Unfortunately, there is no systematic method for identifying these 'accidental' relationships. Usually, by the time you have collected and analysed the vocabulary, and worked for some time on the construction of the thesaurus, you will be sufficiently familiar with the vocabulary to be aware of these pairings.

In the schedule editing we do not normally mark the RTs, but we will use the criteria set out above for determining the RTs when we come to create the individual entries. It should be remembered that, although they differ in many respects from the UF/USE and BT/NT pairs, RTs do share the characteristic of reciprocity. You should never make a RT reference from term A to term B without making a corresponding RT reference from term B to term A.

## Answers to exercises

### Exercise 17.1

Edit the following section of schedule for synonyms and scope notes. You need not write the scope notes, but simply indicate where they might be required.

| | | |
|---|---|---|
| 1. | V | primates UF simiae. apes and monkeys. |
| | VC | monkeys |
| | VE | capuchin monkeys |
| | VF | tufted capuchin monkeys |
| | VG | macaques |
| | VL | rhesus macaques |
| | VM | baboons |
| | VP | apes UF anthropoid apes |
| | VR | chimpanzees |
| | VR/RFM | captive chimpanzees |
| | VS | orangutans UF pongo pygmaeus |
| | VT | gorillas |

There are three sets of synonyms here, marked up with the UF relation. In the first example, I've moved 'primates' into the lead position as the preferred term, because it is both vernacular and also single term (and hence slightly to be preferred over 'apes and monkeys'). There doesn't seem to be anything that requires further explanation.

| | | |
|---|---|---|
| 2. | EL | world  UF  international place |
| | EM | Europe |
| | EMB | Great Britain UF United Kingdom. UK |

> SN  For the purposes of this thesaurus, Great Britain and the United Kingdom can be regarded as synonymous, as the two terms are likely to be used interchangeably in the literature

| | | |
|---|---|---|
| | EME | England |
| | EMF | France |
| | EMG | Germany |
| | EMS | Sweden |
| | EN | Asia |
| | EO | North America |
| | EP | United States UF USA |
| | EPB | Massachusetts |

Another trio of synonym pairs where the choice of preferred term is fairly arbitrary. A scope note should be added under 'Great Britain' to clarify the fact that, although Great Britain and the United Kingdom are not absolutely synonymous, for the purposes of this thesaurus they can be regarded as equivalent. I've also removed the definite article from 'the world'.

### Exercise 17.2
Identify and mark up the narrower terms in the following sections of schedule:

| | | |
|---|---|---|
| 1. | V | primates UF simiae. apes and monkeys. |
| | VC | NT monkeys |
| | VE | NT capuchin monkeys |
| | VF | NT tufted capuchin monkeys |
| | VG | NT macaques |
| | VL | NT rhesus macaques |

*Continued on next page*

***Exercise 17.2*** *Continued*

| VM | NT Baboons |
| VP | NT apes UF anthropoid apes |
| VR | NT chimpanzees |
| VR/RFM | NT captive chimpanzees |
| VS | NT orangutans UF pongo pygmaeus |
| VT | NT gorillas |

You might wonder whether the compound term 'captive chimpanzees' is a proper narrower term. In fact it is, having two broader terms, 'captive animals' and 'chimpanzees', and providing a nice example of polyhierarchy. There are some examples of compound terms whose narrower term status is not so clear.

2.

| EL | world UF international place |
| EM | NT Europe |
| EMB | NT Great Britain UF United Kingdom. UK |
| | SN For the purposes of this thesaurus, Great Britain and the United Kingdom can be regarded as synonymous, as the two terms are likely to be used interchangeably in the literature |
| EME | NT England |
| EMF | NT France |
| EMG | NT Germany |
| EMS | NT Sweden |
| EN | NT Asia |
| EO | NT North America |
| EP | NT United States UF USA |
| EPB | NT Massachusetts |

## Exercise 17.3

Name the RTs and BTs for the compound terms in the following hierarchy:

| | |
|---|---|
| WC | equids |
| WC/LD | equine welfare |
| | BT animal welfare |
| | RT equids |
| WC/RW | working equids |
| | BT equids |
| | BT working animals |
| WCH | horses |
| WCH/JPM | horse maiming |
| | BT maiming |
| | RT horses |
| WCH/RBD | mares |
| WCH/RDP | pregnant mares |
| | BT mares |
| | BT pregnant animals |
| WCH/RW | working horses |
| | BT horses |
| | BT working animals |

# 18 Building a thesaurus 8: creating the thesaurus records

The preparatory work on the vocabulary has now been completed, and all that remains is to create the individual entries that will form the alphabetical display.

## Management of the thesaurus data

At this stage you will need to think about how the thesaurus data will be permanently held and maintained. You will need to create a 'record' for each entry term in the vocabulary, which will consist of:

- the entry term itself
- any notational code or control number
- scope notes
- the separate thesaural relationships, i.e.
  — references to or from preferred and non-preferred terms
  — broader terms
  — narrower terms
  — related terms.

For the purpose of maintaining the thesaurus over time, you may also want to add information about when terms were added or deleted, changes in terms, as well as information about who did what and why. If you also hope to revise or update the systematic structure, you may have to add some information about the level of indentation and other display features. Various means of holding the data will make these tasks easier.

In bringing the vocabulary to its present state I have maintained it as a series of Word files. This method allows easy editing in respect of the insertion, rearrangement and modification of terms in the systematic display, where the context is apparent, but is probably less than ideal for the thesaurus format where the thesaural relationships are the central feature. It's very difficult to sort the records alphabetically to achieve the A–Z format, and you will have to insert each record into the sequence as you go along, which requires a lot of scrolling up and down. Nevertheless, there is no reason why a small vocabulary cannot be maintained as a text file if your resources are limited.

For most situations some sort of database will offer the best solution. There is a more detailed discussion of specialist thesaurus software in Chapter 19, but any general database application could be used. A spreadsheet can also perform quite well for a modest thesaurus, since the relationships between 'fields' in the vocabulary are usually very straightforward.

If you really would prefer to work manually, there is no reason why the records cannot be created on index cards or slips of paper, but of course, unless the thesaurus is to stay in this format, you will have to transfer all the data to whatever system is finally adopted.

## Summary

- A 'record' must be created for each term in the taxonomic structure
- These records can be stored in a variety of ways
- A text file is sufficient for a small thesaurus, but there are limitations on what can be done with the data
- A database application is the best option, although a spreadsheet also works quite well
- Each record will need a number of fields, including the entry term, any notational codes, and the various thesaurus relations
- Other fields can be added as necessary
- The thesaurus can be maintained manually, using index cards or slips.

## Creating the thesaurus records

A full thesaurus entry is created for each term in the vocabulary by working methodically through the systematic display and determining how every term is related to its neighbours. Apart from some judgements about the RTs, this is a fairly mechanical process because of the preliminary organization that has gone into structuring the vocabulary. Here is a sample section of schedule to show how this works:

```
KD          husbandry. husbandry procedures
KE              handling. livestock handling
                    chick handling → WB/RCD/KE
```

| KEF | blindfolding |
| KEM | movement |
| KET | transport. transporting |
| KET/FLV | transport vehicles |
| KEV | loading |

This would first be edited (although when constructing a thesaurus, this would obviously be done as a single process for the whole vocabulary). The basic UF, NT and any SN should be added, and any changes in the choice of preferred term or addition of extra terms can be implemented:

| KD | husbandry UF husbandry procedures |
| KE | NT handling UF livestock handling. stock handling chick handling → WB/RCD/KE |
| KEF | NT blindfolding |
| KEM | NT movement |
| KET | NT transport UF transportation |
| KET/FLV | transport vehicles UF trailers. lorries |
| KEV | NT loading |

I've added some extra synonyms (stock handling, trailers and lorries), and amended the non-preferred term 'transporting' to the noun form 'transportation'. You will also notice that I have not marked the compound terms 'chick handling' and 'transport vehicles' at this stage.

Now we can work through this section of vocabulary one term at a time, creating the individual records as we go, and entering the information into the database or spreadsheet, or onto a slip or card. The main part of this exercise will be the systematic checking for the presence of the various thesaural relationships. Remember that:

- UF marking will generate UF and USE relationships
- NT marking will generate BT and NT relationships
- BT and NT references should be made only one step up or down the hierarchy
- RTs will be scanned by looking at:
  — terms in the same array
  — other coordinate terms
  — compound terms.

Returning to the sample schedule:

| KD | husbandry UF husbandry procedures |
|---|---|
| KE | NT handling UF livestock handling. stock handling chick handling → WB/RCD/KE |
| KEF | NT blindfolding |
| KEM | NT movement |
| KET | NT transport UF transportation |
| KET/FLV | transport vehicles UF trailers. lorries |
| KEV | NT loading |

Taking the first term 'husbandry', and working systematically through the complete set of SN, USE, UF, BT, NT and RT, we end up with:

```
husbandry  SN   -
           UF   husbandry procedures
           USE  -   (there can't be a USE relation if
                     there is a UF)
           BT   -   (this isn't apparent from this small
                     section)
           NT   handling, movement
           RT   -   (no coordinate terms or subordinate
                     compounds visible)
```

This gives the complete record for 'husbandry':

```
husbandry
     UF    husbandry procedures
     NT    handling
     NT    movement
```

At this point I usually tick the term 'husbandry' to show that I've dealt with it, but this is optional – it simply saves having to find your place every time you return to the work, and ensures that no term gets overlooked or omitted.

Taking the next term 'husbandry procedures' we can construct the entry:

```
husbandry procedures
     USE   husbandry
```

Since 'husbandry procedures' is a non-preferred term, its only purpose is as a reference to the preferred term.

The next term 'handling' gives the following results:

```
handling   SN    -
           UF    livestock handling, stock handling
           USE   -
           BT    husbandry
                 (note that only the preferred term is
                 included)
           NT    blindfolding
                 chick handling
                 (because 'chick handling' is a kind of
                 'handling')
           RT    movement
                 (because this is coordinate with
                 'handling')


  handling
           UF    livestock handling
           UF    stock handling
           BT    husbandry
           NT    blindfolding
           NT    chick handling
           RT    movement
```

'Handling' can now be ticked as complete, and the two non-preferred terms entered as:

```
livestock handling
        USE handling

stock handling
        USE handling
```

Continue to work through the vocabulary in this way, storing the information in your file or database as you go. Let's look at some of the individual terms in this section which require more thought about how you deal with them.

'Transport vehicles' is clearly a compound term, created by the combination of 'transport' and 'vehicles' from earlier in the taxonomy. Although it is indented under 'transport' we need to be certain whether it is a NT of transport, or an RT. As it is not a kind or part of 'transport', we can say that the relationship with 'transport' is that of RT. However, it is a kind of 'vehicle', so we can create a BT reference to that term.

The term 'loading', a NT of transport, although not hierarchically related to 'transport vehicles', is coordinate with it and could be a useful RT to add.

The full entry then becomes:

```
transport vehicles
   UF trailers
   UF lorries
   BT vehicles
   RT loading
   RT transport
```

'Chick handling' is a compound term, which we have already identified as a NT of handling. The term itself has been located under the other element of the compound, 'chicks'. Strictly speaking, you would deal with the entry for 'chick handling' when you arrive at that point in the taxonomy, but it is possible that you will have forgotten the BT/NT relationship with 'handling' when you get there. Because it is important to enter both parts of a cross-reference, it is helpful at this stage to create an entry for 'chick handling', even though it will be only partially complete, that is:

```
chick handling
   BT handling
```

When you arrive at its proper location, you can add to the entry any other references that arise from that context.

This can also be a useful approach to the management of RTs which are not in the immediate neighbourhood of the entry term. For example, if it occurs to you that it might be useful to have a reference from 'loading' to 'sport horses' because you know that these animals are frequently loaded, at the same time as you add the RT 'sport horses' to 'loading', open up a record for 'sport horses' and enter the RT 'loading' there. These reciprocal RTs, particularly when the relationship is not reflected in the hierarchy, are in most danger of being overlooked and it is sensible to take some precautions against this happening.

## Summary
- Work through the edited schedule taking one term at a time
- Check through the whole set of thesaural relationships to see what needs to be entered under each
- List the references neatly under the entry term
- Tick or cross off the term to show it's been dealt with
- Look at compound terms carefully to establish whether they are BT/NT or RT
- If you make a reference to a term in another part of schedule, be sure to enter under that term a reciprocal reference to your original term
- Pay particular attention to RTs to make sure that the references are paired.

### Exercise 18.1
Edit the following hierarchy and create full thesaurus records for the terms:

| | |
|---|---|
| JV | veterinary care. animal health care |
| JV/FED | veterinary surgeons. veterinarians |
| JVB | veterinary procedures |
| JVC | administration of drugs |
| JVD | dosing techniques |
| JVF | anaesthesia |
| JVG | euthanasia |

## Presentation of the thesaurus entries
The entries that you create need to conform to the standard thesaurus conventions which we looked at in Chapter 7. Although we have looked at a large number of examples in the preceding sections, it may be helpful to summarize the main aspects of these as follows:

- Scope notes immediately follow the term
- Thesaural relationships are listed in the following order:
  — UF/USE (remember these never occur together)
  — BT
  — NT
  — RT
- If more than one term occurs in any category, the terms are listed in alphabetical order within that category
- It is a matter of individual choice whether you repeat the thesaural relationship code in front of every instance of, say, a narrower term, or simply give it once, as happens for **UF** and **NT** in the example below:

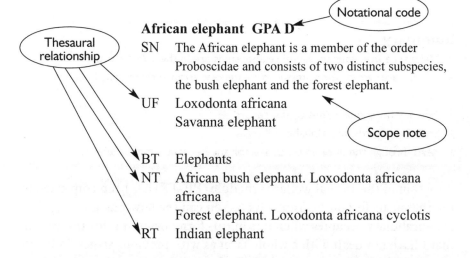

**African elephant  GPA D**

SN   The African elephant is a member of the order Proboscidae and consists of two distinct subspecies, the bush elephant and the forest elephant.

UF   Loxodonta africana
     Savanna elephant

BT   Elephants

NT   African bush elephant. Loxodonta africana africana
     Forest elephant. Loxodonta africana cyclotis

RT   Indian elephant

Notational code

Thesaural relationship

Scope note

The notation used to control order in the animal welfare taxonomy will need to be included in any records of the terms. This is most simply done as shown above, but if your records are held in a spreadsheet or database, you may want to make a separate field for the notational code.

The process of working through the individual entries may seem a tedious business, but as you become more familiar with it, it will become very routine. You may find it possible to dispense with the preliminary schedule editing once you are more experienced, simply using a mental checklist for the different relationships instead, but it is always a good idea to mark the terms as they are dealt with.

## Final editing

When records have been created for every single term in the vocabulary, they are sorted into alphabetical order and the thesaurus display is virtually complete. If the thesaurus is in the form of a database or spreadsheet, you will be able to sort this in various ways, including alphabetical order, but otherwise you will need manually to sort your slips or cards. The alphabetical format will of course act as an index to the systematic format.

As with most vocabulary tools, the mechanical process is never in itself enough to provide a finished product. It is necessary to read through the thesaurus looking for any oddities of verbal forms, or any RT references between terms that have not been generated by the systematic working through of the taxonomic structure.

## Summary

- Make sure that your thesaural relationships are in the correct order
- If there are two or more terms in a category, arrange them in alphabetical order
- Add any notational codes to the record
- Sort the records into alphabetical order
- Read through the finished thesaurus for any necessary manual editing.

A section of the animal welfare schedule (PF–PS) has been converted to the thesaurus format in Appendix 6. You can see how much more space the vocabulary occupies when it is in this format, and it is for this reason that I have not dealt with a whole facet as with previous stages. You will also notice that I have not included records for reciprocal entries where these occur outside PF–PS. This is because the relationships between terms form such a closely interrelated network that it would be impossible ever to impose a limit. Following up every cross-reference and filling out the entry fully would eventually generate the complete alphabetical display.

## Answer to exercise

### Exercise 18.1

Edit the following hierarchy and create full thesaurus records for the terms:

JV            veterinary care UF animal health care
JV/FED        veterinary surgeons UF veterinarians
JVB           NT veterinary procedures
JVC               NT administration of drugs
JVD                   NT dosing techniques
JVF                   NT anaesthesia
JVG                   NT euthanasia

veterinary care
    UF      animal health care
    NT      veterinary procedures
    RT      veterinary surgeons

animal health care
    USE     veterinary care

veterinary surgeons
    UF      veterinarians
    RT      veterinary care

veterinarians
    USE     veterinary surgeons

veterinary procedures
    BT      veterinary care
    NT      administration of drugs

administration of drugs
    BT      veterinary procedures
    NT      anaesthesia
    NT      dosing techniques
    NT      euthanasia

dosing techniques
    BT      administration of drugs
    RT      anaesthesia
    RT      euthanasia

anaesthesia
    BT      administration of drugs
    RT      dosing techniques
    RT      euthanasia

euthanasia
    BT      administration of drugs
    RT      anaesthesia
    RT      dosing techniques

# 19 Managing and maintaining the thesaurus: thesaurus software

We have now been through the entire process of constructing a thesaurus, and have the completed tool held as a collection of individual records for each term in the vocabulary.

Undoubtedly, you will get to a point where you need to add new terms to the thesaurus and to delete obsolescent ones, as well as amending scope notes, instructions, and so on, as the meaning and usage of terms alters over time. These changes need to be carefully managed if the structure of the thesaurus is not to descend into chaos.

## Updating the thesaurus

Because the thesaurus is based on a systematic structure, the addition of new terms is relatively straightforward, since the location of a term is controlled by the system syntax. The process of assigning a new term is the same as the process of organizing the vocabulary during the construction of the thesaurus.

It is necessary to decide, first, which facet a term belongs to, and then to establish if there is an appropriate array, or whether a new one needs to be created. For example, if we want to add the term 'ferrets' to the thesaurus, it clearly must be entered into the animals facet, along with the other mustelidae, as shown here:

| | |
|---|---|
| T | carnivores. carnivora |
| TC | canidae |
| TCF | foxes |
| TCG | blue foxes |
| TCH | coyotes |
| TG | domestic dogs |
| TL | ursidae. bears |
| TL/K | bear farming |

|                  | TM  | mustelidae                  |
|------------------|-----|-----------------------------|
|                  | TMM | mink                        |
|                  | TMN | badgers                     |
|                  | TMO | otters                      |
|                  | TMP | Eurasian otter. lutra lutra |
| Added term →     | TMR | ferrets                     |

The new term must be given a notation, and then a record can be created for it following the general rules in Chapters 17 and 18. The end result should be:

```
ferrets TMR
    BT      mustelidae
    RT      mink
            badgers
            otters
```

Finally, the records for 'mustelidae', 'mink', 'badgers' and 'otters' must be amended to include the appropriate references to 'ferrets'. If you have included a field for history, or editorial changes, you will need to document when the new term was added, and when the other records were amended.

In the same way, when terms are removed from the thesaurus, you must remember not only to delete the record for that term, but also to amend the records that include references to it. Scrupulous attention to detail in the management of the thesaurus records is essential and cannot be stressed too firmly. Whenever a change is made, this must be recorded, and any records on which that change impinges must be corrected.

Compound terms present particular problems. You need to make sure that both parts of the compound are represented in the thesaurus, and locate the term correctly. For example, if we want to add the term 'infected animals' to the thesaurus, we can see that there is an appropriate array (animals by physiological condition) which will accommodate it:

|        | **(animals by physiological condition)** |
|--------|------------------------------------------|
| RDPRM  | pregnant                                 |
|        | pregnant mares → WCH/RDPRM               |
|        | pregnant sows → WF/RDPRM                 |

RDPSB      inbred strains
RDPSG     genetically modified animals

The notation here has been taken from the 'processes' (or physiology) facet, so the term 'infected animals' can be inserted to match the relative position and notation of 'infection' in that facet.

|  |  | **(animals by physiological condition)** |
|---|---|---|
| Added term → | RDLR | infected animals (from RD + LR infection) |
|  | RDPRM | pregnant |
|  |  | pregnant mares → WCH/RDPRM |
|  |  | pregnant sows → WF/RDPRM |
|  | RDPSB | inbred strains |
|  | RDPSG | genetically modified animals |

When creating the new record for 'infected animals', you must remember the RT reference to 'infection', and the reciprocal RT to 'infected animals' must be inserted on the record for 'infection'.

For some compound terms you may need to add concepts in an earlier part of the schedule. For example, if you need to add 'police horses', you might regard this simply as a kind of horse, and therefore only a narrower term of 'horses'. However, it would be structurally more accurate also to add the concept of 'police animals' to the appropriate array, so that the compound is formed in a more logical way, consistent with other compound terms:

|  |  |  |
|---|---|---|
|  | RW | working |
|  |  | working equids → WC/RW |
|  |  | working horses → WCH/RW |
|  | RWG | guard animals |
|  |  | guard dogs → WJD/RWG |
|  |  | guard donkeys → WCR/RWG |
|  |  | guard llamas → WGL/RWG |
| Added term → | RWP | police animals |
|  | RWS | sport |
|  |  | sport horses → WCH/RWS |
|  | RWT | trotting |
|  |  | trotting horses → WCH/RWT |

and hence:

|  | | |
|---|---|---|
| | WCH | horses |
| | WCH/JPM | horse maiming |
| | WCH/RBD | mares |
| | WCH/RDP | pregnant mares |
| | WCH/RW | working horses |
| Added term → | WCH/RWP | police horses |
| | WCH/RWS | sport horses |
| | WCH/RWT | trotting horses |

Maintaining accuracy and consistency in the structure in this way helps to keep the various thesaural relationships correct.

## Automating the thesaurus

In the last chapter we considered how this data should be held permanently, and discussed briefly the suitability of database, spreadsheet, and manual systems. For a thesaurus of any reasonable size, the database seems to be the best method. The nature of the thesaurus records is compatible with a database structure, and the database will allow you to record other sorts of information about the management and maintenance of the thesaurus. The database can also be searched very easily, and the information can be presented in different ways, both on the screen and in print-outs.

If you need to do any of these things at more than a very basic level, you will almost certainly want to consider the use of a specialist thesaurus software package. Such a tool will also provide a more elegant user interface, and more sophisticated management of the thesaurus than you can achieve with a standard database application. It will certainly make the editorial work of thesaurus management and the creation and amendment of records a great deal easier, since much of this will happen automatically.

## Sources of thesaurus software
### Free software

Searching for free software on the web can present problems since most of what appears on the web as free thesaurus software is not in fact for thesaurus management at all. There are a number of free thesauri available as language tools, but these are the vocabularies themselves rather than systems for vocabulary management.

Similarly, some database applications and library management systems have in-built thesauri which may be promoted as features, but these are again actual thesauri used to support searching and retrieval, and not software packages.

Nevertheless, in recent years quite a wide range of thesaurus software has become available, and it's still possible to find some packages which are free to access and download. These have usually been developed by information professionals either for teaching or in conjunction with research projects. On the whole they are relatively unsophisticated, but are entirely suitable for fairly straightforward thesaurus management. Some examples are:

- BEAT Thesaurus software, developed by Josep Sau at the University of Barcelona. This may be freely distributed and used by individuals and can be downloaded from the Willpower Information website at www.willpowerinfo.co.uk/thessoft.htm
- MTM, the management software behind the OECD *Macrothesaurus*, and several other European thesauri, including *Agrovoc* and the *CEDEFOP Thesaurus*. You can find details and a contact address at www.icie.com.pl/
- TAT (Thesaurus administration tool), another research project tool, this time for the EUROVOC project, and downloadable from www.psp.cz/cgi-bin/eng/kps/knih/ee_tat.htm
- TermMaster, created originally for the *Alcohol and Other Drug Thesaurus* by Dagobert Soergel at the University of Maryland, www.clis.umd.edu/faculty/soergel
- Term tree, created for the Museum Documentation Association by Tony Gill, and available as a free download from his website at www.tonygill.com/ttree173.zip
- TheW32, developed by Tim Craven at the University of Western Ontario, Faculty of Information and Media Studies, in conjunction with his teaching. One of a number of freeware packages, it can be found at http://publish.uwo.ca/~craven/freeware.htm.

## Commercial packages

There are a substantial number of commercially produced packages which operate at various levels and are suitable for managing all sizes and types of thesaurus. They range in price from under £500 (there are even one or two at less than £100) to £10,000 plus. It is possible to buy thesaurus software packages which will build a thesaurus from scratch using text analysis and other computational techniques, but these are very expensive and outside the scope of this discussion.

Packages for general thesaurus management fall into two major groups:

- thesaurus management modules which are part of a bigger information management system
- stand-alone thesaurus management software.

Those in the first group will usually cost a great deal more than those in the second, but there are some obvious advantages if you are already using a management system that happens to have a thesaurus module, or if you are about to buy a new system and want the thesaurus management to be part of it. The thesaurus software will interface with the cataloguing module and can link to the cataloguing data as well as taking advantage of any facilities to track user behaviour and search queries. However, if you just need a thesaurus editor, it is unlikely that you will want to purchase a whole system, and there are plenty of choices in the stand-alone category, many of them at a very modest price.

## Directories and evaluative sources

There are several good resources for the listing and evaluation of software. The best is certainly Leonard Will's *Willpower Information*, to be found at www.willpowerinfo.co.uk/thessoft.htm. This is a very substantial listing of all the generally available thesaurus software (plus some slightly more obscure products) with much technical detail and background information. The *Willpower* site also contains much more information about the thesaurus in general.

There are other sites which contain rather briefer considerations of software. Although some of these are no more than links to the product sites, they are useful as starting points. They include:

- American Society of Indexers: section on software for indexers at www.asindexing.org/site/thessoft.shtml. This list has been put together by Jessica Milstead. The same information is replicated at the Australian and New Zealand Society for Indexers website at www.aussi.org/resources/software/thessoft.htm.
- Thesaurus management software compiled by Anne Betz at www.fbi.fh-koeln.de/institut/labor/Bir/thesauri_new/thsoften.htm.

Professional discussion lists are usually a very good source of information about the performance of different packages. Joining one, even if initially you do not contribute much, can tell you a lot about which systems are available, how information professionals use their software, what difficulties they encounter, and how common problems are solved. Such lists are usually very good places to ask for help or advice, which is rapidly forthcoming and normally quite disinterested. In the UK, the Taxonomy list, TAXONOMY@JISCMAIL.AC.UK, is one I would personally recommend.

## Features of thesaurus software

Apart from those very sophisticated systems mentioned above, most software is solely for the management of thesauri, so you should not labour under the misapprehension that the software will build the thesaurus for you. The processes of gathering the vocabulary, deciding on the preferred terms, imposing vocabulary control, and establishing the structure of the subject and the relationships between terms, are all essentially intellectual. However, the software will make the business of managing the thesaurus data much easier, and in some respects it will act as a check on whether the structure is sound. It should also enable you to display the content of the thesaurus in a way that a simple database application will not.

There are certain things that you should be able to assume a package will do. It should:

- provide some sort of template for the records
- support searching of the database
- allow you to view the individual records
- allow you to view in a browse mode either an alphabetical display or systematic display (and ideally both)
- support the reciprocal pairs of USE/UF, BT/NT and RT pairs.

The last requirement is a vital one for thesaurus management. When you create a new record, the software should automatically amend the record of any term to which you make a reference, and include a reciprocal reference to your new term. Although this can be done manually, as described above, automatic editing of this kind will save you a great deal of work, and of course, it will ensure that there are no errors in making the reciprocals. Similarly, when amending or deleting an existing record, the reciprocal relationships should be automatically adjusted or removed.

Beyond these simple requirements, most software packages will offer quite a range of extra features. Often these enhancements are related to the display of the thesaurus data, and the use of more sophisticated user interfaces, particularly in the case of web-mounted thesauri. You need to think carefully which ones are necessary to your own operation, and which simply make the thesaurus look more stylish. Of course, if the thesaurus is accessible to end-users, that might be a valuable feature. Such features are frequently closely linked to financial cost, and might include:

- an ability to expand and collapse hierarchies on screen
- the generation of alternative views of the structure, such as classification trees or concept map visualization
- the capacity to link from one term to another
- the capacity to edit or rearrange the thesaurus on screen using drag and drop technology.

Other features of systems are related to the data structure, and how much and what sort of information can be managed by the software. These are more fundamental to the successful management of the vocabulary, and such factors should be carefully considered if they are a necessary part of your thesaurus operation (and some of these are admittedly situation-specific). Basic operational questions that you need to ask include some about the capacity of the system:

- whether there are limits on the size of the thesaurus (i.e. the number of terms that can be handled)
- whether the software will support several thesauri at once, or if it is intended only for a single thesaurus
- whether different character sets can be used (an important consideration not only for different alphabets, but also for symbols used in scientific documentation).

There are also factors related to the way in which information is held within records, and how much can be accommodated:

- Is there a limit to the number of fields in a record?
- How many thesaural relationships are supported?
- Can the fields be customized to your own requirements? (and if so, whether this can be carried out locally, or must be paid for)
- Are there fields for any administrative or historical data that you want to keep?

- Does the software automatically track changes of this kind (i.e. dates of creation or amendment of records)

A third set of questions is concerned with the way the software operates and interfaces with external resources:

- Is there simultaneous access for more than one user?
- Can the editing be shared?
- Can you import data from external sources such as other thesauri?
- Can you export data in different formats such as HTML or XML to enable web access?

Different software systems exhibit a range of components of these various aspects. The desirability of many of them is closely related to the size of the thesaurus and the size of the information system within which it operates. A very simple package may be ideal for a small specialist organization, whereas a large government department with many users and many interfaces with external bodies will undoubtedly need a much more sophisticated suite of programs.

# 20 Conclusion

We have now covered all the stages in the construction of the thesaurus using facet analysis as the starting point. It should be emphasized that, like any activity involving language, thesaurus construction is not an exact science.

Both the guidelines offered in the standards (which are largely concerned with the form of entry) and the methodology of facet analysis require the thesaurus compiler to exercise personal judgement in the selection and analysis of terms. Often the decisions to be made are not at all easy, because the subtlety and complexity of language does not always permit precise boundaries to be drawn. Don't let this deter you from attempting to construct a thesaurus. The application of method and logic will provide you with a good and efficient tool, even where decisions are necessarily subjective, and a little more experience of working with vocabularies will improve your confidence.

During the time that I was writing this book, the new British standard *Structured Vocabularies for Information Retrieval* (BS 8723) was in preparation, and the first two parts, *Definitions, Symbols and Abbreviations*, and the part relating to thesauri, were published shortly before *Essential Thesaurus Construction* went to press. In the USA, there is also a working party looking at the ANSI/NISO standard and considering many of the same aspects of the modern thesaurus not addressed by the current guidelines. A workshop held at the end of 1999 set some criteria for the working party.

The recommendations of the workshop[1] included the following:

- A new standard for 'thesauri' is needed, and it should be a single standard.
- However, it should not be a standard for 'electronic' thesauri. Essentially all thesauri are digital today, so 'electronic' is superfluous.
- Furthermore, the standard should provide for a broader group of controlled vocabularies than those that fit the standard definition of 'thesaurus'. This includes, for example, ontologies, classifications, taxonomies, and subject headings, in addition to standard thesauri.

- The primary concern is with shareability (inter-operability), rather than with construction or display. Therefore this new standard probably will not supersede Z39.19, but supplement it.
- The standard should focus on concepts, terms and relationships.

The new British standard also addresses these issues, and is notable in that it replaces what was originally a standard for the construction of thesauri with one dealing with different forms of retrieval tools. Parts of BS 8723 yet to be published will be devoted to retrieval vocabularies other than thesauri.

Although it does not concern itself with the details of thesaurus construction, the standard discusses the role of facet analysis in developing the classified display, and acknowledges its usefulness in the generation of hierarchies that conform to the rules for hierarchical relationships in the thesaurus. It will be interesting to see the part that facet analysis will play in the forthcoming sections, for undoubtedly it is a methodology that can generate a whole suite of compatible vocabulary tools from an initial classificatory structure.

While the capacity of machine-driven systems to build vocabularies increases all the time, intellectually created tools still have the edge. Many software designers now understand the principles of facet analysis, and we are beginning to see the merger of the two in some powerful new tools. However, for many small organizations the cost of such sophisticated software exceeds their budgets. A sound methodology for the manual creation of vocabularies is still therefore very necessary, and facet analysis provides such a tried-and-tested approach. On a departmental website for library and information science students I read recently that building a thesaurus for 'things' is much easier than building one for 'ideas'. This is generally true because of the relative difficulty of establishing correct relationships between abstract concepts. Facet analysis makes it much easier to manage the whole spectrum of concepts, including those for abstract ideas. As a basis for creating an integrated set of vocabulary tools it currently has no rival.

## Note

1   *Report on the Workshop on Electronic Thesauri November 4–5, 1999*, National Information Standards Organization, www.niso.org/news/events_workshops/ thes99rprt.html (accessed December 2005).

# Glossary

The Glossary covers a number of specialist and technical terms from the field of indexing and vocabulary construction. It is intended to provide helpful explanations of these terms, rather than precise technical definitions, for novices or those new to the field. I have assumed that not all readers will have a library or information service background.

**abstract noun**   nouns which represent ideas and abstract concepts, as opposed to physical entities, are abstract nouns (e.g. freedom, desire, socialism). Compare with **concrete noun**

**abstracting and indexing service**   a publication (usually periodically produced) which analyses current documentation in a particular subject field, and provides brief summaries of items with a systematic subject arrangement and/or subject index; increasingly these exist in online rather than printed format

**access point**   a term in a vocabulary tool, or a database or equivalent, which allows a user to begin exploring the vocabulary or collection. The term need not itself be used in indexing or description provided it gives cross-references to terms that are

**accession number**   a form of numbering for items in a collection, usually relating to the order in which the items were acquired or processed. An accession number normally has no significance in itself, but acts as a control number or identifier for the item

**agent category**   in facet analysis, one of the fundamental categories of the Classification Research Group (CRG). It accommodates those concepts by means of which actions are carried out, such as tools, equipment, persons and organizations

**alphabetical display**   in a thesaurus, that form of the display which lists the terms alphabetically, each accompanied by cross-references to other terms. Compare with **systematic display**

**alphabetical tool**  a vocabulary tool where the primary arrangement is alphabetical, usually because the tool uses words for indexing rather than codes or notations; examples are **subject heading lists, keyword lists** and **thesauri**

**alphabetico-classed**  a tool or system that uses a mixture of systematic arrangement and alphabetical order. This includes alphabetical arrangement of terms within subject classes (as in MeSH subject headings), or subject classes arranged alphabetically (as in many bookshop shelf arrangements)

**array**  within a facet, a subordinate grouping of concepts that all share some common attribute (the **characteristic** or **principle of division**). Arrays are also referred to as **sub-facets**

**associative term** see **related term**

**authority**  (1) a permanent record of local decisions made about indexing, employed as a reference for future use; (2) an external (usually published) reference source of information used to inform local practice (e.g. for spelling, forms of names, etc.)

**broader term**  for a given term, another term which is more general in meaning, or higher up in a subject hierarchy

**browsing**  searching by scanning the contents of a collection or list rather than trying to retrieve specific items by some known attribute or feature. In digital collections, browsing may be supported by directory style interfaces using systematic arrangement

**by-product category**  in facet analysis, one of the fundamental categories of the Classification Research Group (CRG). It accommodates by-products of an operation and is usually only encountered in technical subjects

**categories**  the fundamental groupings used to sort concepts in facet analysis; they are distinguished by function. The categories of Ranganathan's facet theory comprise personality, matter, energy, space and time. Those of the Classification Research Group (CRG) are: thing, kind, part, property, material, process, operation, patient, product, by-product, agent, space and time

**characteristic of division** see **principle of division**

**child-parent relationship**  the relationship between a term or concept and a more general one. See also **broader term**

**citation order**  the order in which the parts of a compound subject are combined in indexing or description. The choice of citation order will affect the filing order of compounds in any sequence, and, within a particular environment, should be applied consistently

**class**   a set whose members share some common feature. The word 'class' is commonly used for a term in a classification scheme (e.g. the class 'chemistry' or the class 'rabbits')

**classification**   (1) the process of assigning objects to classes; (2) the process of identifying classes and organizing them into a **classification scheme**; (3) the process of assigning a classmark or **subject heading** from a particular scheme to a given document

**classification scheme**   a set of classes organized in a systematic fashion to show the relationships between them. The classification consists of a **vocabulary** (the terms used to represent the classes) and **syntax** (the rules for combining classes). A classification scheme is an example of a **controlled indexing language**

**closed access**   a system where the items making up the collection are stored separately from the areas used by readers, and must be fetched by staff

**combination order**   an alternative name for **citation order**

**compound/complex concept**   a subject or topic that is a combination of more basic elements, and can be **semantically factored** into its constituent parts (e.g. 'impressionism' = 19th century + art movement + Europe)

**compound term**   a term consisting of two or more words (e.g. underwater archaeology, football socks, onion bhaji). The term may also be conceptually compound, although this is not always the case (e.g. hairy armadillos)

**concept**   an idea or notion which is represented by a **term**. 'Concepts' are more commonly referred to in classificatory and taxonomic structures, whereas 'terms' may be preferred in word-based vocabulary tools

**concept map**   a graphical representation of a subject field that shows general relationships between concepts. The concepts are usually depicted within geometric shapes which are joined by lines to indicate any (usually non-specific) relationship between them

**concrete noun**   nouns used for entities of a material or physical kind are concrete nouns (e.g. kangaroo, teapot); contrast with **abstract noun**

**controlled indexing language**   a system used for classifying or indexing documents which uses a more limited set of terms than are found in **natural language**. A controlled indexing language consists of a

**vocabulary** (the terms used for indexing) and **syntax** (the rules for combination of terms). **Thesauri, classifications,** and **subject heading lists** are all examples of controlled indexing languages

**controlled vocabulary**   another name for a **controlled indexing language**

**coordinate class**   classes of equal status in a hierarchy, so that neither is subordinate or superordinate to the other, are called coordinate classes

**count noun**   a noun representing some object that can be counted (e.g. umbrellas, turnips). Count nouns can be pluralized in a thesaurus. Compare with **non-count noun**

**cross-reference**   a reference from one term in a vocabulary to another that allows the user to navigate the vocabulary. In a thesaurus, the cross-references indicate the nature of the relationship between the two terms

**descriptor**   a term used in indexing to indicate the subject content of an item. An individual item might require several descriptors to fully represent its subject. See also **keyword**

**difference**   in a compound term, that part of a term which modifies the **focus,** or essential subject part of the term. The difference often specifies a kind or type of the focus (e.g. in the term 'Christmas pudding', 'pudding' is the focus, and 'Christmas' the difference). The difference is also known as the **modifier**

**disambiguation**   the use of **qualifiers** to clarify terms which are otherwise ambiguous or unclear, usually because they have more than one meaning (e.g. 'shade (shadow)' and 'shade (colour)'). See also **homographs**

**display**   the format of a thesaurus or other vocabulary tool. Many such tools consist of both a **systematic display,** showing the structure of the subject, and an **alphabetical display,** listing the terms in A–Z order

**downward reference**   for a given term, a reference to a more specific term (i.e. one which is lower in the hierarchy). See also **narrower term**

**Dublin Core** a metadata standard for the cataloguing of digital materials, the Dublin Core is probably the best known and most widely used of these systems. It originates from the Online Computer Library Centre in Dublin, Ohio

**energy category**   in facet analysis, one of Ranganathan's fundamental categories. It is used to accommodate concepts which are actions or activities, such as growth, dancing, management, sleeping, worship. Classification Research Group (CRG) categories subdivide it into **operation** and **process** categories

**entity category**   in facet analysis, one of the Classification Research Group (CRG) fundamental categories. It accommodates physical entities such as chemicals, stars, plants and animals, but may also be used for more abstract concepts where these are the major category in the subject (e.g. languages, nations, literary forms, etc.)

**entry term**   a term which appears in the alphabetical listing in a thesaurus. Entry terms may or may not be used in indexing, but they all provide **access points** for the thesaurus user

**equivalence relationship**   a relationship between terms in a thesaurus where the terms are more or less the same in meaning, and only one is chosen for use in indexing. Equivalence relationships exist between synonyms and near synonyms. See also **preferred term** and **non-preferred term**

**exhausting the principle of division**   when organizing terms into an **array**, making sure that every possible value of the common attribute is represented (e.g. an array of 'wines by colour' should include 'red', 'white' and 'rosé')

**expressive notation**   a notation which reflects subject structure, particularly relationships of hierarchy (e.g. a topic deep in a hierarchy has a notation which is longer than a topic higher up)

**facet**   the result of applying one broad principle of division to a subject field. In practice, it is all those concepts in a subject which would be assigned to a particular **fundamental category** (such as materials, operations, agents, etc.). While the categories have generic names, within a given field they become facets of the subject (e.g. the parts category in zoology becomes the parts, organs and systems facet, and the operations category in medicine becomes the treatment or therapy facet)

**facet analysis**   the analysis and organization of the constituent concepts of a subject into **facets** and **arrays**, and the imposition of **citation order** to create a faceted structure

**facet hierarchies**   a term used of online thesauri to describe the individual facets displayed in systematic format

**facet indicator**   a symbol in a compound notational code that indicates either (1) the facet structure of the notation; or (2) the presence of a particular facet

**faceted thesaurus**   a thesaurus built on faceted principles (i.e. generated from a faceted classification)

**factoring**   the breaking down of a compound term into simpler parts.

Factoring may be **semantic** or **syntactic**. It is also known as **splitting**

**filing order**   the order in which indexed items would be arranged in any physical collection or listing. The filing order will naturally follow the order of terms in the vocabulary tool used for indexing (**schedule order**)

**filing value**   the value of symbols used in notational codes. Letters and numbers have a natural filing value, but the filing value of other symbols (such as punctuation marks) must be specified as otherwise their value is unknown to users

**focus**   that element of a compound term which is the essential subject. The focus will be qualified by the **difference** or **modifier** (e.g. in the term 'Fork handles', 'handles' is the focus and 'fork' the difference or modifier)

**fundamental categories**   the set of categories to which concepts are assigned in **facet analysis**. Ranganathan's original set of categories are Personality, Matter, Energy, Space and Time. In more recent developments of facet analysis this number has been increased

**fuzzy searching**   searching that does more than find an exact match for the query terms. The software will support some degree of uncertainty or error in the search input, and still return results

**general-before-special**   the principle that broader or more general subjects should precede more specific subjects in a sequence, particularly when the topics are related in a hierarchical way (e.g. 'vegetables' should precede 'broccoli', and 'winter sports' should precede 'tobogganing'). This principle seems to be axiomatic, and is the basis of most hierarchical structures in subject work

**generic relationship**   sometimes called genus–species relationship, the relationship between an entity and its types or kinds (e.g. between 'trees' and 'oaks', or between 'chairs' and 'armchairs'). In the thesaurus, a **narrower term** in a generic relationship may be marked NTG, and the **broader term** BTG. Compare with **partitive relationship** and **instantive relationship**

**gerund**   a verbal noun that has an '–ing' ending, such as swimming, ploughing, fighting

**hierarchical relationship**   a relationship between neighbouring concepts in a hierarchy, indicating whether they are relatively subordinate, superordinate, or coordinate in status. In a thesaurus, hierarchical relationships are expressed through the medium of **broader** and

**narrower** terms. Hierarchical relationships are sometimes called **paradigmatic** or **semantic relationships**

**hierarchy**   a set of classes or concepts showing the subordinate and superordinate relationships between them. Strictly speaking, a hierarchy should only display **semantic** or **generic relationships** but many vocabularies include other relationships in the hierarchical display

**high-level**   although this term implies detail and precision, in fact it refers to vocabulary tools which operate at a very broad or general level, with relatively few terms or subdivisions

**homographs**   words which have different meanings, but which look exactly the same (although they may be pronounced differently). Homographs require **qualifiers** to distinguish one meaning from another (e.g. 'plant (living organism)' and 'plant (machinery)'). See also **disambiguation**

**including notes**   explanatory notes in a vocabulary that indicate the coverage of a term or class (e.g. 'Puppets including marionettes, glove puppets and shadow puppets'). Including notes are more commonly found in classifications than in other tools

**increasing concreteness**   the principle that abstract concepts should precede concrete concepts in a sequence of topics. Increasing concreteness is one of the guidelines in establishing **schedule order** of facets in a faceted classification

**indexer**   a person who indexes or otherwise describes the subject content of documents or other items in a collection

**indexing**   the act of determining the subject content of items and assigning appropriate subject indexing terms or notations

**information retrieval**   strictly speaking, the process of locating information on a specific topic, usually from a managed collection or database. Information retrieval is currently used in a wider sense to refer to the whole field of information seeking, including searching, search techniques, search tools and other software, and, sometimes, the databases and resources that are searched. **Knowledge organization** (i.e. the subject organization of managed resources, including classification and indexing, and the theory and development of subject tools), is usually distinguished from information retrieval

**information retrieval thesaurus**   a thesaurus used for indexing and retrieval purposes, as opposed to a thesaurus of synonyms and antonyms

**instantive** (or **instantial**) **relationship**   the relationship between a given term or class and a specific individual example or member of it. An example would be the relationship between ships and the *Titanic*, or between murderers and Jack the Ripper. In the thesaurus, a **narrower term** in an instantive relationship may be marked NTI, and the **broader term** BTI. Compare with **generic relationship** and **partitive relationship**

**instructions** notes which tell the indexer how to use a particular term or apply a particular rule

**intelligent searching** searching where the software is able to modify the search by amending the original search terms without intervention of the searcher. This may be done in various ways, including extending the search to use additional terms commonly occurring in the texts retrieved by the original search. Increasingly, a vocabulary tool may lie behind the interface, allowing broadening and narrowing of the search, and searching on synonyms

**inverted order** inversion of the natural word order in compound terms (e.g. 'dancing, ballroom' rather than 'ballroom dancing'). This was common in manual catalogues and indexes, the purpose being to bring the **focus** of the term into the lead position, and to bring together related compounds (e.g. all types of dancing). Online searching makes this practice redundant

**keyword** a descriptor used in indexing. Originally, keyword indexing used terms derived from the text of documents to be indexed rather than intellectually built vocabularies

**keyword list** a list of keywords to be used for indexing documents. The keyword list is usually characterized by a lack of structure in its composition, and does not have cross-references between terms. It may be no more than an alphabetical list of terms taken from documents or previously used in indexing

**keyword system** an indexing system that uses keywords as descriptors, and also the software required to operate the system

**knowledge organization** the organization of resources on a subject basis. This includes the theory and philosophy of subjects and their relationships, the application of this theory to the design and construction of **knowledge organization systems,** and the practical use of such systems to determine and describe the subject content of documents through indexing and classification

**knowledge organization systems (KOS)** systems for the organization of resources on the basis of their subject content. KOS is a very broad concept and includes all the standard kinds of vocabulary tool as well as more elaborate packages with software for search and display

**loan terms**   terms of foreign origin that are now an accepted part of the host language (e.g. pizza or *coup d'état*)

**MARC**   literally, machine readable cataloguing, MARC is a format for creating electronic records for documents, using a series of internationally agreed coded fields. The most recent version, MARC21, is the normal standard for creating bibliographic records in the English-speaking world

**material category**   one of the fundamental categories in facet analysis, it is used to accommodate concepts relating to substances and materials of all kinds, such as chemical compounds, rocks and minerals, building materials and man-made substances

**matter category**   one of Ranganathan's fundamental categories in facet analysis, it corresponds to the **material category** used by the Classification Research Group (CRG)

**metadata**   literally data about data, metadata is the term used for information attached to a document or resource that describes various features of the document, such as its creator, title, date of origin, subject content, and so on. Sometimes metadata can be extracted mechanically from the document, but more usually it is decided upon and assigned by human indexers, who may use a **metadata scheme** for the purpose. Metadata may be stored separately from the items it describes, as in a catalogue or bibliographic database, or, in the case of digital documents, it may form part of the HTML code of the resources themselves

**metadata elements**   the various different fields used in a **metadata scheme**. These usually include author/creator, title of the resource, format, date of creation, subject, and so on

**metadata scheme**   a standard for assigning metadata, it will include a number of fields, or **metadata elements**, together with instructions and explanations of how to apply the scheme. The best known general metadata scheme is the **Dublin Core**, but various systems have been created to accommodate the metadata for more specialized items, such as teaching resources and works of art

**modifier** see **difference**

**multi-word term**   a thesaurus term which contains two or more individual words (e.g. child protection agencies, Fair Isle knitting)

**mutual exclusion**   in an **array** the terms should be mutually exclusive (i.e.

it should not be possible to assign two terms to the same topic). If this can be done, then the **principle of division** has not been properly identified or applied

**name authorities** a published source of, for example, personal or geographic names, that is used to establish the correct form. A name authority can also be created locally by recording decisions so that later occurrences of the name are dealt with consistently

**narrower term** for a given term, another term which is more specific or lower down in the hierarchy

**narrower term generic** a narrower term which is a kind or type of its broader term (e.g. 'chess' and 'board games')

**narrower term instantive** a narrower term which is a specific instance of its broader term (e.g. 'York Minster' and 'cathedrals')

**narrower term partitive** a narrower term which is a part of its broader term (e.g. 'cerebellum' and 'brain')

**natural language** (1) the language used in everyday speech, as opposed to the **controlled vocabulary** used in indexing; (2) specific languages, such as English, Russian, Chinese, etc.

**natural language indexing** indexing using terms decided on by the indexer or taken from the material indexed rather than from a standard indexing language

**navigation** the process of exploring the structure of a vocabulary by following cross-references to locate related concepts

**near synonyms** terms which are near enough in meaning to be treated as synonyms for practical purposes

**node labels** entries in the systematic structure of a thesaurus which indicate the principles by which terms have been grouped. Node label is synonymous with **principle of division**, the term favoured by classificationists

**non-count noun** a noun representing a concept that cannot normally be counted and hence has no plural form (e.g. porridge, inter-planetary travel). Compare with **count noun**

**non-hierarchical relationships** relationships between terms which are not contained one by the other, but which are related in some other way. See **syntactic relationships**

**non-preferred term** a term which will not be used for indexing, but which is retained in the vocabulary so that as many **access points** as possible are provided. A non-preferred term is normally a synonym or near-synonym of a **preferred term**

**notation**   a system of coding that provides a unique reference for each term in the vocabulary, the notation also controls the order of terms in the systematic display. The notation may use letters or numbers, or a combination of both

**noun phrases**   compound terms in which a noun is qualified by some other word, usually an adjective but occasionally another noun or, very rarely, an adverb (e.g. 'artificial snow', 'stuffed toys', 'weapons technology', 'greyhound racing')

**ontology**   a model or representation of a subject field in which the relationships between concepts in the field are specified

**operation category**   one of the fundamental categories in facet analysis. It accommodates concepts that are actions performed on an object by some human agent (e.g. testing, management, training, cooking, dissection)

**paradigmatic relationships**   another way of describing **hierarchical relationships** or **semantic relationships**. Relationships which are part of the permanent structure of the subject rather than the relationships which occur in compound terms (**syntagmatic** or **syntactic relationships**). Examples would include the relationship between 'planets' and 'Saturn', or between 'jewellery' and 'bracelets'

**parent–child relationship**   another way of expressing the **broader term/narrower term** relationship. This term tends to be used in the field of computing

**part category**   one of the fundamental categories in facet analysis. It accommodates concepts which are parts of those concepts in the **entity category** (e.g. in medicine, 'nerves', 'tissues', 'heart', or in vehicle engineering, 'brakes', 'chassis', 'exhaust systems')

**partitive relationship**   a relationship in which one concept is a part of another, a whole–part relationship (e.g. the relationship between 'branches' and 'trees', or between 'Basingstoke' and 'Hampshire'). In the thesaurus, a **narrower term** in a partitive relationship may be marked as NTP, and the **broader term**, BTP. Compare with **generic relationship** and **instantive relationship**

**patient category**   one of the fundamental categories in facet analysis. It accommodates those concepts that are the objects of actions, but are not in the primary entity facet of the subject. It would include objects used in the intermediate stages of manufacturing where the finished article is the primary facet (e.g. in 'the shaping of steel plates to form vehicle bodies', where 'vehicles' are the thing, 'bodies' the part, 'shaping' the operation, and 'steel' the material, 'plates' are the patient of the operation). It is not often encountered outside this kind of field

**personality category**   one of the Ranganathan's fundamental categories in facet analysis. It accommodates concepts which are the main objects of study in a discipline (e.g. 'chemical substances' in chemistry, 'languages' in linguistics, or 'nations' in history)

**polyhierarchy**   a concept which has two containing classes (or a term with two **broader terms**) is said to exhibit polyhierarchy (e.g. 'pet parrots' is a sub-class of 'pets', but also a sub-class of 'parrots', and is in a poly-hierarchical relationship)

**polysemous**   a polysemous term is one having more than one meaning. Terms are usually only considered polysemous if they have some linguistic connection (e.g. 'paper' is polysemous because it can mean the substance paper, a newspaper, an article or essay, wallpaper, and so on). Many terms that are **homographs** are not considered polysemous when their relationship is accidental and arbitrary (e.g. 'Reading (place)' and 'reading (activity)')

**polysemy**   the state of having several different meanings

**population**   the process of expanding a basic subject structure, such as a directory or a vocabulary tool, by inserting into it examples of compound or complex subjects as contained in actual resources. In a digital environment these may be in the form of links to the resources themselves. The process of population can create a much more complicated knowledge structure than the original tool

**post-coordinate indexing**   strictly speaking, a system in which the index terms (for a compound subject) are only brought together at the point of search (as in the case of descriptors or keywords in a database or an online catalogue). The index description is not used to organize the items in the collection, so there is no need to pre-coordinate the terms (i.e. arrange them in any particular order). Compare with **pre-coordinate indexing**

**pre-coordinate indexing**   strictly speaking, a system in which index terms (for a compound subject) are combined by the classifier at the time of indexing because they are used to organize the material in the collection (as in the case of a classification used for shelf order, or subject headings in a file). Pre-coordination is also used to describe a situation when the terms used to describe **compound concepts** are already combined in a published classification schedule or headings list

**predictability**   the capacity of a system to deal with compound subjects in a consistent manner, so that their treatment or location can be estimated by the user. Predictability is an important factor in efficient **information retrieval**

**preferred term**   where several synonyms or near synonyms exist for a given concept, one alone (the preferred term) should be chosen to be used in indexing. The others (the **non-preferred terms**) are retained in the vocabulary, but refer the indexer to the preferred term

**principle of division**   the characteristic or attribute used to group concepts in **arrays** or **sub-facets** (e.g. concepts relating to kinds of person may be grouped by the characteristics gender, age, marital status, etc.). Also known as **characteristic of division**

**process category**   a fundamental category in facet analysis. It is used to accommodate concepts which are actions not performed by a human agent, but which happen spontaneously. Often there is no particular object of the action. Examples include 'change', 'ageing', 'growth', 'circulation'. The process category can often be used to accommodate concepts whose categorical status is very hard to define, but is something like a 'condition' or 'state', such as 'safety', 'security', 'access', 'disease'

**product category**   a fundamental category in facet analysis. It is used to accommodate the products of operations, where these are not in the primary **entity category**. A good example occurs in agriculture, where the crops and animals constitute the primary category, and the product category accommodates concepts such as 'dairy products', 'meat', 'flour', 'eggs', etc.

**property category**   a fundamental category in facet analysis. It is used to accommodate concepts which are properties or attributes of the concepts in the primary facet (e.g. in a subject dealing with materials, concepts such as 'durability', 'hardness', or 'conductivity' would be assigned to the property category)

**qualifier**   a term added to another term in order to clarify its meaning; this is usually necessary where two terms have the same visual form (**homographs**) to distinguish one from the other (e.g. 'burns (injuries)' and 'burns (streams)', or 'occupation (tenancy)' and 'occupation (profession)'). See also **disambiguation**

**quasi-synonyms**   two terms that, although not exact **synonyms**, are close enough in meaning to allow one to be chosen as a **preferred term** in indexing (e.g. 'film' and 'cinema')

**query expansion**   the modification of a query to include additional search terms. This may be achieved by a thesaurus embedded in the search system which automatically selects **synonyms** and/or **broader** and **narrower terms** of the original search terms

**query formulation**   the process of selecting terms for a search. If a thesaurus is embedded in the search system, the searcher can use it to select suitable terms, or it may, for example, automatically substitute preferred terms

**reciprocal references**   in a thesaurus, whenever one term is cross-referenced to another, there must be an equivalent reference from the second term to the original. These pairs are known as reciprocal references

**record**   a document or item in an archive is often referred to as a record. In a library environment, record more usually refers to a representation of an item (e.g. catalogue record, bibliographic record)

**records manager**   an archivist who deals with institutional documentation rather than historical archive material

**related term**   for a given term, another term which is related to it in a non-hierarchical way. Related terms are often in other facets of the vocabulary. Also known as **associative term**

**schedule**   a classification schedule or systematic display of a thesaurus, where the vocabulary is organized to show the structure of the subject and the relationships between terms

**schedule order**   the order of terms or concepts as they appear in the **systematic display** of a vocabulary tool. See also **filing order**

**scope note**   a short explanatory note attached to a term which may define the term or indicate how it is to be used in indexing

**search thesaurus**   a thesaurus which is used to support searching, either by allowing the searcher to choose search terms directly, or as part of the search software. Search thesauri may not themselves have been used to index the items being searched

**semantic content**   the semantic content of a document is its subject

**semantic factoring**   the process of breaking down a compound term into its constituent concepts so that the vocabulary contains only relatively simple terms. Whereas **syntactic factoring** involves only the separation of the terms in the compound, the original term or terms may disappear when semantically factored. For example, 'post-impressionism' may be semantically factored into 'art movement' + 'European' + '20th century'. This will allow documents about post-impressionism to be retrieved in general searches for 20th-century European art movements, at the cost of losing the term itself. Semantic factoring is generally to be avoided

**semantic relationships**   another way of describing **hierarchical** or **paradigmatic relationships**

**sibling relationship**   the relationship between two concepts or terms in the same **array** or **sub-facet,** or which are otherwise of equal status in a hierarchy (e.g. 'apples' and 'pears' are sibling terms in an array of fruit, and 'blonde' and 'brunette' are siblings in the array of hair by colour). In the thesaurus this is more usually referred to as a **related** or **associative term** relationship

**space category**   one of the fundamental categories in facet analysis. It accommodates concepts which are related to place. This will include named places as well as physiographic and other spatial concepts (e.g. Arizona, Milton Keynes, mountain regions, deserts, underwater, western)

**splitting**   the practice of separating a **compound term** into its constituent parts. Splitting has been used in recent thesaurus standards in preference to the term **factoring,** but it is not quite so broad in meaning

**standard**   (1) a published authority stating quality criteria for a product, or the way in which some process should be carried out; (2) a system or tool which is widely adopted for use by a particular community. In the first sense, there are various national and international standards for monolingual and multilingual thesaurus construction

**standard citation order**   the default order for combining terms from different facets in a faceted classification. It was established by the UK Classification Research Group in the middle part of the 20th century. It is considered to be the best general order of combination, but it may need to be varied to suit some subjects

**structured vocabulary**   a vocabulary for document indexing or organization purposes in which the relationships between terms or concepts are recognized

**sub-class**   a subdivision of a class. In the thesaurus, a sub-class is represented by a **narrower term**

**sub-facet**   another word for **array**

**subject heading list**   a formal, usually published, list of **subject headings**

**subject headings**  headings used to organize document records in a catalogue or printed list on the basis of their subject. Unlike thesauri, subject headings include many pre-combined compounds of terms (e.g. 'English 20th-century fiction' or 'Kangaroos in art')

**subject indexing**  the process of deciding on the subjects of documents and assigning appropriate index terms, usually from a **controlled vocabulary**

**subject metadata**  metadata which indicates the subject of a document or other resource

**subordinate class**  in a classification or taxonomy, a class which is lower in the hierarchy than a given class. In the thesaurus, this relationship is represented by a **narrower term**

**superordinate class**  in a classification or taxonomy, a class which is higher in the hierarchy than a given class. In the thesaurus, this relationship is represented by a **broader term**

**synonym control**  the process of identifying synonyms in a vocabulary, and selecting one as the **preferred term** for indexing

**synonyms**  two or more terms that have the same meaning; alternatively, two or more names for the same concept (e.g. 'kiwi fruit' and 'Chinese gooseberry', or 'films' and 'motion pictures'). For indexing purposes, one synonym (the **preferred term**) is selected for use, and the others are cross-referenced to it

**syntactic factoring**  the process of breaking down a compound term into its constituent parts so that the vocabulary contains only relatively simple terms. Unlike **semantic factoring**, syntactic factoring involves only the separation of terms in a compound (e.g. the substitution of two separate terms 'crocodiles' and 'farming' for the compound term 'crocodile farming'). Syntactic factoring is generally to be encouraged. See also **splitting**

**syntactic relationships**  relationships between concepts which are not part of the permanent structure of a subject, but which occur as a result of combining concepts in compound subjects. Syntactic relationships usually exist between terms in two different facets and account for many of the **related terms** in a thesaurus (e.g. 'wheat' and 'harvesting', 'horses' and 'show jumping', or 'cinema' and 'film directors')

**syntagmatic relationships**  another term for **syntactic relationships**

**syntax**  the operating rules of an indexing system (i.e. the way in which concepts or terms are combined, how any notation functions, and so on)

**systematic display**   in a thesaurus, that form of the display which shows how the subject is organized and indicates the relationships between terms, particularly in respect of the hierarchical structure. Compare with **alphabetical display**

**taxonomy**   a systematic or classificatory structure showing the organization of a subject and the relationships between its constituent concepts or classes. It is often used more loosely to mean any sort of subject-related vocabulary

**term**   a word, or group of words, used to label a **concept**

**thesaural relations**   a standard set of categories which accommodate the main types of relationship between terms in a thesaurus, namely **broader term (BT)**, **narrower term (NT)**, and **related term (RT)**. The relations also include the USE and Use For (UF) instructions that indicate **preferred** and **non-preferred terms**

**thesaurus**   a tool for subject indexing of documents or other resources that recognizes and indicates the relationships between the terms which it contains, and in which **vocabulary control** is exercised. A properly constructed thesaurus consists of a **systematic display** of terms, showing the structure of the subject, and an **alphabetical display**, in which the relationships between terms are indicated by the **thesaural relations**. As in the case of **taxonomy**, the term 'thesaurus' is often used more loosely for any sort of subject-related vocabulary

**'thing' category**   one of the fundamental categories of facet analysis. It accommodates concepts which are the principal object of study in the subject or discipline (e.g. metals in metallurgy, or drugs in pharmacology). It corresponds to Ranganathan's **personality category**

**time category**   one of the fundamental categories of facet analysis. It accommodates concepts which are related to time. These include specific dates and time periods, as well as more general temporal concepts (e.g. 17th century, 1984, weekends, Jurassic, winter, nocturnal)

**top term**   in a multi-disciplinary thesaurus, a term for one of the constituent subject areas. Each entry term has a **thesaural relation** TT (for top term) which indicates to which area it belongs (e.g. in a science thesaurus, the term 'armadillo' might have zoology as its TT)

**topic map**   a graphical representation of a subject that shows the structure of the subject, its constituent topics, and the relationships between them

**transliteration**   the process of representing words from a language using one alphabet in another alphabet (e.g. the representation of Russian words in the Roman (rather than Cyrillic) alphabet)

**tree structure**   a representation of a subject domain showing the subdivisions of subjects as branches, rather like a genealogical tree. The tree structure is commonly used in biological taxonomies

**upward references**   for a given term, references to terms higher up in the hierarchy (i.e. more general terms). In the thesaurus, these are usually referred to as **broader terms**

**verbal noun**   the noun form of a verb (e.g. 'management' for 'manage', 'education' for 'educate', 'growth' for 'grow'). Nouns are the preferred form of terms in a thesaurus, and verbs should be converted to this form

**vocabulary**   (1) the terms used in an indexing language as opposed to the **syntax** or operating rules of the language; (2) the indexing language itself, as in **controlled vocabulary**

**vocabulary control**   the management of terms in a **controlled indexing language** in order to limit the number available for indexing. Vocabulary control includes the elimination of synonyms and the choice of **preferred terms**

**vocabulary tool**   a system for the organization and retrieval of resources on a subject basis that consists of the concepts or terms in the subject usually presented in a structured format

**word order**   the order of words in a **compound term**. Before automation, compound terms in a catalogue or index were often inverted to bring the key element to the lead position, and hence group the subdivisions of a topic (e.g. 'cookery, Italian' or 'chemistry, organic'). Now that online systems remove the need for this, natural word order is normally preferred

**word-based tools**   vocabulary tools that use words themselves for indexing, rather than codes or notations (e.g. thesauri, **keyword lists**, and **subject headings**)

# Bibliography

## Standards for thesaurus construction

The following standards provide guidelines for the construction of monolingual thesauri. There are also standards relating to multilingual thesauri, but the construction of the multilingual thesaurus is beyond the scope of this book.

ANSI/NISO Z39.19-1993 (1994) *Guidelines for the Construction, Format, and Management of Monolingual Thesauri*, Bethesda, MD, NISO Press.

BS 8723-1:2005 (2005) *Structured Vocabularies for Information Retrieval – Guide – Part 1: Definitions, Symbols and Abbreviations* London, British Standards Institution.

BS 8723-2:2005 (2005) *Structured Vocabularies for Information Retrieval – Guide – Part 2: Thesauri*, London, British Standards Institution.

## Thesaurus construction manuals

Aitchison, J., Gilchrist, A. and Bawden, D. (2000) *Thesaurus Construction and Use: a practical manual*, 4th edn, London, Aslib.

The standard work in the field of thesaurus construction, and an excellent source of everything to do with the thesaurus. It also has a particularly full bibliography, extending to other types of retrieval tool.

## General surveys of the thesaurus

Thomas, A. R. and Roe, S. E. (eds) (2004) *The Thesaurus: review, renaissance, and revision*, Binghampton, NY, Haworth Press.

A collection of essays on a wide range of aspects of the theory, construction, management and maintenance of the thesaurus. Since so much of what is published on the modern thesaurus is in the journal literature, this work is valuable for the range and depth of its bibliographies and references.

## Websites

Willpower Information at www.willpowerinfo.co.uk

This is a very informative and well maintained website from Leonard Will; a reliable source of information about thesauri, and particularly valuable for its survey of thesaurus software.

## Other sources

A number of references to other works, and to thesauri themselves, can be found in the notes in individual chapters, notably Chapters 3 and 6.

# Appendix I
# Sample titles for thesaurus vocabulary

## Book titles from the online catalogue of the Royal Veterinary College, London

Act to amend the Protection of Animals (Anaesthetics) Act 1964 Great Britain

Animal liberation

Animal theology

Animal welfare in poultry, pig and veal calf production together with the Proceedings of the Committee, Minutes of Evidence and Appendices. Great Britain House of Commons

Eating with conscience: the bioethics of food

Environmental enrichment for captive animals

Ethical case against fur farming: statement by an international group of academics, including ethicists, philosophers and theologians

Guidance on the slaughter of ostriches welfare

Handbook of primate husbandry and welfare

Humane control of animals living in the wild

Human-livestock interactions: the stockperson and the productivity and welfare of intensively farmed animals

Interdepartmental Committee on Slaughterhouses (England and Wales) Interim Report. Great Britain Ministry of Agriculture, Fisheries and Food

Manual of the care and treatment of children's and exotic pets

Recommendation concerning ratites: ostriches, emus and rheas. Standing committee of the European convention for the protection of animals kept for farming purposes

Report on the welfare of broiler breeders

Report on the welfare of farmed fish

Report on the welfare of laying hens

Report on the welfare of pigs kept outdoors

Veterinary, behavioural and welfare implications of bear farming in Asia
Welfare and management of bears in zoological gardens

## Zetoc search on journals, including Animal Welfare, Animal Technology and Welfare and Society and Animals (selected from nos 1–200 of 582 results)

Addressing animal abuse: the complementary roles of religion, secular ethics and the law

Alternatives to nose-ringing in outdoor sows

Animal welfare and contraception of zoo and wild animals

Animal welfare aspects of rodeo events

Animal welfare in large dairy herds

Applying animal learning theory: training captive animals to comply with veterinary and husbandry procedures

Are endocrine disrupting compounds a threat to farm animal health

Aspects of animal welfare with regard to the production of farmed fish in aquaculture systems

Assessing pain in animals – putting research into practice

Assessment of the impact of government animal welfare policy on farm animal welfare in the UK

Assessment of the welfare of working horses, mules and donkeys, using health and behaviour parameters

Automated recording of stress vocalizations as a tool to document impaired welfare in pigs

Behavioural and physiological measures of welfare of pregnant mares fitted with a novel urine collection device

Body weight change as a measure of stress

Boredom with zoo animals – a matter of animal welfare?

Breeding and animal welfare

Can we measure human animal interactions in on-farm animal welfare assessment?

Cat behaviour: social organization, communication and development

Cat overpopulation in the United States

Catching animals who have escaped from their primary enclosure

Changes in ear-pinna temperature as a measure of stress in sheep

Chronic stress in sheep: assessment tools and their use in different management conditions

Cognitive and communication capacities of grey parrots

Comparative study of the influence of social housing conditions on the behaviour of captive tigers

Comparing the behaviour of zoo housed animals with wild conspecifics as a welfare indicator, using the giraffe (Giraffa camelopardalis) as a model

Computer assisted enrichment for zoo-housed orangutans (Pongo pygmaeus)

Confronting cruelty: moral orthodoxy and the challenge of the animal rights movement

Consciousness, emotion and animal welfare: insights from cognitive science

Consistency of piglet crushing in sows

Coordination of French research on animal welfare

Cross-institutional assessment of stress responses in zoo animals using longitudinal monitoring of faecal corticoids and behaviour

Defining, measuring and interpreting stress in laboratory animals

Dog training methods: their use, effectiveness and interaction with behaviour and welfare

Education and training for animal technologists

Effect of blindfolding horses on heart rate and behaviour during handling and loading onto transport vehicles

Effect of breeding schemes on the genetic response of canine hip dysplasia, behaviour traits and appearance

Effect of rearing conditions on the grooming and play behaviour in captive chimpanzees

Effect of supplementary ultraviolet lighting on the behaviour and corticosterone levels of Japanese quail chicks

Effects of mirrors on the welfare of caged rabbits

Effects of novel floorings on dustbathing, pecking and scratching behaviour of caged hens.

Effects of rearing density on rainbow trout welfare, determined by plasmatic and tissue parameters

Effects of road traffic accidents on domestic cats and their owners

Emotion and animal welfare

English almanac and animal health care in the seventeenth century

Enriching the lives of zoo animals and their welfare: where research can be fundamental

Environmental enrichment for ostrich, struthio camelus, chicks

Equine welfare: risk of horses falling in the Grand National

Equipment and requirements for the welfare of trotting horses

Ethics and welfare of animals used in education

Ethics of animal welfare and the idea of animal protection in German laws

Ethics of interventions for the welfare of free-living wild animals

Evaluation of comparison between $CO_2O_2$ and $CO_2$ gas in the euthanasia of mice

Feather pecking in poultry: the application of science in a search for practical solutions

Fish and welfare: do fish have the capacity for pain perception and suffering

Fractal analysis of animal behaviour as an indicator of animal welfare

Group size and space allocation in farmed juvenile blue foxes

Hand-rearing rhesus macaques involving catering for individual needs whilst following a structured hand-rearing schedule

Health and welfare of rehabilitated juvenile hedgehogs

Healthy and happy: animal welfare as an integral part of sustainable agriculture

Hedgehog rehabilitation in perspective

Horse maiming in the English countryside: moral panic, human deviance and the social construction of victimhood

Housing environment alters delayed-type hypersensitivity and corticosterone concentrations of individually housed male C57BL/6 mice

Housing of breeding ostriches in Germany and aspects of animal welfare

How has the risk of predation shaped the behavioural responses of sheep to fear and distress

How tufted capuchin monkeys rank monkey chow in relation to other foods

Human-cat relationship

Impact of the ethical review process for research using animals in the UK

Importance of straw for pig and cattle welfare

Infections in laboratory animals

Influence of a camouflage net barrier on the behaviour, welfare and public perceptions of zoo-housed gorillas

Influence of social status on the welfare of growing pigs housed in barren and enriched environments

Influence of toys on the behaviour and welfare of kennelled dogs

Influence of visual stimulation on the behaviour of dogs housed in a rescue shelter

International regulation of animal welfare: standards for the trapping of wild animals

Investigation into the ways of promoting public understanding of animal welfare in the zoo industry

Investigation on standing stalls for horses with regard to animal welfare

Issues for veterinarians in recognizing and identifying animal neglect and abuse

Juvenile farmed mink with additional access to swimming water play more frequently than animals housed with a cylinder and platform, but without swimming water

Laboratory routines cause animal stress

Legislating a solution to animal shelter euthanasia: a case study of California's controversial SB 1785

Long-term detrimental effects of tooth clipping or grinding in piglets: a histological approach

Measurement of aversion to determine humane methods of anaesthesia and euthanasia

Measuring the value to the public of pig welfare improvements: a contingent valuation approach

Modifying the behaviour of singly caged baboons: evaluating the effectiveness of four enrichment techniques

Movement and mortality of translocated urban-suburban grey squirrels

Nest-building behaviour in male rats from three inbred strains

New individually ventilated cage system for improved rodent care and welfare

Note on the influence of visitors on the behaviour and welfare of zoo-housed gorillas

Nutrition and animal welfare

Peri-natal environmental effects on maternal behaviour, pituitary and adrenal activation, and the progress of parturition in the primiparous sow

Perpetration induced traumatic stress in persons who euthanize non-human animals in surgeries, animals shelters and laboratories

Physical cruelty towards animals in Massachusetts 1975-1996

Pigs and people: sociological perspectives on the discipline of animals in intensive confinement

Preference of domestic rabbits for grass or coarse mix feeds

Preferences of growing ducklings and turkey poults for illuminance

Rattling the cage: towards legal rights for animals

Refined method for acclimatizing and transporting to an offsite designated surgical facility

Refinement in guinea pig housing within the laboratory environment

Refinement of intra-tracheal dosing techniques in rats

Relationship between animal cruelty, delinquency, and attitudes toward the treatment of non-human animals

Review of the welfare of horses and ponies at markets

Salivary cortisol and behaviour in an all-male group of western lowland gorillas

Siberian hamster provides an alternative model for the study of obesity and body weight regulation

Stereotypic swaying and serum cortisol concentrations in three captive African elephants (Loxodonta africana)

Stress in wild-caught Eurasian otters (Lutra lutra): effects of a long-acting neuroleptic and time in captivity

Veterinarian's role in animal welfare

Under-representation of African American employees in animal welfare organizations in the United States

Unraveling the methods of childhood and adolescent cruelty to non-human animals

Use of conjoint analysis to determine the importance of factors that affect the on-farm welfare of the dairy cow

Using science to support ethical decisions promoting humane livestock slaughter and vertebrate pest control

Welfare aspects of chick handling in broiler and laying hen hatcheries

Welfare of badgers subjected to culling: patterns of trap related injury

Welfare of feral cats

Welfare of free-living wild animals in Europe: harm caused by human activities

Welfare of sport horses: role of the rider

Welfare of working equids in Mexico

Welfare of zoo animals

Welfare, husbandry and veterinary care of wild animals in captivity

Zoo animals and their human audiences: what is the visitor effect

## Titles from Animal Welfare Institute Alternative Farming Database (www.awionline.org/farm/alt-farming3.html)

ABCs of rotational grazing

Animal health and welfare in organic agriculture

Behavioural principles of livestock handling

Brush control with goats

Cooperatively producing and marketing all natural beef

Dairy debate: consequences of bovine growth hormone and rotational grazing technologies

Day range poultry: every chicken owner's guide to grazing gardens and improving pastures

Forage needs for meat goats and sheep

Free-range poultry production and marketing

Grass-based dairies hold promise for southern Iowa producers

Guidelines for using donkeys as guard animals with sheep

Help livestock keep their cool: water and shade are keys to comfort

Hog farming that meets the animal's social instincts

Home-range behaviour and social organization in Scottish blackface sheep

Hoop housing for feeder pigs offers a welfare friendly environment compared to a non-bedded confinement system

Hooped shelters for hogs

Livestock guard dogs reduce predation on domestic sheep in Colorado

Livestock guard dogs, llamas and donkeys

Managing manure in harmony with the environment and society

Market growing for wool that comes from predator-friendly ranches: llamas, not guns, protect sheep from coyotes

Milk production and quality of pastured cows rival confinement feeding

Multi-species grazing

Pasture-based poultry production in France

Pig powered composting: livestock can help manage manure on your farm

Producing rare, naturally coloured wools

Put water where you want it: a mobile tank increases your pasture management options

Rearing pigs in species-specific family groups

Red meat can be green

Reducing handling stress improves both productivity and welfare

Seasonal dairy grazing: a case study of six successful dairy farms using seasonal calving and management-intensive grazing

Sheep behaviour under unherded conditions on mountain summer ranges

Shelter and shade: creating a healthy and profitable environment for your livestock with trees

Sows on pasture: reports from sustainable farmers from Minnesota and Iowa

Successful system for housing pregnant sows in groups

Sustainable swine production in the US corn belt

Swedish deep straw farrowing system

Winter range use by cattle of different ages in southwestern Montana

# Appendix 2
## Sample terms for the thesaurus

abuse
acclimatization
act
adolescent
adrenal activation
African American
  employees
African elephants
anaesthesia
anaesthetics
animal abuse
animal behaviour
animal cruelty
animal experiment-
  ation
animal health
animal health care
animal learning
  theory
animal liberation
animal neglect and
  abuse
animal protection
animal rights move-
  ment
animal shelter
animal stress
animal technologists
animal theology
animal welfare

animal welfare organi-
  zations
animals used in edu-
  cation
appearance
aquaculture systems
Asia
assessment
assessment tools
automated recording
aversion
baboons
badgers
barren environments
bear farming
bears
beef
behaviour
behaviour traits
behavioural measures
behavioural responses
bioethics
blindfolding
blue foxes
body weight
body weight
  regulation
boredom
bovine growth
  hormone

breeding
breeding ostriches
breeding schemes
broilers
brush control
cage system
caged hens
caged rabbits
calves
California
calving
camouflage net barrier
canine hip dysplasia
captive animals
captive chimpanzees
captive tigers
captivity
capuchin monkeys
case study
cat behaviour
cat overpopulation
cat owners
catching animals
cats
cattle
cattle welfare
change
chick handling
chickens
chicks

children
children's pets
chimpanzees
chronic
chronic stress
$CO_2$ gas
$CO_2O_2$ gas
coarse mix feeds
cognitive capacity
cognitive science
Colorado
comfort
communication
communication
   capacity
comparative study
comparison
computers
confinement
conjoint analysis
conscience
consciousness
consistency
contraception
cooperation
corticosterone
corticosterone con-
   centrations
corticosterone levels
cortisol
countryside
coyotes
cruelty
culling
cylinders
dairies
dairy cows
dairy farms

dairy herds
day range
deep straw farrowing
   system
delayed-type hyper-
   sensitivity
density
detrimental effects
development
discipline of animals
distress
dog training
dogs
domestic cats
domestic rabbits
domestic sheep
donkeys
dosing techniques
ducklings
ducks
dustbathing
dysplasia
ear-pinnae
education and  train-
   ing
emotion
emus
enclosure
endocrine disrupting
   compounds
England
enriched environ-
   ments
enriching
enrichment
enrichment  tech-
   niques
environmental

enrichment
equids
equine welfare
equipment
escape
ethics
ethics committees
Eurasian otters
Europe
euthanasia
evaluation
exotic pets
faecal corticoids
falling
farm animal welfare
farm animals
farmed [animals]
farmed fish
farmed mink
farrowing
fear
feather pecking
feathers
feeding
feral cats
fish
floorings
food [human]
foods
forage needs
fractal analysis
France
free-living wild
   animals
free-range poultry
fur farming
gardens
genetic response

maternal behaviour
measure
measurement
meat goats
Mexico
mice
milk
milk production
milk quality
mink
Minnesota
mirrors
mobile tank
modification
monkey chow
monkeys
Montana
moral orthodoxy
mortality
mountain summer
  ranges
mountains
movement
mules
multi-species grazing
natural beef
naturally coloured
  wools
neglect
nest-building
neuroleptic
non-bedded confine-
  ment system
non-human animals
nose-ringing
nutrition
obesity
on-farm

on-farm welfare
orangutans
organic agriculture
ostriches
otters
outdoors
outdoor sows
overpopulation
pain in animals
pain perception
parturition
pasture management
pastured cows
pastures
pecking
persons
pest control
pets
physical cruelty
physiological
  measures
pig welfare
piglet crushing
piglets
pigs
pigs kept outdoors
pituitary activation
plasma
platform
play
play behaviour
Pongo pygmaeus
ponies
poultry
poultry production
predation
predator-friendliness
pregnant mares

pregnant sows
primary enclosure
primates
primiparous
producers
production
promotion
protection of animals
Protection of Animals
  (Anaesthetics) Act
  1964
public
public perceptions
public understanding
rabbits
racehorses
rainbow trout
ranches
rare wools
ratites
rats
rearing conditions
rearing density
red meat
rehabilitation [wild
  animals]
religion
rescue shelter
research
research using ani-
  mals
rheas
rhesus macaques
riders
road traffic accidents
rodents
rodeo events
rotational grazing

# Appendix 3
# Facets at stage 1 of analysis

## Agents

Agents is the facet which accommodates all those terms which relate to the means of carrying out operations. This usually includes buildings, equipment, substances and so on, as well as people in the subject, both individual and in the form of groups and organizations. In this list the terms are separated into those three groups. There is some overlap between buildings in the equipment array and organizations, since, for example, a laboratory may exist as a component or as an organization *per se*.

Agents (equipment) is rather broad in nature, as since so many of the terms are to do with buildings and the housing of animals. I've included terms which relate to outdoor management of animals as well; although these are not strictly agents they sit appropriately alongside the 'housing' terms. Other general groups of terms here include feed and foodstuffs, and various drugs and chemicals.

Agents (organizations) contains some terms which could also have been located in the place facet. The concept of organization is used to mean any sort of functional unit with staff and facilities rather than formally constituted societies or bodies.

**Agents (equipment)**
(includes food-
stuffs, buildings,
drugs, etc.)
anaesthetics
assessment tools
cage systems
camouflage net
barriers
$CO_2$ gas
$CO_2.O_2$ gas

coarse mix feeds
computers
cylinders
dairies
enclosure(s)
equipment
floorings
foods
grass
guns
hatcheries

hoop housing
hooped shelters
housing
housing environment
illuminance
individual housing
laboratories
mirrors
mobile tanks
monkey chow
neuroleptics

non-bedded confine-
ment systems
nose-rings
pastures
platforms
primary enclosures
shade
shelter
shelters
single cages
social housing condi-
tions
standing stalls
straw
surgical facilities
swimming water
toys
transport vehicles
trees
ultraviolet lighting
unherded conditions
urine collection
devices

ventilation
water

**Agents
(persons)**
adolescents
African American
employees
animal technologists
cat owners
children
human audiences
persons
producers
public
riders
stockpersons
sustainable farmers
veterinarians
visitors

**Agents
(organizations and
institutions)**
animal rights move-
ment
animal shelters
animal welfare organ-
izations
dairy farms
ethics committees
farms
government
laboratories
markets
ranches
rescue shelters
rodeos
shelters
surgeries
zoo industry
zoological gardens
zoos

## Forms (of document)

Form of a document really has little to do with the subject content, but it
is often desirable to identify, for example, legislation. Case studies and
reports are also usefully indexed as such. Relatively few forms occurred
in the sample vocabulary.

act
case study
law
legislation
Protection of Animals (Anaesthetics) Act 1964
standards

## Operations/actions

Operations is a relatively straightforward facet. It consists of actions upon animals and their environment, both specific (feeding, nose ringing) and more general (management, modification). In general, actions performed by animals (even consciously) are regarded as *processes* while those performed by humans are *operations*. Occasionally a term seems to be both a process and operation (breeding, movement), in which case it may be duplicated.

There are a few 'difficult' terms here which are tricky to categorize. Concepts such as 'criteria', 'measures', 'indicators', etc., are very elusive in terms of their facet status. Usually I would assign such terms to the process facet (which is useful for accommodating concepts that are of the nature of 'problems', 'relations', 'states', 'conditions', etc.) but here these specific terms seem so closely associated with monitoring and performance that they are kept with operations.

abuse
agriculture
anaesthesia
animal abuse
animal cruelty
animal experimenta-
    tion
animal health care
animal liberation
animal neglect and
    abuse
animal protection
animal welfare
aquaculture [systems]
assessment
automated recording
[bear] farming
behavioural measures
blindfolding
body weight regula-
    tion
breeding

breeding schemes
brush control
capture
catching animals
[chick] handling
comparative study
confinement
conjoint analysis
contraception
cooperation
criteria
cruelty
culling
day range
deep straw farrowing
    system
delinquency
deviance
discipline of animals
dog training
    methods
dosing techniques

education and train-
    ing
enriching
enrichment
enrichment tech-
    niques
environmental
    enrichment
ethical decisions
ethical review
euthanasia
evaluation
feeding
fractal analysis
free range
hand rearing
hand rearing schedule
handling
[hedgehog] rehabili-
    tation
[hog] farming
[horse] maiming

humane control
humane methods
humane slaughter
husbandry
husbandry proce-
    dures
indicators
intensive confinement
[international] regula-
    tion
interventions
laboratory routines
livestock handling
loading
longitudinal monitor-
    ing
maiming
management
management condi-
    tions

management intensive
    grazing
market growing
marketing
measures
measurement
modification
movement
multi-species grazing
neglect
nose ringing
organic agriculture
pasture management
pest control
physical cruelty
production
promotion
protection of animals
rehabilitation [wild
    animals]

research
research using animals
rotational grazing
seasonal dairy grazing
slaughter
space allocation
sustainable agriculture
[swine] production
tooth clipping
tooth grinding
training
transport
transporting
trapping
ventilation
veterinary care
veterinary procedures
visual stimulation
welfare indicators

## Parts and properties

These two facets are run together here, only because they have small numbers of concepts and can be conveniently displayed on one page. Both categories are relatively easy to identify, although it should be noted that the animal parts consist of three possible types of concept: regional parts (head, legs, wings, etc.), organs and systems (nervous system, liver, brain, etc.) and constituent elements (cells, tissues, body chemicals, etc.).

Properties are occasionally difficult to distinguish from processes (e.g. hypersensitivity, mortality).

It is immediately evident that the total potential vocabulary is not represented here. In a real situation this would obviously need to be addressed, and the facet expanded considerably. For our purposes in constructing a demonstration thesaurus this need not be done. Of course the complete terminology would constitute a separate field of animal anatomy and generate a much larger thesaurus than can be managed as an exercise. consequently I shall only expand this facet as far as is essential to provide a proper hierarchical context for the terms already here.

**Animal parts**
adrenal [glands]
bovine growth
  hormone
cells
corticosterone
corticosterone
  concentrations
corticosterone levels
cortisol
ear-pinna
endocrine disrupting
  compounds
faecal corticoids
feathers
fur
growth hormone

hips
histology
manure
pituitary glands
plasma
saliva
salivary cortisol
serum
teeth
tissues
trachea
urine
wool

**Animal properties**
appearance
body weight

heart rate
hypersensitivity
mortality
obesity
primiparity
temperature

**(properties of
  groups)**
density
group size

**General properties**
consistency
productivity
predator friendliness

## Place and time

Place and time are the least 'subject-related' of the facets, and many of the concepts here could be applied to any subject field. There is usually no difficulty in identifying time or place concepts, although it should be remembered that, as well as named places and specific times, general spatial and temporal concepts are relevant (e.g. outdoors, mountains, summer, winter).

As with the facets of animals and their parts, only the terms from the sample vocabulary are included, and no attempt is made here to be comprehensive in coverage (although some terms might be added to represent hierarchies accurately).

The notion of place is a little more complex than in some subjects, since the place where animals are kept or managed (farms, markets, laboratories) might be regarded as part of this facet. Generally I have treated places in that sense as agents/facilities because the operational aspects of animal welfare are closely related to the specific local environment.

**Place**

Asia
barren environments
California
Colorado
countryside
England
enriched environ-
    ments
Europe
France
gardens
Germany
Great Britain
home-range

international [place]
Iowa
Massachusetts
Mexico
Minnesota
Montana
mountains
mountain summer
    ranges
on-farm
outdoor
pastures
southern
suburbs
Sweden

UK
United States
urban areas
US corn belt
winter range

**Time**

chronic
long acting
long-term
seasonal
seventeenth century
summer
time in captivity
winter

## Processes

Processes is often the most difficult of the fundamental categories both to
define and to manage. In broad terms a process may be regarded as an
intransitive action (i.e. one with no particular recipient of the action)
such as 'growth', 'feeding', or 'falling'. Sometimes it is defined as an
action that happens 'by itself', i.e. without human agents or intervention.
It is useful in this subject to define processes as actions carried out by animals (whether consciously or otherwise) to differentiate these from those
carried by humans, which are operations. As a consequence, terms such
as 'dustbathing' or 'nest building', which look like operations, are assigned
to this facet.

Process is a useful category for accommodating 'difficult' concepts,
which are not exactly actions but are otherwise hard to categorize. These
include concepts that relate to status, conditions, relationships, or problems of some kind. Examples in this vocabulary are 'aversion', 'influence',
'preference', 'fear', 'stress' and 'victimhood'.

acclimatization
adrenal activation
animal behaviour
animal health
[animal] learning
animal stress
aversion
behaviour
behaviour traits
behavioural responses
boredom
breeding
calving
canine hip dysplasia
cat behaviour
cat overpopulation
cattle welfare
change
chronic stress
cognitive capacity
comfort
communication
communication
    capacity
consciousness
delayed type hyper-
    sensitivity
detrimental effects
development
distress
dustbathing
dysplasia
emotion
equine welfare

escape
falling
farm animal welfare
farrowing
fear
feather pecking
forage needs
genetic responses
grazing
grooming behaviour
growth
handling stress
harm caused by
    human activities
hip dysplasia
human-animal inter-
    actions
human livestock
    interactions
human-cat relation-
    ships
impaired welfare
improvement
individual needs
infections
injuries
maternal behaviour
milk production
milk quality
movement
nest building
nutrition
on-farm welfare
overpopulation

pain in animals
pain perception
parturition
pecking
physiological meas-
    ures
pig welfare
piglet crushing
pituitary activation
play
play behaviour
predation
preference
public perception
public understanding
risk
road traffic accidents
scratching behaviour
seasonal calving
sheep behaviour
social instincts
social organization
social status
stress
stress responses
stress vocalizations
suffering
swaying
translocation
trap related injuries
traumatic stress
victimhood
visitor effect
welfare

## Products

Products is a facet normally encountered only in subjects where some element of 'manufacturing' is present. Although few of the documents selected dealt with the products *per se*, these concepts are important as 'specifiers' of animals, i.e. to generate types of animals 'by product' e.g. beef cattle, fur farming.

| | | |
|---|---|---|
| beef | meat | rare wools |
| dairy [products] | milk | red meat |
| food [human] | natural beef | veal |
| fu | naturally coloured wools | wools |

## Abstract concepts

Although it is not included among the fundamental categories, it is often necessary to create a 'facet' to accommodate general philosophical and theoretical concepts in the subject that are too abstract in nature to be assigned to a category.

This facet may also provide a place for very general relations (known technically as phase relations) and relations with other disciplines. While there is no specific theoretical basis for this, it is common practice in the construction of vocabulary tools.

## (Theory and philosophy)

| | | |
|---|---|---|
| animal theology | ethics | secular ethics |
| bioethics | green [issues] | legal rights of animals |
| conscience | moral orthodoxy | |

## (Phase relations)

| | | |
|---|---|---|
| comparison | (relations with other | religion |
| effect | subjects) | law |
| influence | cognitive science | |

# Appendix 4
# Facets at stage 2 of analysis

## Forms (of document)
case studies
standards
law. legislation
    acts
        Protection of Animals
          (Anaesthetics) Act 1964 →

## Abstract concepts
(phase relations)

comparison
effect
influence

(relations with other subjects)
science
    cognitive science
    ecology. environment
        green issues
religion
    animal theology
ethics. morals. secular ethics
    conscience
    moral orthodoxy
    bioethics
law
    legal rights of animals

## Place and time
**Place**
(by orientation)
    southern

(by local conditions)
    indoor
    outdoor
    barren environments
    enriched environments

(by physiographic features)
    mountains

(by land use)
    gardens
    urban areas
    suburbs
    countryside
    on-farm
    pastures
    ranges
        home-range
        summer ranges
            mountain summer ranges
        winter ranges

(by political place)
    the world. international place
    Europe
        Great Britain. United Kingdom. UK
        England

France
Germany
Sweden
Asia
North America
  United States. USA
    US corn belt
    California
    Colorado
    Iowa
    Massachusetts
    Minnesota
    Montana
    Mexico

**Time**
(general temporal properties)
  long-term. chronic
    long-acting
(duration of time)
  time in captivity
(seasons)
  seasonal
  summer
  winter

(historic time)
  seventeenth century
  twentieth century
    1975–1996

# Agents
(agents – persons)
  (persons by age)
    children
    adolescents
  (persons by ethnic origin)
    African-American
  (persons by occupation)
    (by occupational status)
      employees

animal technologists
producers
stockpersons
sustainable farmers
veterinarians
(persons by relationship with animals)
  owners
    cat owners
  riders
  public
    human audience
    visitors

(agents – equipment)
  drugs
    anaesthetics
      $CO_2$ gas
      $CO_2.O_2$ gas
    neuroleptics
  water
  foods
    grass
    grass-based foods
    coarse mix feeds
    monkey chow
  bedding
    straw
  equipment
    assessment tools
    computers
    handling equipment
      nose-rings
    medical equipment
      urine collection devices
    guns
    vehicles
      transport vehicles

(agents – buildings)
  (services and facilities)
    lighting. illuminance

ultra-violet lighting
ventilation
(parts of buildings)
floorings
(fittings and equipments)
mirrors
platforms
toys
(functional parts)
laboratories
surgical facilities
(types of building by function)
dairies
hatcheries
housing. housing systems
housing environment
individual housing
social housing conditions
(parts of system)
cage systems
single cages
(housing by form)
hoop shelters. hooped
housing
standing stalls. non-
bedded confinement
systems
enclosures
primary enclosures
barriers
camouflage net barriers

external environment
(elements)
shelter
shade
trees
water
mobile tanks
swimming water
pastures

(agents – organizations)
government
government policy
ethics committees

animal rights movement
animal welfare organizations

(organizations by function)
surgeries
shelters (organizations).
animal shelters. rescue
shelters
laboratories
farms. ranches
dairy farms
markets
rodeos
zoos. zoological gardens. zoo
industry

# Operations

(general actions)
analysis
conjoint analysis
fractal analysis
assessment
comparison. comparative study
cooperation
evaluation
intervention
management
measurement
modification
monitoring
criteria
indicators
welfare indicators
measures
behavioural measures
longitudinal monitoring

recording
    automated recording
regulation
    international regulation

education and training (personnel)


animal welfare
animal protection. protection
    humane methods. humane control
rehabilitation (of wild animals)
    hedgehog rehabilitation
animal liberation


animal abuse. abuse
    delinquency
    deviance


    neglect
    animal cruelty. cruelty
        physical cruelty
            maiming
                horse maiming
capture. catching animals
    trapping
confinement
    intensive confinement


veterinary care. animal health care
    veterinary procedures
        anaesthesia
        dosing techniques
        euthanasia
        tooth clipping
        tooth grinding
        nose ringing


environment management
    ventilation
    lighting

space allocation
pest control

environmental enrichment.
    enrichment.
enriching. enrichment techniques
    visual stimulation

research using animals. animal
    experimentation
    laboratory routines

training
    dog training methods
    discipline of animals

farming. agriculture
    aquaculture
    hog farming
    bear farming

    organic agriculture
    sustainable agriculture

husbandry. husbandry procedures
    handling. livestock handling
        chick handling
        blindfolding
        movement
        transport. transporting
            loading
    production. animal production
        poultry production
        swine production
        milk production
    feeding
        body weight regulation
    grazing
        management intensive
            grazing
        multi-species grazing

rotational grazing
seasonal dairy grazing

pasture management
brush control
day range
free range

breeding
    breeding schemes
    contraception
    farrowing systems
        deep straw
        farrowing systems
    hand rearing
        hand rearing schedules
slaughter. humane slaughter
    culling

marketing. promotion
    market growing

# Products
food [human]
    meat
        red meat
            beef
                natural beef
            veal
    dairy foods
        milk
fur
wools
    naturally coloured wools
    rare wools

# Processes
(General processes)

influence
preference
change

acclimatization
growth
development
improvement
detrimental effects
risk
welfare
    needs
        individual needs
    comfort
    impaired welfare
    on-farm welfare

    farm animal welfare
    equine welfare
    pig welfare
    cattle welfare

physiological processes
    adrenal activation
    pituitary activation
    genetic responses
    hypersensitivity
        delayed type hypersensitivity
    stress
        stress responses
        stress vocalization
        chronic stress
        handling stress
        traumatic stress

abnormal physiology. pathology
        harm caused by human activities
        pain [in animals]
            pain perception
        suffering
        (dysfunction)
            dysplasia
                hip dysplasia
                    canine hip dysplasia
        infections
        injuries

trap related injuries
crushing
   piglet crushing

road traffic accidents
translocation
psychological processes. mental processes
  emotion
    fear
    boredom
    aversion
  consciousness
  cognitive processes
    cognitive capacity
    learning
  communication
    communication capacity

animal behaviour
  cat behaviour
  sheep behaviour

  behaviour traits
  behavioural responses

  movement
    swaying
    falling

  feeding
    nutrition
    forage needs

    pecking
    grazing
    predation

  grooming behaviour
    scratching behaviour
    dustbathing

  breeding. breeding behaviour
    parturition
      calving

seasonal calving
farrowing
maternal behaviour
  milk production
    milk quality
  nest building

social behaviour
  interactions
    human-animal interactions.
      human-livestock
        interactions
    public understanding
    public perception
    visitor effect

    human-cat relationship
social instinct
social organization
  social status
play. play behaviour

escape

abnormal behaviour
  feather pecking

# Parts and properties
(properties)
appearance
(size.dimensions)
  body weight
    obesity

temperature
mortality
hypersensitivity
heart rate
primiparity

(parts)
  (components)
    cells

tissues. histology
(bio-chemicals)
  corticosterone
    corticosterone concentrations
    corticosterone levels
    cortisol
  growth hormone
    bovine growth hormone
  endocrine disrupting compounds
(body fluids and products)
  blood
    serum
    plasma
  saliva
    salivary cortisol
  urine
  faeces. manure
    faecal corticoids

(organs and systems)
  endocrine system
    adrenal glands
    pituitary glands
  locomotor system
    skin
      fur
      wool
      feathers
  digestive system
    teeth
  respiratory system
    trachea
  nervous system
    sense organs
      ears
        ear-pinnae

(parts)
  (regions)
    hips

# Appendix 5
# Completed systematic display

## Forms of document
BC          case studies
BD          standards
BL          law. legislation
BT               acts
                         Protection of Animals (Anaesthetics) Act 1964
                           → FGB/EMB/BT

## Philosophy and theory of animal welfare
          (phase relations)
CC         comparison
CE         effect
CF         influence

          (relations with other subjects)
CG         science
CGC       cognitive science
CGE       ecology. environment
CGG         green issues
CR         religion
CRD       animal theology
CT         ethics. morals. secular ethics
CTC       conscience
CTM      moral orthodoxy
CTS       bioethics
CTW     law
CTX      legal rights of animals

## D         Time
          (general temporal properties)
DC         long-term. chronic
DD          long-acting
          (duration of time)
DF         time in captivity

|       | (seasons)   |
|-------|-------------|
| DG    | seasonal    |
| DGS   | summer      |
| DGW   | winter      |

|       | (historic time)        |
|-------|------------------------|
| DP    | seventeenth century    |
| DT    | twentieth century      |

**E**     **Place**

|       | (by orientation) |
|-------|------------------|
| EB    | southern         |

|       | (by local conditions)        |
|-------|------------------------------|
| ECI   | indoor                       |
| ECO   | outdoor                      |
|       | barren environments → FMD    |
|       | enriched environments → FMF  |

|       | (by physiographic features) |
|-------|-----------------------------|
| EFM   | mountains                   |

|       | (by land use)                            |
|-------|------------------------------------------|
| EJG   | gardens                                  |
| EJH   | urban areas                              |
| EJL   | suburbs                                  |
| EJM   | countryside                              |
|       | pastures → FRX                           |
|       | ranges → FRY                             |
|       |     summer ranges → FRY/DGS              |
|       |     winter ranges → FRY/DGW              |
|       |     mountain summer ranges → FRY/EFM/DGS |
|       |     home-ranges → FRYZ                   |

|       | (political place)                    |
|-------|--------------------------------------|
| EL    | the world. international place        |
| EM    | Europe                               |
| EMB   | Great Britain. United Kingdom. UK    |
| EME   | England                              |
| EMF   | France                               |
| EMG   | Germany                              |
| EMS   | Sweden                               |
| EN    | Asia                                 |
| EO    | North America                        |

| EP | United States. USA |
|---|---|
| EPB | Massachusetts |
| EPC | US corn belt |
| EPD | Iowa |
| EPE | Minnesota |
| EPF | Montana |
| EPG | Colorado |
| EPH | California |
| ER | Mexico |

**F**          **Agents**
                (agents – persons)
FB            humans. human beings
                (persons by age)
FCC              children
FCD              adolescents
                (persons by ethnic origin)
FD               African-American
                (persons by occupation)
                   (by occupational status)
FE                    employees
FEB              animal technologists
FED              (by function)
                      producers → KF/FED
                      stockpersons → RHB/FED
                      sustainable farmers → KC/FED
                      veterinary surgeons. veterinarians → JV/FED
                (persons by relationship with animals)
FFG              owners
                      cat owners → WJC/FFG
FFM              riders
FFP              public
FFR                 human audience
FFV              visitors

                (agents – equipment)
FG            drugs
FGB              anaesthetics
FGB/EMB/BT          Protection of Animals(Anaesthetics) Act 1964
FGBC             $CO_2$ gas
FGBD             $CO_2.O_2$ gas
FGN              neuroleptics
FH            water. drinking water

| | |
|---|---|
| FJ | foods |
| FJG | grass |
| FJN | grass-based foods |
| FJS | coarse mix feeds |
| FJT | monkey chow |
| FK | bedding |
| FKB | straw |
| FL | equipment |
| FLB | assessment tools |
| FLC | computers |
| FLH | handling equipment |
| | nose-rings → PFDN/FLH |
| FLM | medical equipment |
| | urine collection devices → PQ/PDZ/FLM |
| FLN | guns |
| FLV | vehicles |
| | transport vehicles → KET/FLV |
| | |
| FM | (agents – buildings/structures/living quarters) |
| FMC | environment generally |
| FMD | barren environment |
| FMF | enriched environment |
| | (services and facilities) |
| FML | lighting. illuminance |
| FMT | ultra-violet lighting |
| FMV | ventilation |
| | (parts of buildings) |
| FN | floorings |
| | (fittings and equipments) |
| FNM | mirrors |
| FNP | platforms |
| FNT | toys |
| | (functional parts) |
| FOL | laboratories |
| FOS | surgical facilities |
| FOT | (types of building/structure by function) |
| | dairies → GL/FOT |
| | hatcheries → WB/PRP/FOT |
| FP | housing. housing systems |
| FPC | housing environment |
| FPD | individual housing |
| FPH | social housing conditions |
| | (parts of system) |
| FPK | cage systems |

| | |
|---|---|
| FPL | single cages |
| | (housing by form) |
| FPM | hoop shelters. hooped housing |
| FPS | standing stalls. non-bedded confinement systems |
| FPT | enclosures |
| FPV | primary enclosures |
| FPW | barriers |
| FPWN | camouflage net barriers |
| | |
| FR | external environment |
| | (elements) |
| FRL | shelter |
| FRS | shade |
| FRT | trees |
| FRW | water |
| FRWM | mobile tanks |
| FRWS | swimming water |
| FRX | pastures |
| FRY | ranges |
| FRY/DGS | summer ranges |
| FRY/DGW | winter ranges |
| FRY/EFM/DGS | mountain summer ranges |
| FRYZ | home ranges |
| | |
| | (agents – organizations) |
| FSB | government |
| FSC | ethics committees |
| | |
| FSD | animal rights movement |
| FSF | animal welfare organizations |
| | |
| | (organizations by function) |
| FSG | animal hospitals. veterinary hospitals. veterinary surgeries |
| FSH | animal shelters. rescue shelters |
| FSL | laboratories |
| FSM | farms. ranches |
| | dairy farms → KF/GL/FSM |
| FSN | markets |
| FSR | rodeos |
| FSZ | zoos. zoological gardens. zoo industry |
| | |
| **G** | **Products** |
| GF | food (human) |
| GH | meat |

| GJ | red meat |
| | beef → WD/RS/GJ |
| | natural beef → WD/RS/KB/GJ |
| | veal → WD/RS/RCD/GJ |
| GL | dairy foods |
| GL/FOT | dairies |
| GN | milk |
| | cow's milk → WD/RN/GN |
| GAP | eggs |
| GS | fur |
| GW | wool. wools |
| GWN | naturally coloured wools |
| GWS | rare wools |

| **H/K** | **Operations** |
| | (general actions) |
| HB | comparison. comparative study → CC phase relations |
| HC | management |
| HD | cooperation |
| | |
| HE | research |
| HF | monitoring |
| HG | criteria |
| HH | indicators |
| | welfare indicators → J/HH |
| HK | measures |
| | behavioural measures → M/HK |
| HL | longitudinal monitoring |
| HM | measurement |
| HN | recording |
| HN/FLC | automated recording |
| | |
| HP | evaluation. assessment |
| HR | analysis |
| HRC | conjoint analysis |
| HRF | fractal analysis |
| | |
| HS | intervention |
| HT | modification |
| HV | regulation |
| HV/EL | international regulation |
| | |
| HW | education and training (personnel) |

| | |
|---|---|
| J | animal welfare |
| J/HH | welfare indicators |
| JB | animal protection. protection |
| JD | humane methods. humane control |
| JH | rehabilitation (of wild animals) |
| | hedgehog rehabilitation → SK/JH |
| JL | animal liberation |
| | |
| JM | animal abuse. abuse |
| | (by cause) |
| JML | delinquency |
| JMV | deviance |
| | |
| JN | neglect |
| JP | animal cruelty. cruelty |
| JPC | physical cruelty |
| JPM | maiming |
| | horse maiming → WCH/JPM |
| | |
| JR | capture. catching animals |
| JRT | trapping |
| JS | confinement |
| JSN | intensive confinement |
| | |
| JV | veterinary care. animal health care |
| JV/FED | veterinary surgeons. veterinarians |
| JVB | veterinary procedures |
| JVC | administration of drugs |
| JVD | dosing techniques |
| JVF | anaesthesia |
| JVG | euthanasia |
| JVH | surgical procedures |
| JVL | cutting. clipping |
| | tooth clipping → PKD/JVL |
| JVR | grinding. rasping |
| | tooth grinding → PKD/JVR |
| JVS | ringing. tagging |
| | nose ringing → PFDN/JVS |
| | |
| JW | environment management |
| | lighting → FML |
| | ventilation → FMV |
| JWC | space allocation. density |
| JWP | pest control |

| | |
|---|---|
| JWR | environmental enrichment. enrichment. enriching. enrichment techniques |
| JWS | visual stimulation |
| | |
| JX | research using animals. animal experimentation |
| JXD | laboratory routines |
| | |
| JY | training |
| | dog training → WJD/JY |
| JYD | discipline of animals |
| | |
| K | farming. agriculture |
| | aquaculture → SE/K |
| | bear farming → TL/K |
| | pig farming. hog farming → WF/K |
| | |
| KB | organic agriculture |
| KC | sustainable agriculture |
| KC/FED | sustainable farmers |
| | |
| KD | husbandry. husbandry procedures |
| KE | handling. livestock handling |
| | chick handling → WB/RCD/KE |
| KEF | blindfolding |
| KEM | movement |
| KET | transport. transporting |
| KET/FLV | transport vehicles |
| KEV | loading |
| KF | production. animal production |
| | poultry production → WB/KF |
| | pig production → WF/KF |
| | |
| KF/FED | producers. animal producers |
| | dairy farming → WD/RN/K |
| | dairy farms → WD/RN/K/FSM |
| KG | feeding. nutrition |
| | body weight regulation → ND/HV |
| KH | grazing |
| KH/DG | seasonal grazing |
| KHB | management intensive grazing |
| KHC | multi-species grazing |
| KHD | rotational grazing |
| | |
| KHE | pasture management |

| | |
|---|---|
| KHF | brush control |
| | |
| KHP | day range |
| KHR | free range |
| | |
| KJ | breeding management |
| KL | breeding schemes |
| KLD | selection of stock |
| KM | contraception |
| KN | mating |
| KN | obstetric management |

farrowing systems → WF/KN/FP
deep straw farrowing systems → WF/KN/FP/FKB

| | |
|---|---|
| KR | hand rearing |
| KRS | hand rearing schedules |
| | |
| KT | slaughter. humane slaughter |
| KV | culling |
| | |
| KW | marketing. promotion |
| KWM | market growing |

| | |
|---|---|
| **L/M** | **Processes** |
| | (General processes) |
| LCD | influence |
| LCE | change |
| LCF | acclimatization |
| LCG | growth |
| LCH | development |
| LCJ | improvement |
| LCM | detrimental effects |
| LCP | preference |
| LCR | risk |
| | |
| LD | health. welfare |

farm animal welfare → RHB/LD
equine welfare → WC/LD
cattle welfare → WD/LD
pig welfare → WF/LD

| | |
|---|---|
| LD/FSM | on-farm welfare |
| | |
| LE | needs |
| LF | individual needs |

| | |
|---|---|
| LG | comfort |
| LH | impaired welfare |
| | |
| LM | physiological processes |
| | adrenal activation → PHD/LM |
| | pituitary activation → PHP/LM |
| | genetic responses → PS/LM |
| | |
| LMC | life cycle |
| | birth → PRP |
| LME | puberty |
| LMF | ageing |
| | |
| LMG | death. mortality |
| LMP | population |
| LMR | overpopulation |
| | |
| LMS | hypersensitivity |
| LMSD | delayed type hypersensitivity |
| LN | stress |
| LN/DC | chronic stress |
| LN/KE | handling stress |
| | traumatic stress → LPT/LN |
| LND | stress responses |
| | stress vocalization → LWV/LN |
| | |
| LP | abnormal physiology. pathology |
| LP/FB | harm caused by human activities |
| LPG | pain [in animals] |
| LPH | pain perception |
| LPS | suffering |
| LPT | trauma |
| LPT/LN | traumatic stress |
| | |
| LQ | (dysfunction) |
| LQD | dysplasia |
| | hip dysplasia → PJD/PFH/LQD |
| | canine hip dysplasia → WJD/PJD/PFH/LQD |
| LQE | translocation |
| LR | infections |
| LS | injuries |
| LS/JRT | trap related injuries |
| LSC | crushing |
| | piglet crushing → WF/RCD/LSC |

| | |
|---|---|
| LSR | road traffic accidents |
| | |
| LT | psychological processes. mental processes |
| LTE | emotion |
| LTF | fear |
| LTG | boredom |
| LTM | aversion |
| LU | consciousness |
| LV | cognitive processes |
| LVC | cognitive capacity |
| LVL | learning |
| LW | communication |
| LWC | communication capacity |
| LWV | vocalization |
| LWV/LN | stress vocalization |
| | |
| M | animal behaviour |
| | cat behaviour → WJC/M |
| | sheep behaviour → WG/M |
| | |
| M/HK | behavioural measures |
| MB | behaviour traits |
| MC | behavioural responses |
| | |
| MD | movement |
| MDC | swaying |
| MDF | falling |
| | |
| MF | feeding |
| MFD | nutrition |
| MFF | forage needs |
| | |
| MFF | pecking |
| MFH | grazing |
| MFP | predation |
| MFP/F | predators |
| | |
| MG | grooming behaviour |
| MGS | scratching behaviour |
| MGT | dustbathing |
| | |
| MP | breeding. breeding behaviour |
| MPM | courtship behaviour |
| | parturition → PRP |

calving → WD/PRP
　　seasonal calving → WD/PRP/DG
　farrowing → WF/PRP

| | |
|---|---|
| MR | maternal behaviour |
| | milk production → PRT |
| | milk quality → PRV |
| MRS | nest building |
| | |
| MS | social behaviour. interactions |
| MS/FB | human-animal interactions. human-livestock interactions |
| | human-cat relationship → WJC/MS/FB |
| | |
| MS/FFP | public understanding |
| MS/FPR | public perception |
| MS/FPV | visitor effect |
| | |
| MSC | social instinct |
| MSF | social organization |
| MSG | social status |
| MSP | play. play behaviour |
| | |
| MT | escape |
| | |
| MV | abnormal behaviour |
| MVP | feather pecking |

# N　Animal anatomy. parts of the body

| | |
|---|---|
| | (properties) |
| NB | appearance |
| NC | (size.dimensions) |
| ND | body weight |
| NDB | low body weight |
| NDF | obesity |
| | |
| NF | temperature |
| | hypersensitivity → LMH |
| | heart rate → PLS/LM |
| | primiparity → PRMN |
| | |
| P | (parts) |
| | (components) |
| PB | cells |

| PC | tissues. histology |
| PD | (bio-chemicals) |
| PDC | corticosterone |
| PDCD | corticosterone concentrations |
| PDCL | corticosterone levels |
| PDCS | cortisol |
| PDG | growth hormone |
| | bovine growth hormone → WD/PDG |
| PDH | endocrine disrupting compounds |
| | body fluids and products |
| PDX | body fluids |
| | blood → PLB |
| | serum → PLC |
| | plasma → PLS |
| | saliva → PK/PDX |
| | salivary cortisol → PK/PDX/PDCS |
| PDZ | waste products |
| | urine → PQ/PDZ |
| | faeces. manure → PK/PDZ |
| | faecal corticoids → PK/PDZ/PDC |

| PF | (regions) |
| PFC | head |
| PFD | face |
| PFDN | nose |
| PFDN/FLH | nose-rings |
| PFDN/JVS | nose ringing |
| PFH | hips |
| PG | (organs and systems) |
| PH | endocrine system |
| PHD | adrenal glands |
| PHD/LM | adrenal activation |
| PHP | pituitary gland |
| PHP/LM | pituitary activation |
| PJ | locomotor system |
| PJD | bones |
| PJD/PFH | hip bones |
| PJD/PFH/LQD | hip dysplasia |
| | canine hip dysplasia → JD/PJD/PFH/LQD |
| PJS | skin |
| PJT | fur |
| PJW | wool |
| PJX | feathers |
| PK | digestive system |

|  | (fluids and products) |
|---|---|
| PK/PDX | saliva |
| PK/PDX/PDCS | salivary cortisol |
| PK/PDZ | faeces. manure |
| PK/PDZ/PDC | faecal corticoids |
| PKD | teeth |
| PKD/JVL | tooth clipping |
| PKD/JVR | tooth grinding |
| PL | circulatory system |
| PLB | blood |
| PLC | serum |
| PLP | plasma |
| PLS | heart |
| PLS/LM | heart rate |
| PM | respiratory system |
| PMF | trachea |
| PN | nervous system |
| PNS | sense organs |
| PNSE | ears |
| PNSEP | ear-pinnae |
| PQ | urinary system |
| PQ/PDZ | urine |
| PQ/PDZ/FLM | urine collection devices |
| PR | reproductive system |
| PRM | pregnancy |
| PRMN | primiparity |
| PRP | parturition. birth |
| PRT | milk production |
| PRV | milk quality |
| PS | genetics |
| PS/LM | genetic responses |

## R/Z   Animals

|  | (animals by gender) |
|---|---|
| RBB | males |
| RBD | neutered males |
| RBF | females |
|  | mares → WCH/RBD |
|  | sows → WF/RBD |
| RBG | neutered females |

|  | (animals by age) |
|---|---|
| RCB | newborn |
| RCD | young. juveniles |

|        |                                      |
|--------|--------------------------------------|
|        | calves → WD/RCD                      |
|        | chicks → WBC/RCD                     |
|        | ducklings → WBD/RCD                  |
|        | piglets → WF/RCD                     |
|        | turkey poults → WBK/RCD              |
| RCG    | growing                              |
| RCM    | mature                               |
| RCW    | aged                                 |

**(animals by physiological condition)**

| RDPRM  | pregnant                             |
|--------|--------------------------------------|
|        | pregnant mares→ WCH/RDPRM            |
|        | pregnant sows → WF/RDPRM             |
| RDPSB  | inbred strains                       |
| RDPSG  | genetically modified animals         |

**(animals by number)**

| RDS  | single animals. solitary animals     |
|------|--------------------------------------|
| RDT  | pairs                                |
| RDT/ | breeding pairs                       |
| RDU  | groups                               |
| RDV  | family groups                        |
| RDW  | social groups. bands. tribes. packs  |
| RDX  | herds. large groups                  |

**(animals by living conditions)**

| RED  | indoors                              |
|------|--------------------------------------|
| REP  | outdoors                             |
|      | outdoor sows → WF/REP                |

| RFB  | wild animals                         |
|------|--------------------------------------|
| RFF  | free-living wild animals             |
| RFG  | wild-caught animals                  |
| RFM  | captive animals                      |
|      | captive chimpanzees → VR/RFM         |
|      | captive tigers → TR/RFM              |
| RFP  | zoo animals. zoo housed animals      |
|      | zoo housed gorillas → VT/RFP         |
| RFS  | feral                                |
|      | feral cats → TS/RFS                  |

| RG   | . domestic animals. domesticated animals |
|------|------------------------------------------|
|      | ★ Where the notion of domestication is inherent in the animal, this concept need not be added. |

|  | domestic cats → WJC |
|  | domestic rabbits → WHR |
|  | domestic sheep → WG |

| RHB | farm(ed) animals. livestock |
|  | farmed fish → SE/RH |
|  | farmed mink → WHM/RH |

| RHB/FED | stockpersons |
| RHB/LD | farm animal welfare |

| RHC | intensively farmed animals |

| RHED | (indoor). housed animals |
| RHEF | caged |
|  | caged hens → WBC/RHEF |
|  | caged rabbits → WHR/RHEF |
| RHEK | kennelled |
|  | kennelled dogs → WJD/RHEK |
| RHEP | (outdoor) |
| RHER | pastured |
|  | pastured cows → WD/RHER |
| RHES | free-range |
|  | free-range poultry → WB/RHES |

**(animals by function)**

| RJ | pets |
| RJ/FCC | children's pets |
| RJX | exotic pets |
| RJY | animals used in education |
| RK | breeding |
|  | breeding ostriches → SFF/RK |
|  | rearing pigs → WF/RK |
| RL | laboratory animals |

| RM | (food production) |
| RN | dairy |
|  | dairy cows → WD/RN |
| RP | egg production. laying |
|  | laying hens → WBC/RP |
| RS | meat |
|  | meat goats → WGG/RS |
|  | veal calves → WD/RS/RCD |
|  | broilers → WBC/RS |

feeder pigs → WF/RS
growing pigs → WF/RS

| | |
|---|---|
| RW | working |
| | working equids → WC/RW |
| | working horses → WCH/RW |
| RWG | guard animals |
| | guard dogs → WJD/RWG |
| | guard donkeys → WCR/RWG |
| | guard llamas → WGL/RWG |
| RWS | sport |
| | sport horses → WCH/RWS |
| RWT | trotting |
| | trotting horses → WCH/RWT |
| RWX | racing |
| | racehorses → WCH/RWX |
| | |
| RX | pests |

**(animals by species)**

| | |
|---|---|
| SB | non-human animals (usually assumed) |
| SC | wild animals |
| | |
| SD | vertebrates |
| SE | fish |
| SE/K | fish farming. aquaculture |
| SE/RH | farmed fish |
| SER | rainbow trout |
| SF | birds |
| SFD | ducks. anatidae |
| SFE | ratites |
| SFF | ostriches |
| SFF/RK | breeding ostriches |
| SFFH | rheas |
| SFFM | emus |
| SFG | gamebirds. gallinaceae. |
| SFH | chickens. domestic fowls. poultry |
| SFK | turkeys |
| SFL | quail |
| SFM | Japanese quail |
| SFP | parrots. psittacidae |
| SFR | grey parrots |

| | |
|---|---|
| SG | mammals |
| SH | rodents |
| SHB | squirrels |
| SHC | grey squirrels |
| SHG | rats |
| SHM | mice |
| SHN | hamsters |
| SHO | Siberian hamster |
| SHP | guinea pigs. cavies |
| SHQ | lagomorphs |
| SHR | rabbits |
| | |
| SJ | insectivora |
| SK | hedgehogs |
| SK/JH | hedgehog rehabilitation |
| | |
| SL | elephants. proboscids |
| SLL | African elephant. loxodonta Africana |
| | |
| SM | hoofed animals. perissodactyla |
| SMB | equids. equidae |
| SMC | horses |
| SMD | ponies |
| SMF | donkeys. asses |
| SMM | mules |
| | |
| SP | even toed ungulates. artiodactyla |
| SPP | pigs. hogs. swine |
| SPQ | camels |
| SPS | llamas |
| SR | ruminants |
| SRB | giraffe. giraffa camelopardalis |
| SRC | bovines |
| SS | cattle |
| SSC | caprines |
| ST | sheep |
| STB | Scottish blackface sheep |
| SW | goats |
| | |
| T | carnivores. carnivora |
| TC | canidae |
| TCF | foxes |
| TCG | blue foxes |
| TCH | coyotes |

| | |
|---|---|
| TG | domestic dogs |
| TL | ursidae. bears |
| TL/K | bear farming |
| TM | mustelidae |
| TMM | mink |
| TMN | badgers |
| TMO | otters |
| TMP | Eurasian otter. lutra lutra |
| TP | felidae. cats |
| TR | tigers |
| TR/RFM | captive tigers |
| TS | domestic cats |
| | |
| V | simiae. apes and monkeys. primates |
| VC | monkeys |
| VE | capuchin monkeys |
| VF | tufted capuchin monkeys |
| VG | macaques |
| VL | rhesus macaques |
| VM | baboons |
| VP | apes. anthropoid apes |
| VR | chimpanzees |
| VR/RFM | captive chimpanzees |
| VS | orangutans. pongo pygmaeus |
| VT | gorillas |
| VT/RFP | zoo-housed gorillas |
| VW | western lowland gorillas |

# W   domestic animals. domesticated animals

| | |
|---|---|
| WB | poultry |
| WBC | chickens |
| WB/PRP | hatching |
| WB/PRP/FOT | hatcheries |
| WBC/RCD | chicks |
| WBC/RCD/KE | chick handling |
| WBC/RHEF | caged hens |
| WBC/RHES | free-range poultry |
| WBC/RP | laying hens |
| WBC/RS | broilers |
| WBD | ducks |
| WBD/RCD | ducklings |
| WBK | turkeys |
| WBK/RCD | turkey poults |

| | |
|---|---|
| WBQ | quail |
| WBR | Japanese quail |
| | |
| WC | equids |
| WC/LD | equine welfare |
| WC/RW | working equids |
| WCH | horses |
| WCH/JPM | horse maiming |
| WCH/RBD | mares |
| WCH/RDP | pregnant mares |
| WCH/RW | working horses |
| WCH/RWS | sport horses |
| WCH/RWT | trotting horses |
| WCH/RWX | racehorses |
| WCP | ponies |
| WCR | donkeys. asses |
| WCR/RW | working donkeys |
| WCR/RWG | guard donkeys |
| WCS | mules |
| | |
| WD | cattle |
| WD/LD | cattle welfare |
| WD/PDG | bovine growth hormone |
| WD/PRP | calving |
| WD/PRP/DG | seasonal calving |
| WD/RCD | calves |
| WD/RHER | pastured cows |
| WD/RN | dairy cattle |
| WD/RN/GN | cows' milk |
| WD/RN/K | dairy farming |
| WD/RN/K/FSM | dairy farms |
| WD/RN/RDX | dairy herds |
| WD/RS | beef cattle |
| WD/RS/GJ | beef |
| WD/RS/KB | organic beef farming |
| WD/RS/KB/GJ | natural beef |
| WD/RS/RCD | veal calves |
| WD/RS/RCD/GJ | veal |
| WD/RS/RN | dual-purpose breeds |
| | |
| WF | pigs. hogs. swine |
| WF/K | pig farming. hog farming |
| WF/KN | obstetric management |
| WF/KN/FP | farrowing systems |

| | | |
|---|---|---|
| WF/KN/FP/FKB | | deep straw farrowing systems |
| WF/LD | pig welfare | |
| WF/PRP | farrowing | |
| WF/RBD | sows | |
| WF/RBD/REP | outdoor sows | |
| WF/RDP | pregnant sows | |
| WF/RCD | piglets | |
| WF/RCD/LSC | piglet crushing | |
| WF/RK | rearing pigs | |
| WF/RS | growing pigs | |

| | |
|---|---|
| WG | sheep |
| WG/M | sheep behaviour |
| WGD | Scottish blackface sheep |
| WGG | goats |
| WGG/RS | meat goats |
| WGL | llamas |
| WGL/RWG | guard llamas |

| | |
|---|---|
| WH | fur-bearing animals |
| WHM | mink |
| WHM/RH | farmed mink |
| WHR | rabbits |
| WHR/RHEF | caged rabbits |

| | |
|---|---|
| WJ | pets. animals in the home |
| WJC | cats |
| WJC/FFG | cat owners |
| WJC/M | cat behaviour |
| WJC/MS/FB | human-cat relationship |
| WJD | dogs |
| WJD/JY | dog training |
| WJD/PJD/PFH | hip bones |
| WJD/PJD/PFH/LQD | canine hip dysplasia |
| WJD/RHEK | kennelled dogs |
| WJD/RWG | guard dogs |
| WJR | rabbits |
| WJS | small rodents |

# Appendix 6
# Thesaurus entries for sample page

* Entries are made for terms from PF to PLS/LM on pages 268–9 of Appendix 5. Note that where RTs are made to terms not on pages 268–9 e.g. from 'hip dysplasia' to 'dysplasia', the reciprocal entries (which would be only partial) are not included here.

**adrenal activation**                PHD/LM
    **BT**   physiological processes
    **RT**   adrenal glands
    **RT**   pituitary activation

**adrenal glands**                PHD
    **BT**   endocrine system
    **RT**   adrenal activation
    **RT**   pituitary gland

birth
    **USE** parturition

**blood**                PLB
    **BT**   circulatory system
    **NT**   plasma
    **NT**   serum
    **RT**   heart

**bones**                PJD
    **BT**   locomotor system
    **NT**   hip bones

**circulatory system**                PL
    **NT**   blood
    **NT**   heart
    **RT**   endocrine system

**digestive system**                PK
    **NT**   teeth
    **RT**   faeces
    **RT**   feeding
    **RT**   foods
    **RT**   saliva

**ear pinnae**                PNSEP
    **BT**   ears

**ears**                PNSE
    **BT**   sense organs
    **NT**   ear pinnae

**endocrine system**                PH
    **NT**   adrenal glands
    **NT**   pituitary glands
    **RT**   circulatory system
    **RT**   endocrine disrupting
           compounds
    **RT**   urinary system

**face**                PFD
    **BT**   head
    **NT**   nose

**faecal corticoids**  PK/PDZ/PDC
    **BT**   corticosterone
    **RT**   faeces

**faeces**                PK/PDZ
    **UF**   manure
    **BT**   waste products
    **RT**   digestive system
    **RT**   faecal corticoids

**feathers**  PJX
    **BT**   skin
    **RT**   birds

**fur** PJT
    **BT**   skin
    **RT**   wool
    **RT**   fur farming

**genetic responses** PS/LM
    **BT**   physiological processes
    **RT**   genetics

**genetics** PS
    **RT**   genetic responses
    **RT**   reproductive system

**head** PFC
    **NT**   face

**heart** PLS
    **BT**   circulatory system
    **RT**   blood
    **RT**   heart rate

**heart rate** PLS/LM
    **BT**   physiological processes
    **RT**   heart

**hip bones** PJD/PFH
    **BT**   bones
    **BT**   hips
    **RT**   canine hip dysplasia
    **RT**   hip dysplasia

**hip dysplasia** PJD/PFH/LQD
    **BT**   dysplasia
    **RT**   canine hip dysplasia
    **RT**   hip bones

**hips** PFH
    **NT**   hip bones
    **RT**   canine hip dysplasia
    **RT**   hip dysplasia

**locomotor system** PJ
    **NT**   bones
    **NT**   skin
    **RT**   movement

manure
    **USE**  faeces

**milk production** PRT
    **RT**   milk quality
    **RT**   parturition
    **RT**   reproductive system

**milk quality** PRV
    **RT**   milk production

**nervous system** PN
    **NT**   sense organs
    **RT**   psychological processes

**nose** PFDN
    **BT**   face
    **RT**   nose ringing
    **RT**   nose rings

**nose ringing** PFDN/JVS
    **BT**   ringing
    **RT**   nose
    **RT**   nose rings

**nose rings** PFDN/FLH
    **BT**   handling equipment
    **RT**   nose
    **RT**   nose ringing

**parturition** PRP
    **UF**   birth
    **RT**   milk production
    **RT**   pregnancy

**pituitary activation** PHP/LM
    **BT**   physiological processes
    **RT**   adrenal activation
    **RT**   pituitary gland

**pituitary gland** PHP
    **BT**   endocrine system
    **RT**   adrenal glands
    **RT**   pituitary activation

**plasma** PLP
    **BT**   blood
    **RT**   serum

**pregnancy** PRM
    **RT**   obstetric management
    **RT**   parturition
    **RT**   primiparity
    **RT**   reproductive system

**primiparity** PRMN
    **RT**   pregnancy

**reproductive system** PR
    **RT**   breeding management
    **RT**   genetics

**RT** milk production
**RT** pregnancy
**RT** parturition

**respiratory system**                    PM
  **NT** trachea

**saliva**                                PK/PDX
  **BT** body fluids
  **RT** digestive system
  **RT** feeding
  **RT** salivary cortisol

**salivary cortisol**           PK/PDX/PDCS
  **BT** cortisol
  **RT** saliva

**sense organs**                          PNS
  **BT** nervous system
  **NT** ears
  **RT** communication

**serum**                                 PLC
  **BT** blood
  **RT** plasma

**skin**                                  PJS
  **BT** locomotor system
  **NT** fur
  **NT** wool
  **NT** feathers

**teeth**                                 PKD
  **BT** digestive system
  **RT** feeding
  **RT** tooth clipping
  **RT** tooth grinding

**tooth clipping**                    PKD/JVL
  **BT** cutting
  **RT** teeth
  **RT** tooth grinding

**tooth grinding**                    PKD/JVR
  **BT** grinding
  **RT** teeth
  **RT** tooth clipping

**trachea**                               PMF
  **BT** respiratory system

**urinary system**                        PQ
  **RT** circulatory system
  **RT** urine
  **RT** urine collection devices

**urine**                             PQ/PDZ
  **BT** waste products
  **RT** urinary system
  **RT** urine collection devices

**urine collection devices**   PQ/PDZ/FLM
  **BT** medical equipment
  **RT** urine

**wool**                                  PJW
  **BT** skin
  **RT** fur
  **RT** naturally coloured wools
  **RT** rare wools

# Index

Readers should note that index entries refer only to the main text of the book. Terms in the Animal Welfare thesaurus are not included in the index, but an alphabetical list of those terms is contained in Appendix 2.